Lecture Notes in Information Systems and Organisation

Volume 26

Lecture Notes in Information Systems and Organization—LNISO—is a series of scientific books that explore the current scenario of information systems, in particular IS and organization. The focus on the relationship between IT, IS and organization is the common thread of this collection, which aspires to provide scholars across the world with a point of reference and comparison in the study and research of information systems and organization. LNISO is the publication forum for the community of scholars investigating behavioral and design aspects of IS and organization. The series offers an integrated publication platform for high-quality conferences, symposia and workshops in this field. Materials are published upon a strictly controlled double blind peer review evaluation made by selected reviewers. LNISO is abstracted/indexed in Scopus

More information about this series at http://www.springer.com/series/11237

Nearchos Paspallis · Marios Raspopoulos
Chris Barry · Michael Lang
Henry Linger · Christoph Schneider
Editors

Advances in Information Systems Development

Methods, Tools and Management

 Springer

Editors
Nearchos Paspallis
School of Sciences
University of Central Lancashire
Larnaca
Cyprus

Marios Raspopoulos
School of Sciences
University of Central Lancashire
Larnaca
Cyprus

Chris Barry
Cairnes School of Business and Economics
National University of Ireland Galway
Galway
Ireland

Michael Lang
Cairnes School of Business and Economics
National University of Ireland Galway
Galway
Ireland

Henry Linger
Faculty of Information Technology
Monash University
Melbourne
Australia

Christoph Schneider
Department of Information Systems
City University of Hong Kong
Kowloon
Hong Kong

ISSN 2195-4968   ISSN 2195-4976   (electronic)
Lecture Notes in Information Systems and Organisation
ISBN 978-3-319-74816-0   ISBN 978-3-319-74817-7   (eBook)
https://doi.org/10.1007/978-3-319-74817-7

Library of Congress Control Number: 2018930115

Printed on acid-free paper

This Springer imprint is published by the registered company Springer International Publishing AG part of Springer Nature
The registered company address is: Gewerbestrasse 11, 6330 Cham, Switzerland

Preface

The **International Conference on Information Systems Development** (ISD) is an academic conference where researchers and practitioners share their knowledge and expertise in the field of information systems development. As an Affiliated Conference of the Association for Information Systems (AIS), the ISD conference complements the international network of general IS conferences (ICIS, ECIS, ACIS, AMCIS, PACIS, and HICSS). The ISD conference continues the tradition started with the first Polish-Scandinavian Seminar on Current Trends in Information Systems Development Methodologies, held in Gdansk, Poland in 1988. This seminar has evolved into the International Conference on Information Systems Development.

Throughout its history, the conference has focused on different aspects, ranging from methodological, infrastructural, and educational challenges in the ISD field to bridging the gaps between industry, academia, and society. Advancements in information systems foster technological developments. The deployment of the resulting technologies in all areas of society, including public and private sectors, the community, and in the home, is greatly beneficial. ISD has always promoted a close interaction between theory and practice that has set a human-centered agenda focused on advancing the methods, tools, and management of IS.

This volume is a selection of papers from ISD2017, the 26th Information Systems Development conference hosted by the School of Sciences, University of Central Lancashire—Cyprus (UCLan Cyprus), and held in Larnaca, Cyprus on September 6–8, 2017. All accepted conference papers have been published in the AIS eLibrary, which is accessible at http://aisel.aisnet.org/isd2014/proceedings2017. This volume contains extended versions of the best papers, as selected by the ISD2017 Proceedings Editors.

The theme of the conference was *Advances in Methods, Tools and Management*. It focused on the latest developments in ISD and particularly on methods and tools used to design, create, and maintain information systems. The ISD2017 conference attracted contributions in the general area of information systems development, as well as in more specialized topics including IS methodologies and modeling,

vi   Preface

management of IS development, ISD education, human–computer interaction (HCI) in ISD, cognitive science, and security and privacy in ISD.

ISD2017 focused on these and associated topics in order to promote research into theoretical and methodological issues and ways in which these advances enable better synergies between theory and practice. We believe that the innovative papers assembled in these lecture notes will inform the reader of important contributions in this regard.

Larnaca, Cyprus   Nearchos Paspallis
Larnaca, Cyprus   Marios Raspopoulos
Melbourne, Australia   Henry Linger
Galway, Ireland   Chris Barry
Galway, Ireland   Michael Lang
Kowloon, Hong Kong   Christoph Schneider

Conference Organization

Conference Chairs
Nearchos Paspallis
Marios Raspopoulos

International Steering Committee
Chris Barry
Michael Lang
Henry Linger
Christoph Schneider

Track Chairs
Information Systems Methodologies and Modelling
Malgorzata Pankowska

Managing is Development
Emilio Insfran

ISD Education
Irene Polycarpou
Tihomir Orehovački
Mark Freeman

Human Computer Interaction (HCI) in ISD
Dijana Plantak Vukovac
Panayiotis Zaphiris

Cognitive Science
Andreas Andreou
Jaroslav Pokorny

Security and Privacy in ISD
Christos Douligeris
Eliana Stavrou

General Topics in ISD
Michael Lang
Gabriel Panis
Andreas Pamboris

Reviewers

Aleksandra Lazareva
Alena Siarheyeva
Ana Castillo-Martinez
Andreas Christoforou
Andreas Gregoriades
Andreas Lanitis
Andreas Panayides
Andri Ioannou
Andrina Granic
Berislav Andrlic
Carlos Torrecilla-Salinas
Chris Barry
Christodoulos Efstathiades
Christoph Schneider
Christos Karpasitis
Christos Kyrlitsias
Daniel Rodriguez
Danijel Radošević
Darko Etinger
David Fonseca
Despina Michael-Grigoriou
Dimitris Karagiannis
Dominique Blouin
Dragutin Kermek
Florina Livia Covaci
Geir Horn
George Sielis
Georgia Kapitsaki
Georgios Stylianou
Giancarlo Guizzardi
Gustavo Rossi
Hasan Alyamani
Igor Balaban
Javier Gonzalez Huerta
Javier Gutiérrez
Jennifer Pérez

Jesus Garcia-Molina
Joan Lu
Joanna Palonka
João Barata
John Sören Pettersson
Josephina Antoniou
Karel Richta
Luis Fernandez-Sanz
Maja Cukusic
Manuele Kirsch Pinheiro
Maria Christofi
Maria Jose Escalona
Maria Terzi
Mario Jadric
Marios Belk
Marios Raspopoulos
Maristella Matera
Mariusz Żytniewski
Muhammad Binsawad
Nearchos Paspallis
Nicolas Tsapatsoulis
Nikola Marangunić
Nikolina Žajdela Hrustek
Nina Rizun
Ovidiu Noran
Panagiotis Germanakos
Panayiotis Andreou
Panayiotis Charalambous
Paola Beltran
Paris Kaimakis
Parisa Aasi
Peter Bellström
Peter Pocta
Priscila Cedillo
Raphael Oliveira
Romain Rouvoy

Silvia Abrahao   Van Dong Phung
Snježana Babić   William Song
Sotirios Chatzis   Xavier Bellekens
Stéphane Galland   Zlatko Stapic

Contents

Contributors

Juan Aguado-Delgado University of Alcalá, Alcalá de Henares, Spain

Héctor R. Amado-Salvatierra Galileo University, Guatemala City, Guatemala

Henrik Andersson Karlstad University, Karlstad, Sweden

Andreas S. Andreou Cyprus University of Technology, Limassol, Cyprus

Lorena Arcega Universidad San Jorge, Saragossa, Spain; University of Oslo, Oslo, Norway

João Barata CTCV - Technological Center for Ceramics and Glass, Coimbra, Portugal; CISUC, University of Coimbra, Coimbra, Portugal; ESTGOH, Polytechnic Institute of Coimbra, Oliveira do Hospital, Coimbra, Portugal

Guillermo Beltrán Systems and Computing Engineering Department, Universidad de los Andes, Bogotá, Colombia

Moshiur Bhuiyan Service Consulting, Enterprise Cloud Systems, Sydney, NSW, Australia

Muhammad Binsawad King Abdulaziz University, Jeddah, Saudi Arabia

Carlos Cetina Universidad San Jorge, Saragossa, Spain

Sotirios P. Chatzis Cyprus University of Technology, Limassol, Cyprus

Panayiotis Christodoulou Cyprus University of Technology, Limassol, Cyprus

Lena Y. Connolly National University of Ireland, Galway, Ireland

Paulo Rupino da Cunha CISUC, University of Coimbra, Coimbra, Portugal

Jorge Echeverría Universidad San Jorge, Zaragoza, Spain

Francisco J. Estrada-Martínez University of Alcalá, Alcalá de Henares, Spain

Simone Fischer-Hübner Karlstad University, Karlstad, Sweden

Jaime Font Universidad San Jorge, Saragossa, Spain; University of Oslo, Oslo, Norway

Lesley Gardner University of Auckland, Auckland, New Zealand

Anand Subhashchandra Gonnagar ESTGOH, Polytechnic Institute of Coimbra, Oliveira do Hospital, Coimbra, Portugal

Oscar González-Rojas Systems and Computing Engineering Department, Universidad de los Andes, Bogotá, Colombia

Mª Teresa Gómez López Universidad de Sevilla, Seville, Spain

Juan E. Gómez-Morantes Systems Engineering Department, Pontificia Universidad Javeriana, Bogotá, Colombia

Øystein Haugen Østfold University College, Halden, Norway

Igor Hawryszkiewycz University of Technology, Sydney, Australia

José R. Hilera University of Alcalá, Alcalá de Henares, Spain

I. Holubová Charles University, Prague, Czechia

Farzaneh Karegar Karlstad University, Karlstad, Sweden

Aneesh Krishna Department of Computing, Curtin University, Bentley, WA, Australia

Michael Lang National University of Ireland, Galway, Ireland

Daniel Lindegren Karlstad University, Karlstad, Sweden

Mateus Mendes ESTGOH, Polytechnic Institute of Coimbra, Oliveira do Hospital, Coimbra, Portugal; Institute of Systems and Robotics of the University of Coimbra, Coimbra, Portugal

Rafael M. Gasca Universidad de Sevilla, Seville, Spain

T. Novella Charles University, Prague, Czechia

Salvador Otón University of Alcalá, Alcalá de Henares, Spain

Luisa Parody Universidad de Sevilla, Seville, Spain

Óscar Pastor Universitat Politècnica de València, Valencia, Spain

Udayangi Perera Muthupoltotage University of Auckland, Auckland, New Zealand

John Sören Pettersson Karlstad University, Karlstad, Sweden

Van Dong Phung University of Technology, Sydney, Australia

P. W. C. Prasad School of Computing and Mathematics, Charles Sturt University, Sydney, NSW, Australia

Francisca Pérez Universitat Politècnica de València, Valencia, Spain

Rajip Raj Thapa School of Computing and Mathematics, Charles Sturt University, Sydney, NSW, Australia

Cristian Timbi-Sisalima Universidad Politécnica Salesiana, Cuenca, Ecuador

Doug J. Tygar University of California, Berkeley, USA

Ángel Jesús Varela Vaca Universidad de Sevilla, Seville, Spain

Malin Wik Karlstad University, Karlstad, Sweden

Analysing the Relationships Between Digital Literacy and Self-Regulated Learning of Undergraduates—A Preliminary Investigation

Udayangi Perera Muthupoltotage and Lesley Gardner

Abstract Advances in technology access allow undergraduates to personalize their learning to their individual interests via the creation and use of informal personal learning environments (PLEs). A comprehensive understanding of how every day digital technologies are adapted and used to create such PLEs and their impact on acquisition and development of students' digital literacy (DL) and self-regulated learning (SRL) skills, is still lacking. This paper presents the initial exploratory quantitative phase, of a longitudinal mixed methods study planned to identify and describe the relationship between DL and SRL skills of students, when using PLEs. Structural equation modelling was used to analyze data collected from 202 participants in online surveys. The results confirm that DL components effect some SRL sub-processes and some evidence was obtained for reciprocal relationships. Implications for Information Systems theory and practice are discussed together with future research opportunities.

Keywords Digital literacy · Self-regulated learning · Personal learning environments

1 Introduction

Ubiquitous access to 'everyday digital technologies' [1] enables technology to be seamlessly incorporated into the lives of current undergraduate students [2]. These technologies include social or entertainment technology (such as web 2.0 tools),

A prior version of this paper has been published in the ISD2017 Proceedings (http://aisel.aisnet.org/isd2017/proceedings2017).

U. Perera Muthupoltotage (✉) · L. Gardner
University of Auckland, Auckland, New Zealand
e-mail: u.muthupoltotage@auckland.ac.nz

L. Gardner
e-mail: l.gardner@auckland.ac.nz

digital media tools, programming tools, software applications and all manner of digital devices. Students are able to customize their learning to their personal interest via the construction of technology based informal personal learning environments (PLE) [3], using these technologies. Such PLEs, encompass an extensive collection of freely available tools and services accessible on the students' personal digital devices. Components and content of the PLE is altered to fit individual learning needs [4] and it is rarely limited to a single technology or even device [5].

For example, students are constantly accessing information via online search in various formats such as text and multimedia in and outside of their classes. They are using informal and formal social networks such as Facebook and LinkedIn to connect with friends and peers to share, verify, validate and supplement learning. They discuss and reflect on information collaboratively using a multitude of internet based communication tools such as Twitter or Skype. Collection and sharing of information and artefacts via file sharing and synchronization tools such as Evernote and Dropbox also abounds. Many are also creating and generating information via participation in forums, blogs and wiki's. Thus, these students are creating PLEs to supplement many of their learning needs on their own, using tools and technologies of their choice [4]. The study of such PLEs have gained increasing interest [6]. There is scope, however, for consideration of the learning opportunities afforded by the combined use of various tools and technologies to construct an informal PLE [7]. How learning actually takes place when students select their own digital technologies to engage in informal learning activities initiated and controlled purely by them, together with how the use of such PLEs impact the digital and learning skills of students also warrants further study [8].

Self-regulated learning (SRL) encompasses a vital aspect of the PLE [9]. Prior research shows that the creation and use of a PLE allows learners to regulate their own learning, thereby significantly enhancing their learning outcomes [2].

Moreover, PLEs are shown as a context of developing a working knowledge of digital technology and understanding of how it can be effectively used for educational purposes. i.e. 'Digital Literacy' (DL) skills [10]. Researchers acknowledge that the lack of digital literacy skills could impact learning skills and performance of students [11].

Assume a common scenario of a student trying to use the online search tools of his/her PLE for accessing information to supplement learning. The student should be able to effectively plan the search task while demonstrating an ability to monitor and evaluate the impact of the search results on the required learning. These are some component skills of SRL [12]. Moreover, the student should also exhibit an ability to competently use the search tools, while being knowledgeable of issues related to web based activities such as plagiarism. These are aspects of DL. Without successfully applying both skill sets the student would not be able to complete the search task effectively. Moreover, previous research posits a positive correlation between DL and SRL skills of learners [13] and that DL requires effective SRL [14].

Following a similar line of reasoning, we suggest the further examination of these interactions between DL, SRL and informal PLEs via a broad mixed methods study. This paper presents one component of a proposed larger study. The specific aim of this paper is to investigate the direct relationships between DL and academic SRL skills of undergraduates within the context of their technology based informal PLEs.

We develop and empirically test structural models for the explanation and prediction of relationships between DL components of students and component skills of self-regulated learning. This research contributes to the Information Systems literature in investigating and clarifying how different digital skills of students could impact their academic self-regulatory behaviours. It investigates if the interaction with technology for learning and different digital skills developed herein might be changing student SRL behaviours. Via empirical evidence, we hope specifically to understand and describe how technological adoption in learning settings can improve self-regulated learning.

In the subsequent sections relevant literature on PLE, DL and SRL within the context of informal learning is reviewed. This review guides the development of our research model. Next, we describe our research methodology and discuss the data analysis process and results. The paper concludes with a discussion of our results, expected contributions and directions for future research.

2 Related Work

2.1 Personal Learning Environments (PLE)

Personal learning environments, considered as a form of Technology-Enhanced Learning (TEL), are characterized by the principles of learner autonomy, ownership and empowerment [15]. Contemporary practice acknowledges the PLE to be a diffuse concept, thought to innately embody the private and unique nature of its user. However, the relative novelty of the PLE concept and the different ways of implementing, demands for more empirical research in order to validate the usefulness of students' PLEs in diverse informal settings.

In [16] it is noted that researchers seem to consider the PLE mainly from a technology oriented perspective while a few studies, take a different standpoint, viewing the PLEs primarily as an educational concept [17]. For these researchers a PLE is not a software application or collection of tools, but more of a new method of using technologies for learning.

Consequently, in this study the PLE is viewed as a concept, recognized as a new approach to the use of digital technologies in learning [18]. It is defined as comprising of all the different tools undergraduates use in their everyday life for learning. This definition reflects the core concepts of these environments: self-regulation and adaptation to personal needs [19], by including frequently used technologies and tools for providing a natural connection between formal and informal learning [20].

2.2 Digital Literacy (DL)

The term, Digital literacy (DL), while used in an erratic manner in literature [21], is a very broad concept, not restricted to any particular skill set, technology form or information and concentrates on personal capabilities and attributes [22].

According to [23] DL consists of: photo-visual literacy; reproduction literacy; branching literacy; information literacy; socio-emotional literacy and real-time thinking skill. These multiple literacies were incorporated into technical, cognitive and social-emotional dimensions of online and offline learning with digital technologies [24]. The technical literacy dimension includes having the relevant technical and operational skills to use digital technologies for learning. The cognitive literacy dimension is associated with critical thinking applied to searching, evaluating and selecting information and digital tools and technologies for learning, while being knowledgeable about related ethical, moral and legal issues. The social-emotional literacy dimension involves using online resources in a responsible manner, observing 'netiquette' such as showing respect while avoiding misinterpretation and misunderstanding and showing an awareness of privacy and individual safety concerns.

In keeping with these conceptualizations, digital literacy in this paper, refers to the collection of literacies associated with the usage of digital technologies. Technologies could include desktops, mobile devices (e.g. laptops, tablets, smartphones, PDAs), Web 2.0 technologies and other collaborative resources on the internet as well as any open source or commercially available software packages.

We adopt Ng's [24] digital literacy framework to underpin our conceptualization of digital literacy. This framework effectively draws together the broad definitions of digital literacy present in literature, while imbuing the varying literacy concepts referred to above. It has particular value because of its emphasis on different types of digital literacies envisioned as undergraduates' skills, which is the main focus of our study. Further, it is in keeping with our own conception of DL as skills that students autonomously acquire outside formal education via the use of a PLE.

2.3 Self-Regulated Learning (SRL)

Self-Regulated Learning (SRL) is defined as self-generated thoughts, feelings, and actions that are planned and cyclically adapted to the attainment of personal learning goals [25]. It is stated that the component skills include: (1) goal setting, (2) determining and implementing good strategies for realizing the goals, (3) monitoring performance consistently for improvement, (4) reorganization of one's physical and social environment to be attuned with one's goals, (5) efficient time management, (6) appraising one's methods and related results, and (7) acclimating future methods [12].

Contemporary research acknowledges SRL to be a core skill for students to succeed in informal learning environments [16]. Moreover, the use of technology is acknowledged to foster SRL in higher education contexts [20]. While the psychological and pedagogical theories around SRL precede the dawn of the PLE, SRL is regarded as an essential characteristic of the PLE. Consequently, SRL is supported within the PLE through gathering independent resources in a manner that realizes an explicit learning goal. The PLE, therefore, allows learners to regulate their own learning, hence augmenting their learning outcomes [2].

Measuring self-regulation in learning involves the process of assessing how well students have developed the array of features consisting of (1) planning, (2) cognitive, (3) monitoring, and (4) regulating strategies. Santoso et al. [26], as indicated by multiple measurement models of SRL present in contemporary literature [27].

These features, can be measured through the use of the Academic Self-Regulated Learning Scale (A-SRL-S) [28]. This is a self-report measure based on the conceptualization and factors of the SRL framework detailed in [29]. It consists of seven sub-processes. (1) Memory strategy pertains to strategies used for memorizing and retaining information [30]. (2) Goal-setting involves setting specific proximal goals for oneself [12]. (3) Self-evaluation is the constant reflection on and rectification of one's learning methods [29]. (4) Seeking assistance is actively obtaining help from teachers or peers to supplement learning [30]. (5) Environmental structuring is restructuring one's physical and social context to make it compatible with one's goals [12]. (6) Learning responsibility is ascribing causation to results, and adapting future methods [29]. (7) Organizing involves monitoring performance selectively for signs of progress while managing personal time use efficiently [12].

As such the A-SRL-S scale successfully addresses all features shared across often used multiple SRL models and is deemed suitable to represent the SRL construct as applicable in this research.

2.4 Connections Between Digital Literacy and Self-Regulated Learning

Present day university students are required to be digitally literate, by possessing a working knowledge of digital technology and understanding it's usage for learning. But it must be accompanied by, among other aspects, strategies that promote, self-regulated learning [31]. In [32] we discussed the indication of significant relationships between DL skills of students and their SRL skills using contemporary literature.

However most studies, when investigating these relationships, employed an experimental approach where a given technology was imposed on the students, and did not investigate how their current technological portfolio being used in daily life (i.e. everyday technologies) could have or is having an impact on their SRL skills.

The generalizability of the findings of studies conducted in the formal classroom to an informal learning context is also limited. Therefore there is a lack of empirical evidence regarding how technology use affects SRL skills of students when learning within informal settings via the construction of PLEs. There is also a need to understand the self-regulatory processes of students engaged in the use of such learning environments.

Therefore we define the guiding mixed methods research question (RQ) for this study as follows:

RQ. To what extent and in what ways are the digital literacy skill levels of undergraduate students and their self-regulated learning skills interrelated?

In the quantitative phase of investigating this RQ, it is hypothesized that each individual component of digital literacy has a significant positive effect on each individual component of self-regulated learning. We also hypothesize that each individual component of self-regulated learning has a significant positive effect on the different components of digital literacy.

The focal objective for the qualitative phase, in investigating this RQ, is to explore and explain how the acquisition and use of technology within an informal PLE influences the development of digital literacy skill and SRL strategies of undergraduates.

It must be noted that this paper presents only the quantitative phase of investigating our research question. The following sections detail the research model and methodology used in this study.

3   Research Methodology

3.1   Research Model

In specifying the research model for this study, there were two alternative possibilities available. The first was to specify a non-recursive model which allowed for causal paths to backtrack between the digital literacy constructs and the self-regulated learning constructs. The related literature, however, does not justify such a model, as prior studies, where some relationships have been established, have used multiple different conceptualizations of DL components and SRL components. Making the collective findings inconclusive for validating the specification of a non-recursive relationship between the DL and SRL. Moreover the specification of a non-recursive model necessitates the satisfaction of multiple assumptions before they can be statistically validated making the evaluation process more difficult [33].

Therefore, the second possibility which was specifying two alternate recursive models, and evaluating these separately was adopted for this study. This was deemed the most suitable for this study due to the exploratory nature of the study. It was proposed that two alternate models would be specified and path analysis used for identifying significant paths which indicated relationships between DL components and SRL component from DL to SRL and SRL to DL.

3.2 Data Collection Instruments

Measurement scales for DL were drawn from the instrument used by Ng [24] consisting of technical literacy (TL) (6 items), cognitive literacy (CL) (2 items), social emotional literacy (SEL) (2 items).

The seven factor structure from the A-SRL scale [28] was used for measuring self-regulated learning. (1) memory strategy (MS) (14 items), goal-setting (GS) (5 items), self-evaluation (SE) (12 items), seeking assistance (SA) (8 items), environmental structuring (ES) (5 items), learning responsibility (LR) (5 items), and organizing (O) (6 items).The A-SRL scale was originally developed, used and proved with college students and allows measurement of SRL behavioural strategies. Unlike other measures for SRL which focus primarily on motivation (e.g. [34]), the focus of this instrument is situation specific SRL behaviours, as suitable for this study. Using a self-report instrument here, also allows us to view key variables through the eyes of actual students, which can capture data that an outside observer may miss.

However in addressing validity issues arising from using self-report measures, we assume that the participants, have the ability to verbally understand and report their thoughts and feelings. But this may not always be the case and can lead to measurement error [35]. To ensure face and internal validity as well as consistency, a pilot test was conducted among 18 first and second year undergraduate students, 5 postgraduate students and 2 academic staff members before it was released via email to the target population.

3.3 Data Collection

Data collection was performed online by using the survey application Qualitrics. As the study presented in this paper is a component of a larger study it was decided that the survey would be conducted in two parts. The digital literacy constructs, together with attitude, frequency of technology use, level of usage, digital skills development approaches, proficiency levels in technology use, usage ratings and perceptions of usefulness of various technologies were included in first survey together with social demographics of the respondents. The A-SRL scale items were included in a second survey. The respondents of the first survey were asked to indicate willingness to participate in the second survey and second survey was emailed to respondents who agreed to continued participation in the research.

This increased the risk of number of respondents decreasing from the first survey to the second. Moreover as the first and second survey responses would need to be matched to the relevant respondent, it was not possible to conduct the surveys anonymously. However, length of surveys are generally found to have a negative linear relation with response rates in web surveys [36] and thirteen minutes or less completion time is considered as the ideal length to obtain a good response rate from college students [37]. Therefore administering the survey in two parts was considered a good strategy for reducing optimizing and satisfying behaviour among respondents [38].

Moreover the separation of the two surveys is also a means of controlling common method bias arising from common sources, where the measurement of predictor and criterion variables have been separated by introducing a time lag between their measurement [39]. Other procedural remedies which were adopted to minimize common method bias in the surveys was to display each section separately to allow the participants to realize that they were viewing a different set of questions. The first survey was emailed across to a random sample of undergraduate students enrolled in courses within the Business Faculty of a top university in the Asia-Pacific region. A total of 287 complete responses was obtained for the first survey, of which 264 were usable. 243 students indicated agreement to fill in second survey. However, only 215 responses were obtained for the second survey when it was emailed across, of which 202 were usable.

4 Data Analysis

Structured equation modelling (SEM) was the technique selected for investigating the interested phenomena. SEM enables characterization of real-world processes better than simple correlation-based models and is better suited for the mathematical modelling of complex processes [40]. Moreover, SEM assesses the supposed causation among a set of dependent and independent constructs via the structural model while evaluating the loadings of measurements on their expected latent constructs in the same analysis. Thus, SEM is acknowledged to be a more rigorous analysis of the proposed research model.

SEM techniques are divided into two types as variance based and covariance based [40]. The former is thought to yield robust results regardless of sample size and normality issues [41]. Hence, due to the small sample size used in this study and its focus on investigating behavioural relationships, variance-based SEM or PLS-based SEM [41] was the technique adapted. Further, PLS-based SEM can be used in an exploratory study, where the theoretical knowledge is relatively limited [42]. Data analysis was conducted using WarpPLS 6.0 [43].

4.1 Measurement Model Evaluation

The fit of the internal structure of our model, which draws on prior developed constructs, was established through the more rigorous validity criteria of a reflective measurement model specified in WarpPLS.

Reliability and internal consistency for the measurement model was evaluated using Cronbach alpha and Composite reliability (CR). Both measures were considered as Cronbach alpha alone, is thought to under-estimate reliability [44]. A cut off value of 0.70 was adopted for both measures [45]. The CR together with Cronbach alpha for all constructs showed a value above 0.70. Convergent validity aims to ensure that each indicator of a given construct shares a high proportion of its variance. Indicator reliability was established by checking all cross loadings to be above 0.70 [45] where all indicators fulfilled this criteria. Next, the average variance extracted (AVE) values for each construct were examined. According to [45] any constructs showing an AVE of less than 0.5 are subject to insufficient convergent validity. All AVE values were greater than this threshold and convergent validity is established. Table 1 depicts associated measures.

Discriminant validity is the degree to which a latent variable differentiates from other latent variables. In order to establish discriminant validity we examined the cross loadings to ensure that all indicators have the highest loading on the designed construct and lower loading values on the other constructs. It was seen that the last indicator for TL, 'I have good digital skills' had it highest loading on the CL construct. Consequently this indicator was dropped from subsequent analysis. Additionally the Fornell Larker criterion [46] was applied where the square root of each constructs' AVE value needs to be greater than its correlation with any other construct.

Table 2 below provides the results for square root of AVE on the diagonal together with the correlations among the three constructs as off diagonal elements. It is seen that the discriminant validity requirements are met.

In [39] the Harman Single Factor technique is recommended for assessing common method bias. If the single factor which is introduced in this manner (common latent factor) explains more than 50% of the variance, then common method bias may be present [47]. When this technique was used factor analyses produced a single factor which accounted for 37.64% of the variance in the constructs. Although being simple this method does not statistically control for common method variance. It is also sensitive to the number of variables involved with greater chance for multiple common method factors to exist in larger models [8].

Table 1 CR, Cronbach alpha (α), and AVE values for the constructs

	TL	CL	SEL	MS	GS	SE	SA	ES	LR	O
CR	0.96	0.93	0.964	0.986	0.967	0.983	0.972	0.944	0.961	0.969
α	0.948	0.849	0.924	0.985	0.958	0.981	0.967	0.925	0.948	0.961
AVE	0.827	0.869	0.93	0.838	0.856	0.825	0.814	0.77	0.83	0.838

Table 2 Correlations and square root of AVE for the constructs

	TL	CL	SEL	MS	GS	SE	SA	ES	LR	O
TL	**0.91**									
CL	0.897	**0.932**								
SEL	0.886	0.822	**0.964**							
MS	0.67	0.66	0.633	**0.916**						
GS	0.82	0.752	0.769	0.662	**0.925**					
SE	0.641	0.601	0.556	0.629	0.633	**0.908**				
SA	0.67	0.643	0.672	0.542	0.616	0.56	**0.902**			
ES	0.637	0.645	0.545	0.635	0.667	0.433	0.473	**0.878**		
LR	0.778	0.745	0.703	0.739	0.783	0.765	0.711	0.708	**0.911**	
O	0.731	0.699	0.678	0.721	0.749	0.729	0.699	0.622	0.836	**0.92**

Note Square root of AVE in bold

The examination of full collinearity variance inflation factors (VIFs) is another method that is recommended for identifying common method bias [48]. The average full collinearity VIF (AFVIF) for the measurement model was 4.629, where the acceptable level recommended is less than 5, although it would have been ideal if this value was less than 3.3.

4.2 Structural Model Evaluation and Discussion

Having established the validity and reliability of the measurement model the next step was to evaluate the structural model. The size and significance of the path coefficients examined the hypothesized relationships and the level of influence (*p*-value). The coefficient of determination could be evaluated from the R2 value to measure the predictive accuracy. Effect size was also examined to understand the level of impact from one construct to another.

The two structural models corresponding to the two research models were evaluated using the warp3 PLS regression algorithm, which tries to identify a relationship defined by a function whose first derivative is a U-curve, as found in most natural and behavioural phenomena [49]. After estimating *p*-values with both bootstrapping and jack-knifing resampling techniques, bootstrapping with 100 re-samples was selected as the technique which provided the most stable coefficients.

The analysis results suggested that technical literacy (TL) had significant impacts on all of the sub-processes of SRL as indicated in Table 3. Cognitive literacy (CL) had significant impacts on all of the sub-processes of SRL except Goal Setting (GS). Social emotional literacy (SEL) had significant positive impact on Goal Setting (GS), Seeking Assistance (SA) and Environment Structuring (SA) sub-processes only. Unexpectedly, SEL was seen to have a significant negative

Table 3 Path coefficients, significance levels, total effects, effect sizes and R-squared for DL component effects on SRL sub-processes

Path		MS	GS	SE	SA	ES	LR	O
TL →	ß	0.275***	0.621***	0.450***	0.218***	0.486***	0.557***	0.412***
	effect size	0.187	0.515	0.3	0.147	0.325	0.451	0.309
CL→	ß	0.355***	0.047	0.118*	0.182**	0.324***	0.22***	0.274***
	effect size	0.241	0.036	0.074	0.119	0.212	0.17	0.2
SEL→	ß	0.089***	0.184**	(−0.135)*	0.326***	0.124*	0.063	0.101
	effect size	0.057	0.143	0.082	0.22	0.07	0.046	0.07
	R^2	0.485	0.694	0.292	0.487	0.607	0.667	0.579

Note $*p < 0.05$, $**p < 0.01$, $***p < 0.001$

Table 4 Path coefficients, significance levels, total effects, effect sizes and R-squared for SRL sub-processes effects on DL components

Path		TL	CL	SEL
MS →	ß	0.09	0.116*	0.153*
	effect size	0.061	0.077	0.098
GS→	ß	0.46***	0.35***	0.499***
	effect size	0.382	0.27	0.389
SE→	ß	0.073	0.065	0.023
	effect size	0.049	0.041	0.014
SA→	ß	0.223***	0.215***	0.319***
	effect size	0.16	0.147	0.225
ES→	ß	0.065	0.137*	0.044
	effect size	0.042	0.089	0.025
LR→	ß	0	0.052	−0.009
	effect size	0	0.04	0.007
O→	ß	−0.087	0.027	0.028
	effect size	0.069	0.02	0.02
	R-squared	0.625	0.684	0.764

Note $*p < 0.05$, $**p < 0.01$, $***p < 0.001$

impact on Self Evaluation (SE). The expected variance in each SRL sub-processes due to digital literacy components are shown in the last row of Table 3.

Analysis indicated that most SRL sub-processes did not have a significant positive impact on digital literacy components as shown in Table 4. GS, SA, MS and ES were the four sub-processes which had an impact on CL. SEL was affected significantly positively by GS, SA and MS, while TL appeared to be the least affected by SRL sub-processes, with only GS and SA having a significant positive impact. The expected variance in each DL component due to the sub-processes of SRL are shown in the last row of Table 4.

Our results indicate that possessing the applicable technical and operational skills to employ digital technologies for learning has a statistically significant positive effect on all of the self-regulation sub-processes, supporting our initial hypothesis. While the small p-value (≤ 0.001) indicates strong evidence to support this effect, the effect sizes of TL on SRL processes are within the small to medium range for the sample of undergraduates considered [50]. Further TL has the highest impact on how students set achievable learning goals (GS). The next highest impacts of TL is on taking responsibility for students learning actions and adapting (LR), closely followed by reorganization of their physical and social environment to ensure compatibility of goals (ES). A possible reason might be the prolific use of organizers and schedulers accessible on their mobile phones and other devices integrated on to their PLEs for planning and management of their activities. Further, communication tools such as Skype and messenger partnered with sharing mechanisms for artefacts produced such as Dropbox, enables fast feedback on tasks together with seamless collaboration. Moreover, web based formal an informal social network environments partnered with forums and blogs enable the restructuring of students' social environment to suit their goals.

There is significant evidence that the relationship between TL and GS is reciprocal. Possibly goal setting behaviours change the level of operational digital skills that students acquire and demonstrate and should be investigated further. Another possible indication of a reciprocal relationship is seen between TL and SA. However contrary to our initial hypotheses' each individual subcomponent of SRL does not affect TL.

CL which encompasses critical thinking applied to information and tool usage has the highest statistically significant positive impact on strategies used for remembering and recalling information (MS), again closely followed by its impact on ES. However the effect size is comparatively small.

It is also interesting that GS behaviours, an activity which one would assume needs critical thinking is not statistically affected at all by CL. However GS behaviours have a small yet significant positive impact on CL. This could mean that the manner in which students set achievable goals for themselves, changes the manner in which they select tools to be incorporated on to their PLEs and thereafter interpret information obtained.

There is indication of a possible reciprocal relationship between CL and SA, however the effect sizes in both cases are very small. Again contrary to our initial hypothesis SE, LR and O have no significant impact on CL.

SEL show its highest statistically significant positive impact on strategies used for obtaining assistance from teachers or peers to supplement learning (SA). A possible explanation is that demonstrating responsible behaviour and 'netiquette' when connecting with others over the social tools, such as social networks of ones PLE is important to ensure that assistance can be readily obtained from peers. Indeed this relationship appears to be reciprocal where the amount of help obtained seems to increase the level of responsible and strategic behaviour shown online by students.

While SEL does not have a very large impact on GS, goal setting behaviour does positively affect SEL, again providing indication of reciprocity. Surprisingly SEL shows a small yet significant negative impact on the student's self-evaluation

(SE) strategies. Perhaps this is an indication of the challenges that connection with peers for education via social media bring across, such as lack of privacy and real friendship [51].

5   Conclusion and Outlook

Our research examined two models of the extent to which SRL sub-processes and DL constructs influence each other. Empirical analysis applying PLS-SEM technique confirmed that there are indeed some significant influences of some DL components on some SRL sub-processes and vice versa, while providing indication of a few reciprocal relationships between the constructs examined. Therefore we can add further empirical validity and clarity to the claims that the use of technology impacts SRL skills [52] and show that some SRL skills are instrumental in developing DL skills [53]. Further, our findings shed light on the specific digital literacy skills that undergraduates cultivate by using information systems for construction of PLEs. We also provide an opening for a comprehensive dialogue among researchers interested in understanding the patterns, contexts and consequences of technology adoption for learning and its specific effects on students' self-regulatory behaviours. Further, the measurement model could confirm that the DL and SRL constructs we used have appropriate reliability and validity and could encourage other researchers in incorporating these constructs in their research. Moreover, as we have not considered cultural attributes here, this research is ripe for replication in other cultural settings to determine if the relationships remain constant across different settings.

From a practical perspective our findings have some technological implications given the current interest in encouraging self-regulated learning in the classroom [54]. While there is interest in what teaching and learning practices and behaviors could encourage students to enhance self-regulated learning skills, our findings indicate that the daily interaction with technology itself is having an impact on the university students self-regulated learning skills. Technological interaction has a positive impact on self-regulatory strategies such as goal setting, environment structuring and learning responsibility. A closer examination of the particular affordances of technology which encourages these behaviors could then pave the way for identifying ways to better utilize those affordances. Accurate identification and understanding of the technological affordances for self-regulated learning would provide design guidelines for educational technology which could enhance self-regulated behavior among users.

Next, our exploratory analysis paves the way for further research. A qualitative analysis incorporating the examination of mind maps of actual PLEs constructed by students, combined with face to face interviews could help in explaining and clarifying the above findings. Some of our preliminary findings indicate that using their PLEs, students engage in motivational and behavioral SRL processes as well as metacognitive SRL processes. We have also been able to identify specific affordances that technological tools integrated into a PLE offers students. These preliminary findings have been reported in [55] and further analysis is presently underway.

Moreover, future work should be conducted with a control group of participants who will not be exposed regularly to technological tools via their university courses to eliminate single group threats which are a limitation of this study. Further a confirmatory study is propositioned to test specific hypothesis of the reciprocal relationships indicated in this exploratory study via a non-recursive research model and a larger sample. The effects of moderators such as gender, level of usage of tools, time spent using technology and proficiency levels and mediation effect of attitude towards learning with technology on the relationships between DL an SRL also warrant further investigation.

References

1. Vivian, R., Barnes, A.: Social networking: from living technology to learning technology? Curric. Technol. Transform. Unkn. Future Proc. Ascilite Syd. 1007–1019 (2010)
2. Fruhmann, K., Nussbaumer, A., Albert, D.: A psycho-pedagogical framework for self-regulated learning in a responsive open learning environment. In: Proceedings of the International Conference eLearning Baltics Science (eLBa Science 2010), pp. 1–2. Fraunhofer (2010)
3. Tausend, J.: How students use technology outside of the classroom, EdTech Magazine. http://www.edtechmagazine.com/higher/article/2013/08/how-students-use-technology-outside-classroom. Accessed 04 Aug 2015 (2013)
4. Fiedler, S.H.D., Väljataga, T.: Personal learning environments: concept or technology? Int. J. Virtual Pers. Learn. Environ. 2(4), 1–11 (2011)
5. Tess, P.A.: The role of social media in higher education classes (real and virtual)—a literature review. Comput. Hum. Behav. 29(5), A60–A68 (2013)
6. Pettenati, M.C.: Roadmap to PLE—a research route to empower the use of personal learning environments (PLEs). Interact. Des. Archit. 2010(9–10), 11 (2010)
7. Keppell, M.J.: Personalised learning strategies for higher education. In: The Future of Learning and Teaching in Next Generation Learning Spaces. International Perspectives on Higher Education Research, pp. 3–21. JAI Press, Bingley, WA. United Kingdom (2014)
8. Eichhorn, B.R.: Common Method Variance Techniques. Clevel. State Univ. Dep. Oper. Supply Chain Manag. Clevel. OH SAS Inst. Inc. (2014)
9. Mikroyannidis, A., Connolly, T.: Chapter 02. Introducing Personal Learning Environments to Informal Learners: Lessons Learned from the OpenLearn Case Study|Open Educational Resources, Open Educational Resources and Social Networks. http://oer.kmi.open.ac.uk/?page_id=1254#.VYzLgfmqpBc. Accessed 26 June 2015 (2012)
10. Laakkonen, I., Taalas, P.: Towards new cultures of learning: personal learning environments as a developmental perspective for improving higher education language courses. Lang. Learn. High. Educ. 5(1) (2015)
11. Margaryan, A., Littlejohn, A., Vojt, G.: Are digital natives a myth or reality? University students' use of digital technologies. Comput. Educ. 56(2), 429–440 (2011)
12. Zimmerman, B.J.: Becoming a self-regulated learner: an overview. Theory Pract. 41(2), 64 (2002)

13. Yang, M., Kim, J.: Correlation between digital literacy and self-regulated learning skills of learners in university e-learning environment. Adv. Sci. Technol. Lett. **71** (Education 2014), 80–83 (2014)
14. Greene, J.A., Moos, D.C., Azevedo, R.: Self-regulation of learning with computer-based learning environments. New Dir. Teach. Learn. **2011**(126), 107–115 (2011)
15. Buchem, I.: Editorial for the Special Issue on Personal Learning Environments. Spec. Ed. Pers. Learn. Environ. Curr. Res. Emerg. Pract. **15**(2) (2014)
16. Bembenutty, H.: New directions for self-regulation of learning in postsecondary education. New Dir. Teach. Learn. **2011**(126), 117–124 (2011)
17. Valtonen, T., Hacklin, S., Dillon, P., Vesisenaho, M., Kukkonen, J., Hietanen, A.: Perspectives on personal learning environments held by vocational students. Comput. Educ. **58**(2), 732–739 (2012)
18. Gallego, M.J., Gamiz, V.M.: Personal Learning Environments (PLE) in the academic achievement of university students. Aust. Educ. Comput. **29**(2) (2015)
19. Kravcik, M., Klamma, R.: Supporting self-regulation by personal learning environments. In: Advanced Learning Technologies (ICALT), 2012 IEEE 12th International Conference on, pp. 710–711. IEEE (2012)
20. Dabbagh, N., Kitsantas, A.: Personal learning environments, social media, and self-regulated learning: a natural formula for connecting formal and informal learning. Internet High. Educ. **15**(1), 3–8 (2012)
21. Eshet, Y.: Digital literacy: a conceptual framework for survival skills in the digital era. J. Educ. Multimed. Hypermedia. **13**(1), 93–106 (2004)
22. Bawden, D.: Origins and concepts of digital literacy. In: Digital Literacies: Concepts, Policies and Practices. Peter Lang, New York (2008)
23. Eshet, Y.: Thinking in the digital era: a revised model for digital literacy. Issues Informing Sci. Inf. Technol. **9**(2), 267–276 (2012)
24. Ng, W.: Can we teach digital natives digital literacy? Comput. Educ. **59**(3), 1065–1078 (2012)
25. Zimmerman, B.J.: Chapter 2—attaining self-regulation: a social cognitive perspective. In: Zeidner, M.B.R.P. (ed.) Handbook of Self-Regulation, pp. 13–39. Academic Press, San Diego (2000)
26. Santoso, H.B., Lawanto, O., Becker, K., Fang, N., Reeve, E.M.: High and low computer self-efficacy groups and their learning behavior from self- regulated learning perspective while engaged in interactive learning modules. J. Pre-Coll. Eng. Educ. Res. J-PEER. **4**(2) (2014)
27. Butler, D.L., Cartier, S.C.: Multiple complementary methods for understanding self-regulated learning as situated in context. In: Meetings of the American Educational Research Association (2005)
28. Magno, C.: Assessing academic self-regulated learning among Filipino college students: the factor structure and item fit. Int. J. Educ. Psychol. Assess. **5** (2010)
29. Zimmerman, B.J., Martinez-Pons, M.: Construct validation of a strategy model of student self-regulated learning. J. Educ. Psychol. **80**(3), 284–290 (1988)
30. Paris, S.G., Byrnes, J.P.: The constructivist approach to self-regulation and learning in the classroom. In: Zimmerman, B.J., Schunk, D.H. (eds.) Self-Regulated Learning and Academic Achievement, pp. 169–200. Springer, New York (1989)
31. Azevedo, R.: Understanding the complex nature of self-regulatory processes in learning with computer-based learning environments: an introduction. Metacognition Learn **2**(2–3), 57–65 (2007)
32. Perera Muthupoltotage, U., Gardner, L., Peiris, A.: Investigating the interrelationship between undergraduates' digital literacy and self-regulated learning skills. In: ICIS 2016 Proceedings. Dublin, Ireland (2016)
33. Crano, W.D., Brewer, M.B., Lac, A.: Principles and Methods of Social Research. Routledge (2014)

34. Pintrich, P.R., Smith, D.A.F., Garcia, T., Mckeachie, W.J.: Reliability and predictive validity of the Motivated Strategies for Learning Questionnaire (MSLQ). Educ. Psychol. Meas. **53**(3), 801–813 (1993)

35. Roth, A., Ogrin, S., Schmitz, B.: Assessing self-regulated learning in higher education: a systematic literature review of self-report instruments. Educ. Assess. Eval. Account. 1–26 (2015)

36. Fan, W., Yan, Z.: Factors affecting response rates of the web survey: a systematic review. Comput. Hum. Behav. **26**(2), 132–139 (2010)

37. Handwerk, P.G., Carson, C., Blackwell, K.M.: On-line versus paper-and-pencil surveying of students: a case study. In: 40th Annual Meeting of the Association of Institutional Research (2000)

38. Krosnick, J.A., Presser, S.: Question and questionnaire design. Handb. Surv. Res. **2**, 263–314 (2010)

39. Podsakoff, P.M., MacKenzie, S.B., Lee, J.-Y., Podsakoff, N.P.: Common method biases in behavioral research: a critical review of the literature and recommended remedies. J. Appl. Psychol. **88**(5), 879–903 (2003)

40. Gefen, D., Straub, D., Boudreau, M.-C.: Structural equation modeling and regression: guidelines for research practice. Commun. Assoc. Inf. Syst. **4**(1), 7 (2000)

41. Chin, W.W., Marcolin, B.L., Newsted, P.R.: A partial least squares latent variable modeling approach for measuring interaction effects: Results from a Monte Carlo simulation study and an electronic-mail emotion/adoption study. Inf. Syst. Res. **14**(2), 189–217 (2003)

42. Chin, W.W.: How to write up and report PLS analyses. In: Vinzi, V.E., Chin, W.W., Henseler, J., Wang, H. (eds.) Handbook of Partial Least Squares, pp. 655–690. Springer, Berlin Heidelberg (2010)

43. Kock, N.: Using warpPLS in e-collaboration studies: an overview of five main analysis steps. Int. J. E-Collab. IJeC. **6**(4), 1–11 (2010)

44. Hair, J.F.J.H., Hult, G.T.M., Ringle, C.M., Sarstedt, M.: A Primer on Partial Least Squares Structural Equation Modeling. SAGE Publications, Inc. (2016)

45. Babin, B.J., Anderson, R.E.: Multivariate Data Analysis. Prentice Hall, Upper Saddle River, NJ (2009)

46. Fornell, C., Larcker, D.F.: Evaluating structural equation models with unobservable variables and measurement error. J. Mark. Res. **18**(1), 39–50 (1981)

47. Podsakoff, P.M., Organ, D.W.: Self-reports in organizational research: problems and prospects. J. Manag. **12**(4), 531–544 (1986)

48. Kock, N., Lynn, G.: Lateral collinearity and misleading results in variance-based SEM: an illustration and recommendations. J. Assoc. Inf. Syst. **13**(7) (2012)

49. Kock, N.: Using warpPLS in e-collaboration studies: descriptive statistics, settings, and key analysis results. Int. J. E-Collab. IJeC. **7**(2), 1–18 (2011)

50. Sawilowsky, S.: New effect size rules of thumb. J. Mod. Appl. Stat. Methods. **8**(2) (2009)

51. Zaidieh, A.J.Y.: The use of social networking in education: challenges and opportunities. World Comput. Sci. Inf. Technol. J. WCSIT. **2**(1), 18–21 (2012)

52. Greene, J.A., Yu, S.B., Copeland, D.Z.: Measuring critical components of digital literacy and their relationships with learning. Comput. Educ. **76**, 55–69 (2014)

53. Shopova, T.: Digital literacy of students and its improvement at the university. J. Effic. Responsib. Educ. Sci. **7**(2), 26–32 (2014)

54. Zumbrunn, S., Tadlock, J., Roberts, E.D.: Encouraging self-regulated learning in the classroom: a review of the literature. Metrop. Educ. Res. Consort. MERC. 1–28 (2011)

55. Perera Muthupoltotage, U., Gardner, L.: Undergraduates Perception of Informal Personal Learning Environments: Affordances for Self-regulated Learning. Presented at the 28th Australasian Conference on Information Systems. Hobart, Tasmania (in press)

Application of RFID Technology to Reduce Overcrowding in Hospital Emergency Departments

Rajip Raj Thapa, Moshiur Bhuiyan, Aneesh Krishna and P. W. C. Prasad

Abstract Australian hospital Emergency Departments (ED) are experiencing challenges due to overcrowding despite the government's regular initiative of improved model of care. Australian Triage model of care within ED has not been able to prove reflective for ramification of the issues associated with overcrowding. This paper explores the opportunity for the use of Radio Frequency Identification (RFID) technology in hospital ED to reduce overcrowding. The Australian ED model of care with Triage scale and improved patient journey were studied. The best possible RFID integration was sought and evaluated against health care domain's model of care. Potential indicators of suitability were ED length of stay, ED wait times. Ambulance diversions were studied and contrasted from the start of the patient journey to the end of the patient's treatment cycle, to find opportunities for the implementation of RFID technology. Based on the results of the study, it is recommended that RFID implementation be tested in actual scenarios to realise the potential benefits.

A prior version of this paper has been published in the ISD2017 Proceedings (http://aisel.aisnet.org/isd2014/proceedings2017).

R. R. Thapa · P. W. C. Prasad
School of Computing and Mathematics, Charles Sturt University,
Sydney, NSW 2010, Australia
e-mail: rajiprajthapa@gmail.com

P. W. C. Prasad
e-mail: cwithana@studygroup.com

M. Bhuiyan
Service Consulting, Enterprise Cloud Systems, Sydney, NSW 2560, Australia
e-mail: moshiurb@ecloudsys.com

A. Krishna (✉)
Department of Computing, Curtin University, Bentley, WA 6120, Australia
e-mail: a.krishna@curtin.edu.au

© Springer International Publishing AG, part of Springer Nature 2018
N. Paspallis et al. (eds.), *Advances in Information Systems Development*,
Lecture Notes in Information Systems and Organisation 26,
https://doi.org/10.1007/978-3-319-74817-7_2

Keywords Radio frequency identification (RFID) · Healthcare
Emergency departments (ED) · Length of stay · Patient waiting times
Hospital information system (HIS)

1 Introduction

RFID (Radio Frequency Identification) technology has been widely used in the
Healthcare sector for better, more reliable and secure quality services. RFID systems have been integrated into hospital information systems and are being used for
full automation of patient identification, staff allocation, patient's medication and
patient management. RFID's generated information has been illustrated for its
potential applications in healthcare environment.

Emergency Department (ED) is the first point of contact for critical patient care.
The flow of patient is very high and each patient has their own vital needs for
getting emergency treatment. Organisational flow and workforce empowerment in
emergency department is very limited. Service being delivered to patient is not
sufficient and efficient. The scheduling of ED care is always interrupted and
changes when the patients are sent in continuous manner. When huge number of
patients are present, it's very cumbersome to manage the staff and supplies in ED.

The main objective of Healthcare organizations' is to deliver top quality patient
treatments and, whenever possible, cures. Delivering fast and effective quality
medical services are a top priority for Emergency Departments (EDs), with issues of
speed and efficiency foremost on the agenda. Overcrowding in EDs is common and
the need to treat patients under such conditions may lead to medical errors. A study
into overcrowding conducted at emergency departments showed that the patient
waiting time was too long and only limited numbers of patients were seen within
the time frame of ATS scale. In the Australian context, ED overcrowding in Sydney
has resulted in ambulance diversions to different hospitals [1]. It is clear these issues
need to be resolved. Even though the Australian Government has implemented the
Australasian model of care which brought about an improved patient journey to
Emergency Departments, overcrowding is still the biggest challenge faced by
Australian hospitals and patient waiting times are unacceptably high [2]. An
improved Australasian triage scale with RFID infusion and an improved patient
journey model is the expected outcome of this project.

The organization of this paper is as follows: Sect. 2 discusses the literature
review and the motivation for the proposal. An existing solution to issues in ED
along with proposed model is discussed in Sect. 3. Section 4 deals with the evaluation of the proposed framework, Sect. 5 explores the evaluation of the proposed
model in more depth, Sect. 6 discusses the limitations and finally, Sect. 7 provides
concluding remarks and some recommendations for future implementation of RFID
technology in the area.

2   Background

EDs are the primary point for unplanned admissions into hospitals. The number of patients admitted to EDs in Australia has increased substantially. During a study from 2012–2013 conducted by the Australian Institute of Health and Welfare there were over 6.7 million patient admissions to public EDs with the number increasing again to 7.4 million by 2014. Increasing numbers of presentation to the ED have resulted in overcrowding which has been raising issues to deliberate quality patient care [3]. Findings have suggested the detrimental outcomes of ED crowding such as an increased length of stay [4], increased patient waiting times [5] and increased ambulance diversions which then lead to increased mortality and decreased patient quality care [6].

In 2009, the Australian Government had introduced the National Emergency Access Targets (NEAT) to enhance the drive for the service model of care. The Australian Triage Scale (ATS) was then employed to decrease the patient waiting times in EDs. ATS is based on a numbering system for patient classification which considers the level of complexity of the health condition affecting the patient when they arrive at the ED [7].

As it can be seen in the study, to improve healthcare related operations, surgical operations or emergency care services, it is important to realize the entirety of the patient's treatment cycle in hospital. A patient's treatment cycle consists of six stages as follows: [8]

Admission: At the time when patients are admitted, information is recorded with a unique ID number.

Examination: Once the patient is formally admitted, the patient is taken to the department handling diagnostics and treatment facilities. RFID technology is used to identify the right treatment for the right patient. RFID is applied to address many potential errors including contraindicated medications, this is because its database can be utilized to track the patient's medications and to raise a red flag when there is a problem. The right medication is then matched to the right patient by identifying the patient's unique ID [9].

Patient care: During the patient care stage and further critical assessments, all relevant information is recorded and examined.

Recovery: After treatment, patients are managed during recovery.

Discharge: After it has been determined that the hospital care is complete, the patient is issued post-hospital care instructions.

Billing: Billing information is processed and the statements are sent to the relevant parties.

Each piece of information is crucial and needs careful monitoring. RFID usage can be applied at each level of the patient's treatment. If embedded within the Hospital Information System, it provides huge benefits for time management and, therefore, for the patients [10]. Overcrowding and its associated issues in an ED have been highlighted since late 1980s. This is because the lengthier patient overcrowding in an ED has the potential to halt the quality care and adequate service. EDs with such critical issues are more prone to medical errors, posing a threat to patients' safety. Technological innovations such as RFID tagging of patients has the potential to solve many of the issues raised here [11].

Australia has been using the Fast Track Service Delivery Model which allocates patients into different streams to provide them with the commenced care rather than having them waiting for care. This subdivision of care is to decrease the full load in ED and to partition the level of patient care, achieving higher efficiency. Patient's extended stay and bed occupancy are, thus, solved and this system provides a solution to the issue of patient overcrowding. Adopting the Fast Track Service Delivery Model and classifying the patients during triage has resulted in significant improvements but the ED still has a high load of patients. This strategy can be extrapolated through a technological adaptation and this is where RFID comes in handy [3]. To rectify the solution, every element of the ED needs to be accessed for a logical system analysis and design. Emergency staff, emergency medical supplies, emergency system design and advanced level of framework are required to be surveyed for a precise understanding of what is happening in the ED.

Service delivery improvement suggestions with other sectors in government could be applied to the health domain [12–14]. Grace HO has mentioned the Australian healthcare challenges in terms of its screening of technology. Royal Melbourne Hospital, for example, is using handheld computers and an hTrak application in its operating theatres, cardiology and radiology departments. This system allows medical equipment such as surgical devices like scalpels, scissors to be tracked and traced during surgery. It also provides a system for item-level billing to patients. Another example is Queensland's Redcliffe Hospital which has implemented a kiosk-based automated arrival system. These systems have been shown to increase the data accuracy and to reduce human error. The system allows patients to, among other things, scan the bar-coded appointment letter, which they would have received in the mail, at a kiosk to register their arrival at the hospital. The kiosk will then show the patient where their specific clinic's waiting room is, allowing admin and clinical staff at the hospital to have fewer manual processes to complete, thereby improving the equality and timeliness of the service. These leading examples confirm that the way the patient data can be accessed can significantly increase the workflow efficiency and minimize chances of medical errors [15].

RFID systems have already been implemented in many hospitals globally specially to track patients' movements throughout different hospital services. Medical staff are often given RFID tags on their badges for collecting workflow data so that inefficiencies in current hospital operations can be traced. The key feature of RFID tagging is, to minimise adverse drug events, which is the general public's health concern. Steer et al. [16], conducted an interesting study using RFID that introduced a novel method of monitoring offload time and identifying variance within emergency departments. The authors recognized the fact that emergency services crews often wait for ED beds to become available to offload their patients. However, there is no national benchmark for emergency medical services turn-around or offload times, or method for objectively and reliably measuring these issues [16]. Our paper proposes the use of RFID in reducing the overcrowding within the emergency medical services. Lai et al. [17] discussed patients' medication administration system and highlighted the importance of the re-engineering of this process with the RFID integration [17]. Their study provides some insight into the integration of RFID in the existing hospital system to improve hospital management and medication safety. The tagging functionality of RFID can assist health professionals to prescribe and handle medication, thus helping to prevent deaths caused by the adverse reactions of the drugs prescribed. The benefits of RFID tagging have been known for long but it is now able to extend its benefits to EDs where overcrowding is the challenge. As Australian population is ageing, the need for care is increasing. Emergency crowding is one of the biggest challenge Australian Hospitals are currently facing [18].

One way to meet the demands of emergency care is the optimization of EDs and hospital bed capacity. The recent 'National Health Reform Agreement on improving Public Hospital Services' has included a measure to improve this. The National Emergency Access Target (NEAT) is aimed to improve access to emergency care via reducing access block and its associated negative outcomes. This requires that once a patient has arrived at the ED, the patient's admission, referral to treatment in an inpatient unit or discharge should all happen within four hours. Effective patient discharge and ward transfer mechanisms can facilitate the timely transit of the emergency patient into a hospital bed also improving the time to inpatient acceptance for ED patients. In NSW, the target is not being achieved. ED overcrowding has been increasing for over 20 years [19]. Evidence from initiatives to address overcrowding have suggested that there is a need for system change practices and for a better use of resources to maintain the quality of care delivered. Some areas for improvement include:

- ED front processes, which involve patient arrival and triage, registration, bed or clinical area placement, review by nurse and medical assessment, are not being streamlined. This results in lengthy waiting times between each of these processes.
- The patient is assessed by a senior medical officer only after spending considerable time with junior medical staff or other clinical providers, thus leading to delays in decision making and in treatment implementation.
- Another scenario is the frequent bed block within ED due to a failure in the identification of the patient's subsequent needs.
- Lack of differentiation of patients in ED waiting room.
- Delay in review and acceptance of emergency admissions by the inpatient team due to factors such as competing work demands and lower prioritisation of new admissions.
- Lack of available beds in hospital resulting in access block, overcrowding and no treatment bed spaces available in the ED.
- Hospital back end processes are not streamlined which is resulting in delayed discharge and the least sick patients are occupying the designated inpatient beds while new emergency admitted patients queue in the ED awaiting an inpatient bed.

Table 1 Australasian triage scale

ATS category	Treatment acuity maximum waiting time	Performance indicator threshold (%)
ATS 1	Immediate	100
ATS 2	10 min	80
ATS 3	30 min	75
ATS 4	60 min	70
ATS 5	120 min	70

Emergency models of care in New South Wales (NSW)

A Models of Emergency Care (MOC) document was created in 2006 as part of the clinical services redesign program for NSW health. The model of care document was aimed at assisting the EDs and hospitals in providing the ideal patient journey as developed by the NSW Health Emergency Care Taskforce. These models of care summarized the set of possible ED processes and included experiences from NSW EDs, other jurisdictions and published literature. In 2014–2015, 7.4 million patients presented themselves to 290 Australian Public Hospital emergency departments as reported to National Non-Admitted Patient Emergency Department Care Database (NNAPEDCD). This result corresponds to over 20,000 presentations each day [20].

Use of Australasian Triage Scale (ATS)

ATS is a five-point scale used for prioritizing patients at Emergency departments in NSW. Triage is defined as the process of categorizing Emergency Department patients as per their need for medical care and assessment. It involves prioritization of the assessment of ED patients who need immediate care as per their clinical severity and urgency compared with patients with less urgent illness who can wait longer to be seen, or those who need a referral to a more appropriate healthcare setting. ATS triage scale is represented in Table 1.

3 RFID Integration in the Emergency Department Patient Flow Model (Proposed Model)

RFID technology is used from the start of the patient's journey to the ED as shown in Fig. 1, first to be implemented in the ambulance arrival modes. The paramedics in the ambulance will first assess the patient and monitor the severity of their health condition.

The patient is then tagged with RFID, meaning information is fed for a patient's classification. Categorization of the patient as per the Australasian Triage scale is then carried out and the information is exchanged between the communication

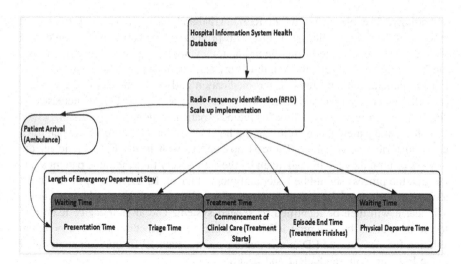

Fig. 1 Patient flow progress with feasibility of RFID implementation

channels to nearby hospital EDs for clinical intervention. All data, from the type of emergency severity to an assessment of the level of care needed, is recorded in the RFID information system. The database is updated with the patient's conditions and the required special care. If the emergency department in the nearest hospital has the specialized care to meet the patient's needs, the information is communicated to the ambulance team about the availability of the requested care. This eliminates the screening of nearby hospitals and the emergency patient is taken only to hospitals that have the required specialized care. One of the main problems that Australian hospitals have been facing—Ambulance Diversion from hospitals—is solved, leading to better patient care. For example, cardiac arrest patients are directly taken to hospitals having specialized cardiac care emergency departments.

Australian triaging classification is now carried out in the ambulance by the ambulance team when inputting the patient's information into RFID. This will increase the efficiency in the already adopted model of care in NSW. Currently, triage takes place in hospitals when the patient arrives at ED. This arduous task, which is often a burden to the already overworked triage nurses at the hospital, will now be delegated to the ambulance unit. With the help of RFID, the triage step is now faster. Now when the patients arrive at ED, their treatment with clinical experts can start immediately.

Through all the different stages of the patient's treatment cycle in hospital from admission to discharge, RFID needs to be scanned and read. Additional information is being added every time the patient moves along phases within the hospital during the treatment phase. The right medication and the right treatment for the right patient can all be ensured, being the key to reducing hospital generated mistakes. Patient movement is traced and all parameters should be justified. Staff overload and a chaotic intake in ED is reduced to a minimum through adopting RFID technology. The placement of an RFID wristband on each patient provides an efficient feature for resolution of the main problems EDs currently encounter. As the patient is being tagged from the moment they are first in an emergency through the whole treatment cycle, the length of stay and bed occupancy are easy to check. For the patient, that ensures that the medication and treatment required are being provided in an accurate and more timely manner; as for the ED, it increases its ability to estimate its availability for the next patient waiting for treatment.

If the same patient needs to revisit the hospital ED in the future, RFID can trace every historical detail again. There is no need to wait in the ED to redo all the process or until they are triaged again by the staff. Every time the same patient visits the ED, the process should be faster and more efficient. RFID can also be deployed as an alarm triggered for patient falling to disease or general poor health conditions. The alarm will then be identified by related systems and an ambulance team will locate the patient by scanning RFID signaling. Every process leads to a potential solution for the issues of ED overcrowding and mishaps. RFID implementation will make ED stages more efficient and faster.

The quality of patient progression through the ED has a significant role in predicting a patient's treatment cycle. An analysis of the patients' waiting times and length of stay helps to answer queries about why patient overcrowding has been a prevailing factor in Australia. RFID implementation throughout the whole treatment cycle provides the technological innovation to counter the problems of long waiting times and overcrowding. The Australasian Triage classification system, adopted by the Australian government, is the only method that has addressed the issue of patient overcrowding to date which is shown by Fig. 2. The Australian model of care has proven to be successful in delivering the right solution but RFID integration for data information and exchange along with the already present Australasian Triage scaling is the best way to avoid overcrowding and lengthy waiting times. Clinical teams can assess patients as soon as they arrive at the emergency care. All information is exchanged via the RFID and its tracking application is used throughout the patient's treatment process. Proposed RFID model can be seen from Fig. 3 in better details.

RFID system deployment from different perspectives of users is reflected by the use case diagram analysis in Fig. 4.

Process Description:

- Patient have RFID accessories
- Wrist bands with RFID tags for monitoring or tracking the patient's health condition
- Update of the health record or report in emergency department at hospital
- Emergency department staffs will prepare themselves for examination of the patient. It will be easy to manage the medical doctors and other allied health professionals
- Medication, emergency surgeries, waiting times, length of stay will be easily handled

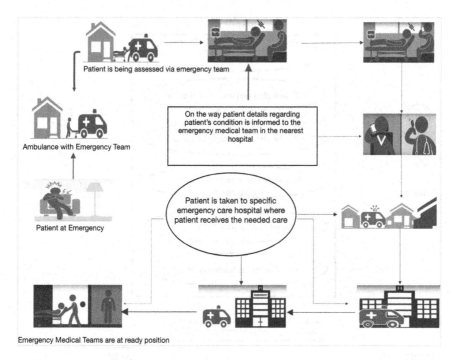

Fig. 2 Patient journey to hospital current practice

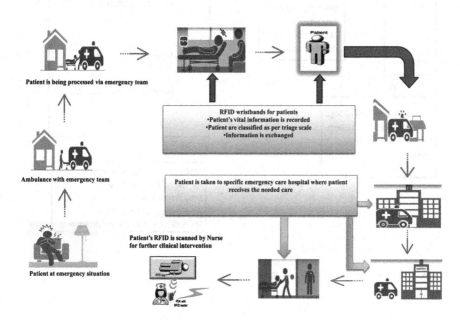

Fig. 3 Proposed RFID implementation in patient journey

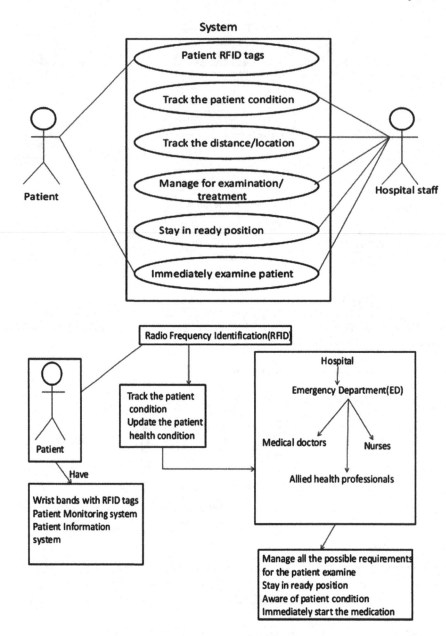

Fig. 4 Use case diagram of RFID integration in Emergency Departments

- Hospital staff at the emergency department will be in a ready position before the patient arrival which not only will improve the patient care with right treatment but also provides a system relay station pool for efficient workflow ultimately resulting in patient waiting times reduction.

Qualitative benefit analysis about the implementation of RFID in emergency department results in waiting times: Before and after the application of RFID in Emergency care.

Process	Before	After
Pre-hospital	Emergency ward is unaware of: What's the number of patient that will be sent on the way? At what time they will be arriving? What kind of injuries the patients are having? It's very hard to deploy the medical resources and staff including the specialist physicians from different departments	Emergency medical technician in ambulance has enough time to get along with the patients on the way to hospital. Medical technician can input the basic information like patient ID, elementary triage and injuries types into RFID wrist loop. At the same time, information will be transferred to Emergency Room (ER) by wireless communication. Data receiver will take the information and series of activities are planned at ER
Emergency room	It is hard to analyse and compare many patients in crowded chaotic emergency, which requires the physician to ask patient basic information again Hospital will be required to upload the information about patient's status and empty bed at the same time. This will add the pressure and confusion in the ER which can lead to mishaps	RFID deployment can support the ER manager by real-time control. Medical staff will have a proper flexible environment for making right decisions and care. Chaotic working pressure and patient waiting times are well balanced leading to good quality care

4 RFID Efficiency Indicators

For the successful implementation of the RFID technology implementation in EDs, it is mandatory to have a comprehensive analysis with solution being offered. Justification of the RFID technology adoption from the perspective of ED, a coherent study is needed with clinical outcomes. ED overcrowding is the result of complex interwoven processes comprising various critical stages and system functionalities. Understanding the systematic process of the patient journey and the treatment lifecycle of patients in ED is crucial for developing and understanding the RFID implementation. The effects of ED overcrowding are numerous and negatively impact treatment. Fine tuning the ED system flaws using opportunities for increasing efficiency outcomes with RFID technology is desirable for theory and practice.

Evaluations of the critical parameters need to be carried out in order to bind together elements of problems in emergency and to establish the scope of the study. Work efficiency with characterization of work load, human empowerment, patient waiting times and length of stay are the key elements for evaluation of the model for RFID implementation in EDs.

Going beyond the scope of the traditional research application, RFID wristbands for patients can lead to waiting times reduction making patient management more sustainable. Here, this paper is presents justification of the implementation model based on expected outcomes in conjunction with the current NSW health government strategy. The practical implementation of the proposed RFID model is not possible during this paper preparation. Furthermore, RFID has only been implemented as a tracking technology in health care; it has not been studied for resolution of patient overcrowding at EDs. This paper henceforth only justifies the proposed model based on outcomes expected as the result of RFID implementation in EDs and comparing it with NSW health government report on ED overcrowding model. Selection of the parameters for justifying the proposed model defines the sustainability and scope of the implementation work. Patient wait times, length of ED stay, patient presentation, and patient classification during triage are considered and selected for proving the strength of the proposed RFID framework. Efficacy and results of the proposed framework will be analyzed based upon these critical parameters.

Australian Emergency Department data are accessed and studied for the identification of a coherent solution.

From the Australian hospital statistics (2014–2015) as shown in Table 2, 11.4% presentation were presented at emergency department and 35% at urgent triage category. From the perspective of study, it is vital to understand how many patient presentations do receive patient care.

Also, from the number of patients who have visited the hospital for emergency care and assessment as shown in Table 3, only 6% of cases receive treatment within less than 1 h and 38% of the populations are required to wait 4 h or more which is the key factor in Emergency Department patient waiting times and overcrowding.

It is expected that with RFID implementation as a potential solution, more number of patients presenting will be seen within 1 h. If more patients are being

Table 2 Emergency Department visit AIHW data based on Triage category 2014–2015

Triage category	Type of visit (%)
Of the 7.4 million emergency department presentation	Resuscitation = 0.7
	Emergency = 11.4
	Urgent = 35.0
	Semi-urgent = 42.5
	Non-urgent = 10.3

Table 3 AIHW treatment time statistics

Treatment time	Number of presentations	Proportion of presentations percentage (%)
Less than 1 h	32,555	6
1 h to <2 h	79,046	16
2 h to <3 h	102,556	20
3 h to <4 h	98,178	19
4 h or more	191,571	38
Total	506,965	100

Table 4 Emergency Department patient visit as per triage category and arrival mode

Triage category and arrival mode	Total	Total percentage (%)
Resuscitation • Ambulance total = 49,035	41,216	84
Emergency • Ambulance total = 843,443	384,137	45
Urgent • Ambulance total = 2,578,398	872,058	33
Semi-urgent • Ambulance total = 3,130,356	467,807	15

seen within fewer hours, then more patients can be treated and this will reduce patient waiting times. The result after RFID implementation should reflect this approach with presenting emphasis on more number of patients should be seen in reduced wait time.

RFID Implementation for Ambulance Service

RFID implementation in ambulances as proposed in the study is justified by the data shown by the Australian Hospital Statistics based on patient arrival modes in Hospitals as shown in Table 4. Patient's first point of contact in an emergency is the emergency team ready for the transportation from the point of casualty to a point of care. Patients are taken to EDs by ambulance. RFID implementation in ambulances to facilitate patient information and tracking in the proposed RFID framework leads to efficient patient management.

Patient Wait Time

The time from the point of patient presentation in ED to the commencement of treatment is the wait time [21]. Australian Institute of Health and Welfare (AIHW) have presented the patient waiting times as per

- The proportion of presentations seen on time
- The 50th percentile waiting time (median waiting time where 50% of presentation has commenced clinical care)
- The 90th percentile waiting time (where 90% of presentation has commenced clinical care).

Integration of RFID technology at the ED should decrease the waiting time and increase the number of patient seen quicker, so that more patients can be seen on time through this increase in workflow efficiency. Medical teams will be spared time which can be utilized for seeing a higher number of patients. Staff pressure is reduced as teams are well acquainted with the emergency scenario.

Time of Stay
Patient stay time in emergency department is the overall time spent in an ED from admission to discharge.

AIHW, 2015 has categorized stay time calculation as:

- Presentation ending in admission
- Presentation not ending in admission
- All presentation.

RFID integration in Emergency Department potentially decrease the time of stay.

5 Limitations

RFID technology has been previously used in EDs for the reduction of over-crowding and patient waiting times. It has always been used as the traditional technology to track patients and medications. While some research has pointed to RFID usage in EDs for surgical equipment tracking, it has not been studied for the measures of overcrowding and patient waiting times in EDs. This research has conducted an in-depth review of studies and system designs that have key agenda of RFID implementation at EDs. The Australian population is ageing and there is a tremendous increase in emergency department presentations at the hospitals. Patient overcrowding and patient waiting times are still the most pressing unresolved problem faced by the NSW government. An RFID design framework has been presented here along with the rationale for an Australasian Triage scale but have not been practiced yet. More research on practical implementation is needed to justify the real applicability of the RFID based proposal as suggested in this paper. This paper provides motivation for future research on RFID and its usage in EDs in Australian Hospitals. The outcome mentioned are "expected outcome", our future work will address this expectation by either introducing a pilot implementation and a value stream mapping exercise in an emergency department setting.

6 Conclusion

This paper has identified major opportunities for RFID technology usage in Emergency Departments. The primary focus was on the successful implementation of RFID in EDs at Australian hospitals to address issues relating to patient over-crowding, patient waiting times, medication errors and patient monitoring system. Literature surveyed has indicated that there is an opportunity to integrate RFID in EDs. The review has presented an overview of the scenarios and complications found in EDs. To predict the usability of RFID technology at Australian hospitals primarily focused on New South Wales (NSW), cases and model of care that has already been implemented by the NSW government in practice were studied and a logical approach for RFID technology integration was developed based on facts and research.

This paper has summarized key facts and components from current and proposed RFID integration at the Emergency Departments in NSW. RFID possibility of integration at Emergency department in NSW is based on the dynamic functionality of the technology and its potential for application. The current NSW emergency care model was studied and its potential for RFID adoption was fully explored. The ED study showed the need for RFID technology which is also justified by different research studies into RFID integration in healthcare. In terms of challenges to its adoption, several studies have suggested pathways for successful deployment of RFID in EDs. RFID, currently used only as a traditional tool for tracking has a wide range of applicability in EDs and this paper is a first step towards future analysis and research. Future work needs to include practical implementation and consideration of different approaches for RFID application in EDs in Australian Hospitals. Bed blocks have been the raising issues in current scenario of Australia which have led many patients stranded at hospitals waiting to get admitted. RFID technology has the potential vibe to embrace the challenges faced by EDs.

References

1. Derlet, R.W., Richards, R.J.: Overcrowding in the nation's emergency departments: complex causes and disturbing effects. Ann. Emerg. Med. **35**(1), 63–68 (2000)
2. Robinson, C., Verrall, C., Houghton, L., Zeitz, K.: Understanding the patient journey to the emergency department—a South Australian study. Australas. Emerg. Nurs. J. **18**(5), 75–82 (2015)
3. Australian Institute of Health and Welfare, A.I.O.H.A. (Ed.), Australian Hospital Statistics 2013–14: Emergency Department Care. Health Services Series no. 58. Cat. no. HSE 153. AIHW, Canberra (2014)
4. Travers, J.P., Lee, F.C.: Avoiding prolonged waiting time during busy periods in the emergency department: is there a role for the senior emergency physician in triage? Eur. J. Emerg. Med. **13**, 342–348 (2006)

5. Terris, J., Leman, P., O'connor, N., Wood, R.: Making an IMPACT on emergency department flow: improving patient processing assisted by consultant at triage. Emerg. Med. J. **21**, 537–541 (2004)
6. Elder, E., Johnston, A.N.B., Crilly, J.: Improving emergency department throughput: an outcomes evaluation of two additional models of care. Int. Emerg. Nurs. **25**(3), 19–26 (2016)
7. Hodge, A., Hugman, A., Varndell, W., Howes, K.: A review of the quality assurance processes for the Australasian Triage Scale (ATS) and implications for future practice. Australas. Emerg. Nurs. J. **16**, 21–29 (2013)
8. Cangialosi, A., Monaly, J.J.E., Yang, S.C.: Leveraging RFID in hospitals: patient life cycle and mobility perspectives. IEEE Commun. Mag. **45**, 18–23 (2007)
9. Hu, L., Ong, D.M., Zhu, X., Liu, Q., Song, E.: Enabling RFID technology for healthcare: application, architecture, and challenges. Telecommun. Syst. **58**, 259–271 (2015)
10. Kuo, F., Fu, C.J., Liu, L., Jin, M.H.: The implement of RFID in emergency medicine. In 2007 9th International Conference on e-Health Networking, Application and Services, pp. 125–130 (2007)
11. Arkun, A., Briggs, W.M., Patel, S., Datillo, P.A., Bove, J., Birkhahn, R.H.: Emergency department crowding: factors influencing flow. W. J. Emerg. Med. **11** (2010)
12. Fortuito, A.M., Haque, F., Shabnam, L., Bhuiyan, M., Krishna, A., Withana, C.: Enhancing public service delivery through organisational modeling. CoRR abs/1606.03548 (2016)
13. Wijesinghe, N., Bhuiyan, M., Prasad, P.W.C.: Service delivery innovation in judicial domain context. JSW **12**(2), 101–113 (2017)
14. Fortuito, A.M., Haque, F., Shabnam, L., Bhuiyan, M., Krishna, A., Withana, C.: Citizen's charter driven service area improvement. APSEC, 401–408 (2015)
15. Ho, G.: Can technology help overcome Australia's healthcare challenges? Australian Broadcasting Corporation (ABC)—technology and games. Available: http://www.abc.net.au/technology/articles/2012/04/27/3490209.htm (27 April 2012, 20 August)
16. Steer, S., Bhalla, M.C., Zalewski, J., Frey, J., Nguyen, V., Mencl, F.: Use of radio frequency identification to establish emergency medical service offload times. Prehospital Emerg. Care **20**(2), 254–259 (2016)
17. Lai, C.-L., Chien, S.-W., Chen, S.-C., Fang, K.: Enhancing medication safety and reduce adverse drug events on inpatient medication administration using RFID. WSEAS Trans. Commun. **7**, 1045–1054 (2008)
18. Health, Q.: Fast track service delivery model. Improving our hospital services in Queensland. https://www.health.qld.gov.au/improvement/improving-services/sdm-fast-track.asp (2013, December)
19. Forero, R., Hillman, K.M., McCarthy, S., Fatovich, D.M., Joseph, A.P., Richardson, D.B.: Access block and ED overcrowding. Emerg. Med. Australas. **22**, 119–135 (2010)
20. A. I. O. H. A. Welfare: emergency department care 2014–15. Available: http://www.aihw.gov.au/hospitals-data/national-non-admitted-patient-emergency-department-care/ (2015, 21 August)
21. Hing, E., Bhuiya, F.A.: Wait Time for Treatment in Hospital Emergency Departments, 2009. Citeseer (2012)

Assessing the Performance of Automated Model Extraction Rules

Jorge Echeverría, Francisca Pérez, Óscar Pastor and Carlos Cetina

Abstract Automated Model Extraction Rules take as input requirements (in natural language) to generate domain models. Despite the existing work on these rules, there is a lack of evaluations in industrial settings. To address this gap, we conduct an evaluation in an industrial context, reporting the extraction rules that are triggered to create a model from requirements and their frequency. We also assess the performance in terms of recall, precision and F-measure of the generated model compared to the models created by domain experts of our industrial partner. Results enable us to identify new research directions to push forward automated model extraction rules: the inclusion of new knowledge sources as input for the extraction rules, and the development of specific experiments to evaluate the understanding of the generated models.

Keywords Conceptual models · Natural language requirements
Model extraction

A prior version of this paper has been published in the ISD2017 Proceedings (http://aisel.aisnet.org/isd2014/proceedings2017).

J. Echeverría (✉) · F. Pérez · C. Cetina
Universidad San Jorge, Zaragoza, Spain
e-mail: jecheverria@usj.es

F. Pérez
e-mail: mfperez@usj.es

C. Cetina
e-mail: ccetina@usj.es

Ó. Pastor
Universitat Politècnica de València, Valencia, Spain
e-mail: opastor@pros.upv.es

© Springer International Publishing AG, part of Springer Nature 2018   33
N. Paspallis et al. (eds.), *Advances in Information Systems Development*,
Lecture Notes in Information Systems and Organisation 26,
https://doi.org/10.1007/978-3-319-74817-7_3

1 Introduction

Software requirements specifications are prevalently expressed using Natural Language (NL) [1]. The transition from requirements expressed in NL to a domain model is an important step to obtain a precise and analyzable specification [2]. Automated model extraction from NL requirements has been studied for a long time, with a large body of literature already existing in the area such as [3–8].

Automated model extraction applies model extraction rules. Nevertheless, crucial aspects about the existing Automated Model Extraction Rules (AMER) remain under-explored such as the AMER that are triggered to build a domain model, and the differences between the model generated by applying the AMER and the models generated by domain experts for a given NL requirements specification. These differences can be accentuated in many industrial situations [9].

However, the large majority of existing work on model extraction is evaluated over exemplars and in artificial settings. Evaluations on model extraction in real settings remain scarce. This work, which is conducted in an industrial context, takes a step towards addressing this gap by assessing the performance of the AMER. This allows us to evaluate whether the result obtained from the AMER is closer to the results obtained from the domain experts.

In this work, we design a process made up of four steps in order to compare the model generated according to the AMER with the models generated by the domain experts of our industrial partner, which is a worldwide provider of railway solutions. First of all, a model is generated from a requirements specification using AMER. In the second step each one the domain experts of our industrial partner generated a model from a requirements specification. Next, in the third step, some Natural Language Processing (NLP) techniques are applied to homogenize the words used in all models. Finally, we obtain as results both a report with the occurrences of each AMER triggered by the requirements, and a report with the performance measurement in terms of precision, recall and F-measure values.

Our results show that 10 of 18 AMER are triggered, providing insights about the rules that are capable of deriving a model from NL requirements in realistic settings.

Moreover, our results of performance show an average value of 78.75% in terms of recall and 75.55% in terms of precision. Furthermore, results enable us to identify new research directions to push forward the AMER: It is necessary to consider new knowledge sources that can play the role of tacit knowledge, and it is necessary to perform specific experiments to evaluate the understanding of models generated by the AMER.

The paper is structured as follows: Section 2 provides the required background on the AMER. Section 3 describes our process. Section 4 shows the results, and Sect. 5 presents a discussion of the results. Section 6 deals with the threats to validity. Section 7 summarizes the works related to this paper. Finally, Sect. 8 concludes the paper.

2 Background

The AMER used in this work appear in [10]. The authors summarize the literature on model extraction from unrestricted NL requirements and identify a set of extraction rules. These AMER are shown in Fig. 1. These AMER are organized into four categories based on the nature of the information they extract: concepts, associations and generalizations, cardinalities, and attributes. These categories are defined as follows:

- **Concepts** are the items in the real world that the domain experts are trying to discover for building a domain model.
- **Associations and generalizations** describe a naturally occurring relationship between specific concepts.
- **Cardinalities** are measures of the number of links between one concept and another concept in a relationship.
- **Attributes** are defined as descriptive pieces of information about concepts.

The above AMER have two limitations: (1) they do not cover link paths [11], these rules enable the extraction of relations between concepts that are only indirectly related, and (2) they do not fully exploit the results from NLP tools, these tools provide detailed information about the dependencies between different segments of sentences.

Concepts

Rule	Description	Example
A1	All NPs in the requirements are candidate concepts.	Requirement in Fig. 3:: **PLC**, and **pantograph**
A2	Recurring NPs are concepts.	Requirement in Fig. 3:: **pantograph**
A3	Subjects in the requirements are concepts.	Requirement in Fig. 3:: **PLC**
A4	Objects in the requirements are concepts.	"The PLC changes the pantograph":: **pantograph**
A5	Gerunds in the requirements are concepts.	"Stopping is activated by the PLC":: **Stopping**

Cardinalities

Rule	Description	Example
C1	If the source concept of an association is plural / has a universal quantifier and the target concept has a unique existencial quantifier, then the association is many-to-one.	"All arriving trains shall contact the control station":: [Arriving Train] contact ▶ [Control Satation] * 1
C2	If the source concept of an association is singular and the target concept is plural / quantified by a define article, then the association is one-to-many.	"The train closed the doors":: [Train] close ▶ [Door] 1 *
C3	If the source concept of an association is singular and the target concept is singular then the association is one-to-one.	"The train closed the door":: [Train] close ▶ [Door] 1 1
C4	An explicit number before a concept suggests a cardinality	"The train closed 3 doors":: [Train] close ▶ [Door] 1 3

Associations & Generalizations

Rule	Description	Example
B1	Transitive verbs are associations.	Requirement in Fig. 3:: [PLC] set up ▶ [Pantograph]
B2	A verb with a preposition is an association.	"The signal is sent to PLC":: [Signal] send to ▶ [PLC]
B3	<R> in a requirement of the form "<R> of <A> is <B>" is likely to be an association.	"The control of the doors is PLC":: [PLC] control ▶ [Door]
B4	"contain", "include", [...] suggest aggregations / compositions.	"The PLC contains a circuit":: [Circuit]————◇[PLC]
B5	"is a", "may be", "kind of", [...] suggest generalizations.	"The door may be automatic door or manual door":: [Automatic Door] [Manual Door] —▷ [Door]

Attributes

Rule	Description	Example
D1	"identified by", "recognized by", "has", [..] suggest attributes.	"A door is identified by the door id":: **Door id** is an attribute of **Door.**
D2	Genetive cases suggest attributes.	Door's side:: **Side** is an attribute of **Door.**
D3	The adjective of an adjectivally modified NP suggests an attribute.	"large train":: **Size** is an attribute of **Train**
D4	An intransitive verb with an adverb suggests an attribute.	"The train arrives in the morning at 10 AM":: **Arrival time** is an attribute of **Train.**

Fig. 1 Automated model extraction rules

There is a large body of literature about the automated extraction of models from NL requirements, the large majority of existing work on model extraction is evaluated over no real environments. Thus, there is a need to conduct evaluations in industrial contexts. For this reason, our work aims to cover the lack of evaluations to analyze the models generated from requirements specifications written in NL in real contexts. Our aim is to compare the models generated using the AMER with the models generated by the domain experts in an industrial context.

3 Process

In order to compare the model generated according to the AMER with the models generated by the domain experts, we design a process made up of four steps, marked I–IV in Fig. 2. First, the requirements specification in NL is taken as input to generate a model by applying the AMER. Second, the domain experts take as input the requirements specification to generate a model for each domain expert. Third, NLP techniques (e.g., Parts-Of-Speech Tagging and root reduction) are applied to homogenize the words used in both the model generated according to the AMER and the model generated by the domain experts. Finally, we obtain as results both a report with the occurrences of each extraction rule triggered by the requirements, and a report with the performance measurement in terms of precision and recall values by comparing the natural language processed model obtained from the AMER with the natural language processed model obtained from each domain expert.

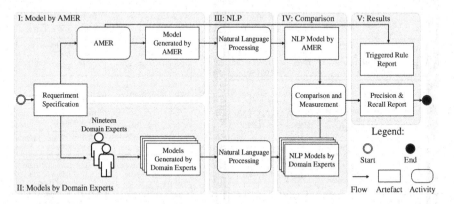

Fig. 2 Process overview

3.1 Model Generated by the AMER

To generate the model by applying the AMER (see Fig. 1) it is necessary to provide as input a requirements specification. In this work, the requirements specification provided as input was stated by a domain expert, who is not involved in this paper. The requirements specification is made up of four requirements, which have an average length of 28 words. In general, requirements are expressed using NL text in a large number of software projects, and the railway domain is no exception [12]. NL is used to specify requirements due to its high degree of understandability among all of the stakeholders in industrial projects [13].

In the requirements, we identify the units of interest that are noun phrases and verbs. A noun phrase (NP) is a unit that can be the subject or the object of a verb. A verb (VB) appears in a verb phrase (VP) alongside any direct or indirect objects, but not the subject. Verbs can have auxiliaries and modifiers (typically adverbs) associated with them. After the NPs and VBs are identified, we find grammatical dependencies between individual words in a sentence, e.g., the subject and the object. Finally, we apply the AMER shown in Fig. 1, which are organized in four categories (concepts, associations and generalizations, cardinalities, and attributes), in order to construct the model. The model obtained as a result of applying the AMER to the requirements specification has 67 elements.

The upper part of Fig. 3 shows an example of a requirement in which the main units of interest to apply the AMER are highlighted (e.g., nouns and verbs), whereas the lower part of Fig. 3 shows the model obtained as a result of applying the AMER.

The AMER are applied to generate the model associated to the requirement of Fig. 3 as follows:

- A3: The statement of A3 claims *"Subjects in the requirements are concepts"*, then **PLC** is a concept.
- A2: The statement of A2 claims *"Recurring NPs are concepts"*, then **Pantograph** is a concept.

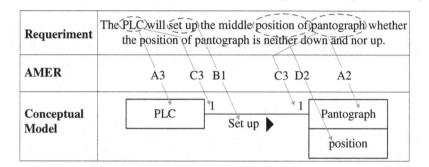

Fig. 3 Example of model generation by applying the AMER

- B1: The statement of B1 claims *"Transitive verbs are associations"*, then **set up** shows an association between **PLC** and **Pantograph**.
- C3: The statement of C3 claims *"If the source concept of an association is singular and the target concept is singular then the association is one-to-one"*, then the association between **PLC** and **Pantograph** is one-to-one.
- D2: The statement of D2 *claims "Genitive cases suggest attributes"*, then **position** is an attribute of **Pantograph**.

3.2 Models Generated by Domain Experts

To generate models by domain experts, this step involved 19 domain experts from our industrial partner. They are experts in developing software and requirements. In their daily work, these experts develop software from requirements. They have spent a mean of 6.65 years working as software engineers. The domain experts stated that they spent a mean of 3.36 h per day interpreting requirements.

We involved 19 domain experts rather than one because it would not be fair to consider only one domain expert as the oracle (the ground truth). According to the literature [14, 15], several different solutions (models) can be provided for the same problem (requirements specification). Hence, we compare the model generated by several domain experts with the model generated by the AMER. This comparison will allow us to evaluate whether the result of the AMER is close to some of the models generated by the domain experts. In addition, we perform the comparison in a real world industrial context, which is a step towards addressing the existing gap of obtaining results in an industrial context (the large majority of existing work on model extraction is evaluated over samples or artificial settings).

In this step, each domain expert had to interpret each of the requirements in NL provided as input. As a result of this interpretation, the subjects had to build a software model that captures all the ideas articulated in the requirements. To avoid a possible ceiling effect, there was no time limit in interpreting requirements. As a result of this step, 19 different software models were obtained. These models required an average of 62 min to be built and they have an average of 72.94 elements. Figure 4 shows an example of a requirement and its corresponding model generated by a domain expert. All requirements and the software models generated by domain experts are available at http://svit.usj.es/requerimentinfluenceexperiment.

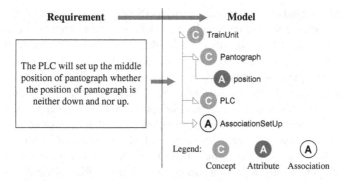

Fig. 4 Example of a model generated by a domain expert from a requirement

3.3 Natural Language Processing

Once the models generated by the AMER and the models generated by domain experts are obtained, we apply to them NLP techniques to homogenize the words used in the models with the aim of comparing them. Figure 5 shows the process to homogenize the words used in the models.

The whole compendium of NLP techniques used in this work are syntactical analysis, root reduction, and human in the loop as follows:

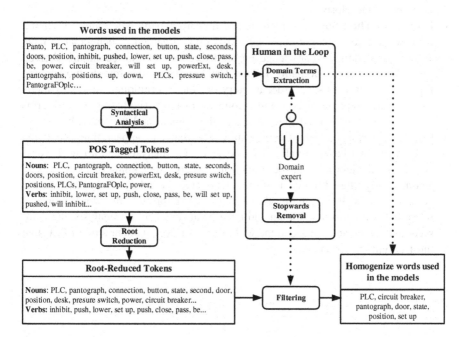

Fig. 5 NLP techniques to homogenize the words used in the models

1. **Syntactical Analysis**. Syntactical Analysis (SA) techniques split the words used in the models, analyzing the specific roles of each one of them and determining their grammatical load. In other words, these techniques determine the grammatical function of each word (e.g.: nouns, verbs, adjectives, adverbs, etc.). These techniques, often referred to as Parts-Of-Speech Tagging (POS Tagging) techniques allow engineers to implement filters for words that fulfill specific grammatical roles in a sentence, usually opting for nouns, since these words are the ones that carry the relevant information about descriptions of features and actions [16]. Words like verbs, adverbs, and adjectives are often filtered out and disregarded. For example, some of the POS Tagged Tokens obtained as outcome of syntactically analyzing a model are the nouns PLC, seconds, button and doors; and the verbs pushed and close.

2. **Root Reduction**. Through the usage of semantic techniques such as Lemmatizing, words can be reduced to their semantic roots or lemmas. Thanks to lemmas, the language of the models is unified, avoiding verb tenses, noun plurals, and strange word forms that interfere negatively with the comparison process. Prior to carrying out Root Reduction (RR) techniques, it is imperative to use SA techniques, due to the fact that RR techniques are based on word dictionaries that are built upon the grammatical role of words in a sentence. The unification of the language semantics is an evolution over pure syntactical role filtering that allows for a more advanced filtering of words in models. For example, some of the Root-Reduced tokens obtained as outcome of the previously POS Tagged tokens are the nouns PLC, second, button and door; and the verbs push and close.

3. **Human-In-The-Loop**. The inclusion of domain experts is a widely discussed topic within the SE community since it is often regarded as beneficial to have some sort of domain knowledge embedded. Some of the techniques derived from humans are Domain Terms Extraction, Stopwords Removal and Equivalence of Terms. In order to carry out these techniques, domain experts provide three separate lists of terms: one list of terms (both single-word terms and multiple-word terms) that belong to the domain and that must be always kept for analysis, a list of irrelevant words that can appear throughout the models and that have no value whatsoever for the analysis, and a list of words that are equivalent and can be unified in models. Both kinds of terms can be automatically filtered in or out of the final query, depending on the needs of the domain experts. For example, the domain experts provide the word door as a word that belong to the domain and must be always kept for analysis, the word second as irrelevant word, and the word system as a equivalent term of PLC that must be unified for analysis.

3.4 Comparison of Models

The model generated by the AMER and the models generated by the domain experts are then compared in order to get a confusion matrix. A confusion matrix is a table that is often used to describe the performance of a classification model on a test data (the model generated by the AMER) for which the true values are known (from each model generated by a domain expert). In our case, each solution outputted is a model composed of a subset of the model elements. Since the granularity will be at the level of model elements, each model element presence or absence for each category of the AMER (concepts, associations and generalizations, cardinalities, and attributes) will be considered as a classification. The confusion matrix distinguishes between the predicted values and the real values classifying them into four categories:

- True Positive: values that are predicted as true (in the model generated by the AMER) and are true in the real scenario (the model generated by a domain expert). That is, True Positive are the model elements included in both, the model generated by the AMER and the domain experts.
- False Positive: values that are predicted as true (in the model generated by the AMER) but are false in the real scenario (the model generated by a domain expert). False Positive are the model elements included in the model generated by the AMER and not included in the model generated by domain experts.
- True Negative: values that are predicted as false (in the model generated by the AMER) and are false in the real scenario (the model generated by a domain expert). True Negative are the model elements included in neither the model generated by the AMER nor the domain experts.
- False Negative: values that are predicted as false (in the model generated by the AMER) but are true in the real scenario (the model generated by a domain expert). That is, False Negative are the model elements not included in the model generated by the AMER and included in the model generated by the domain experts.

From the values in the confusion matrix we create a report including three performance metrics (Recall, Precision, and F-measure) of both, from the model generated by the AMER and from each model generated by a domain expert for each category of the AMER (concepts, associations and generalizations, cardinalities, and attributes).

Recall is the number of model elements retrieved (True Positive) divided by the number of the model elements generated by the domain experts (True Positive + False Negative):

$$Recall = \frac{True\ Positive}{True\ Positive + False\ Negative} \tag{1}$$

Precision is the number of model elements retrieved (True Positive) divided by the elements of the models generated by the AMER (True Positive + False Positive):

$$Precision = \frac{True\ Postive}{True\ Positive + False\ Positive} \qquad (2)$$

F-measure combines Precision and Recall to obtain the harmonic mean, the value of F-measure is defined as follows:

$$F-measure = 2 * \frac{Precision^* Recall}{Precision + Recall} \qquad (3)$$

A Recall value of 0% means that there are no model elements of a category obtained from the model generated by the domain expert that matched those of the model generated by the AMER. On the other hand, a Recall value of 100% means that all the model elements of a category from the model generated by the domain expert are present in the model generated by the AMER.

A Precision value of 0% means that there are not model elements of a category obtained from the model generated by the AMER that matched those of the model generated by the domain expert. On the other hand, a Precision value of 100% means that all the model elements of a given extraction rule category from the model generated by the AMER are present in the model generated by the domain expert. Finally, a value of 100% Precision and 100% Recall for a category of the AMER implies that the same model has been generated by both the domain expert and the AMER.

4 Results

In this section, we present both the results with the occurrences of each extraction rule from the requirements, and the results of performance measurement in terms of precision and recall values for each domain expert and for each category of the AMER (Concepts, Associations and Generalizations, Cardinalities, and Attributes).

Figure 6 shows a chart with the 18 different the AMER in the x axis and the occurrences of each extraction rule in the y axis that have been triggered to obtain the model generated by the AMER. As the graph shows, 11 rules from the four categories have been triggered in total. The rules with more occurrences since they have been triggered in all the requirements are: A1 (all NPs in the requirements are candidate concepts), A3 (subjects in the requirements are concepts), and B1 (transitive verbs are associations). This makes the category Concepts as the most applied in requirements even it is achieved by using only 60% of the rules. By contrast, the categories that have triggered the maximum number of different rules (75%) are Cardinalities and Attributes.

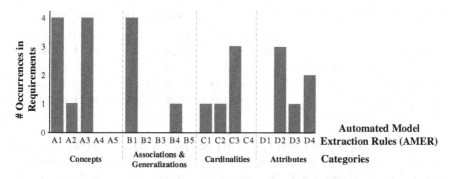

Fig. 6 Automated model extraction rules (AMER) in requirements

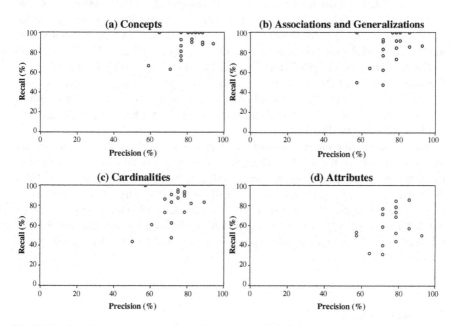

Fig. 7 Recall and precision values for each category and domain expert

Figure 7 shows four charts with the results of the performance measurement in terms of recall and precision values after comparing the model obtained by the exaction rules with each model obtained by a domain expert. Each chart represents a category of the AMER (*Concepts, Associations and Generalizations, Cardinalities*, and *Attributes*), whereas each point in the charts represents the value of the two performance indicators (recall on the y axis and precision on the x axis) for each domain expert.

Figure 7a related to *Concepts* shows that when the domain experts generated the models from requirements, most of Recall values are higher than Precision values

Table 1 Mean values and standard deviations for precision, recall, and the F-measure

	Recall ± (σ)	Precision ± (σ)	F-measure ± (σ)
Concepts	89.02 ± 11.95	79.26 ± 8.40	83.53 ± 8.66
Associations and generalizations	83.17 ± 16.64	74.81 ± 9.02	78.07 ± 11.10
Cardinalities	81.08 ± 16.73	72.56 ± 9.15	75.90 ± 11.19
Attributes	61.72 ± 17.96	75.56 ± 9.32	66.75 ± 13.37

(13 of 19). The ranges of values related to *Concepts* are [63.16%,100%] for Recall and [58.82%,94.12%] for Precision. Similarly, Fig. 7b related to *Associations and Generalizations* shows that the domain experts achieved higher Recall values than Precision values in their models. This fact appears in 12 models of 19. The ranges of values related to *Associations and Generalizations* are [47.62%,100%] for Recall and [57.14%,92.86%] for Precision. The results related to *Cardinalities* are similar to previous ones, Fig. 7b shows that when the domain experts generated the models, most of Recall values are higher than Precision values (12 of 19). Related to *Cardinalities*, the range of values of Recall is [43.75%,100%] and the range of Precision is [50%,89.29%]. Finally, Fig. 7d shows that the tendency is opposite to the previous categories. The number of models with higher values of Precision is 12. The ranges values related to *Cardinalities* are [31.25%,85.71%] for Recall and [57.14%,92.86%] for Precision.

Table 1 shows the mean values of recall, precision and F-measure of the graphs for each category of the AMER. The category *Concepts* obtains the best results in recall and precision, providing an average value of 79.26% in precision and 89.02% in recall. In recall, the next best result is obtained by *Associations and Generalizations* (83.17%) followed by *Cardinalities* (81.08%) and *Attributes* (61.72%). In precision, the next best result is obtained by *Attributes* (75.56%) followed by *Associations and Generalizations* (74.81%) and *Cardinalities* (72.56%).

5   Discussion

The recall values of 100% (see the points in the 100% line of Fig. 7) indicate that the AMER has fully covered the model elements created by a domain expert. However, recall values lower than 100% indicate that the AMER has not covered all the model elements of the domain expert. By analyzing these results, we detected that in cases where the AMER does not reach 100% of recall it is because the domain experts create the models using as input both the requirements specification and their own tacit knowledge about the domain.

Domain experts leverage tacit knowledge to specify: concepts in 12/19 models, associations in 14/19 models, cardinalities in 17/19 models, and attributes in 19/19 models. Especially in the case of attributes, research in the AMER should consider as input to its rules other knowledge sources (such as domain ontologies or reference architectures) in order to achieve the performance of domain experts.

For the categories *Concepts, Associations and Generalizations*, and *Cardinalities* in the models generated by the domain experts the most values have higher values of recall than values of precision. On the contrary, the values in the category *Attributes* are higher for precision than recall. These data and the achieved values corroborate the need to use ontologies, reference architectures or similar techniques. This is especially relevant in the case of category *Attributes*.

For the same requirements specification, several different models may be considered solutions equally valid by different domain experts [14, 15]. For example, the same domain expert can use more model elements than another domain expert to specify the same requirement. Precision values below 100% may reveal that models created by the AMER have a different modeling style than domain experts. However, precision values lower than 100% may also reveal that the models created by the AMER specify aspects that domain experts considered non-relevant to be specified.

By analyzing the comparisons between the model created by the AMER and the models created by domain experts, we detected that precision values lower than 100% were produced by differences in modeling style. Neither concepts (79.26%), associations (74.81%), cardinalities (72.56%), nor attributes (75.56%) can exactly match the modeling style of any of the 19 domain experts.

Achieving that the modeling style of the AMER is aligned with the modeling style of a domain expert can be beneficial to facilitate the domain expert's understanding. However, in industrial environments, the same model is consumed by multiple actors (such as domain experts, engineers or testers) and each actor may have different modeling preferences. Therefore, it is necessary to perform specific experiments in order to evaluate the understanding of the AMER modeling style for the different actors that consume the models in an industrial environment.

6 Threats to Validity

This section describes the threats that we have avoided, the threats that we could not avoid but that we mitigated, and the threats that we could not tackle. We use the classification of threats to validity of [17]; this classification distinguishes four aspects of validity:

Construct validity: The first identified threat of this type was the author bias, this threat means that the people that define the artifacts can subjectively influence the obtainment of the results that they are looking for. In order to mitigate this threat, the requirements specification was designed by a domain expert who was external to the design of the experiment and who was not involved in this paper. The second threat was the task design, this threat appears when the tasks can be correctly performed just by chance. To mitigate this threat the requirements specification did not have a true/false answer; the domain experts had to generate a model; this is very difficult for them to answer correctly if they do not understand the requirements. The third identified threat was the hypothesis guessing, this threat means that the subject may guess the hypotheses and work to fulfill them. To mitigate this, we did not talk with the domain experts about the evaluation goals.

Internal validity: The first identified threat of this type was the history, this threat appears when different treatments are applied to the same object at different times. We mitigated this threat by applying the AMER to the requirements specification without knowledge about the models generated by domain experts. The second identified threat was the subject motivation, this threat appears when the subjects are not motivated to participate in the experiment. The experiment was affected by this threat since the domain experts were recruited as part of their daily work (they were not volunteers).

External validity: The first identified threat of this type was the statistical power, this threat appears when the number of subjects is not enough to generalize results. Our experiment was affected by this threat, because the number of subjects (19) was not high enough to generalize results. However, it is important to note that the role of the subjects (domain experts in an industrial environment) makes an interesting contribution in an area where most experiments are conducted with students or artificial problems. The second identified threat was the object dependency, this threat appears when the results may depend on the objects used in the experiment and they cannot be generalized. We mitigated somewhat by using requirements specification were real requirements that were extracted from the company's catalog.

Reliability: The first identified threat of this type was the data collection, the data collection was not always done in the same way. This was mitigated by applying the same mechanized procedure. In addition, we tested the data coherence when the domain experts finished each generated model. Finally, the last identified threat was the reliability of measures, this threat appears when there is no guarantee that the outcomes will be the same if a phenomenon is measured twice. To mitigate this threat, we used measurements accepted by the research community such as precision and recall.

7 Related Work

Several works have dealt with processing requirements specifications for model building. These works aim to extract conceptual models from texts with NL requirements. One example of these works was developed by Robeer et al. [18], who propose to automatically derive conceptual models from user stories that are written in NL. Sagar and Abirami [7] also proposed an automatic transformation from functional specifications in NL to conceptual models. The proposal is based on the analysis of grammatical constructs. The result of the transformation is the construction of an entity-relationship diagram with notations. Ferrari et al. [19] conducted an evaluation of a tool (named CAR) that supports a textual definition of requirements. The evaluation was done using metric completeness, where the experiments compare the completeness of requirements using CAR versus using no tool. The authors of that paper are also the subjects of the study. These empirical studies had not been conducted in an industrial context involving real domain experts as our work does.

In [10] Arora et al. present an automated approach based on NLP for extracting domain models from unrestricted requirements. This approach is developed by bringing together existing extraction rules in the software engineering literature, extending these rules with complementary rules from the information retrieval literature, and proposing new rules to better exploit results obtained from modern NLP dependency parsers. In [20] Ambriola et al. present the tool CIRCE, an environment for the analysis of NL requirements. The tool is based on a transformational paradigm. The result of all the transformations is a set of models for the requirements document, for the system described by the requirements, and for the requirements writing process. Furthermore, Yue et al. [8] propose a method and a tool called aToucan to automatically generate a UML analysis model comprising class, sequence and activity diagrams from a use case requirements and to automatically establish traceability links between model elements of the use case requirements and the generated analysis model. Even though these works provide empirical data on building models from textual requirements, they do not address the performance of the AMER as our work does.

Ben Abdessalem Karaa et al. [21] explain their vision of an approach for class diagram generation from user requirements expressed in NL. Their approach amalgamates the statistical and pattern recognition properties of NLP techniques. To validate their approach the authors implemented a tool named ABCD. Elbendak et al. [4] present a tool, Class-Gen, which can partially automate the identification of objects/classes from NL requirements specifications for object identification. Ibrahim et al. [5] propose a method and a tool to facilitate requirements analysis process and class diagram extraction from textual requirements supporting NLP techniques. They propose a tool (named RACE) that assists analysts by providing a way to produce the class diagram from their requirements. Thakur and Gupta [22] propose a systematic, automated approach to identify the domain elements from textual specifications. The approach uses a language model to interpret the sentences, and identifies the domain elements using the semantic relationships between the words in the sentences obtained from Type Dependencies. These works do not evaluate their approach in a real context with real requirements as our work does.

8 Concluding Remarks

The transition from a requirements specification expressed in NL to a domain model is an important step that can be performed using the AMER. However, crucial aspects remain under-explored in real settings. To address this gap, we have designed a process to assess the AMER performance in terms of recall, precision and F-measure by comparing the model generated by the AMER with the model generated by different domain experts of our industrial partner.

In contrast to current research efforts in the AMER (which develop more and more rules to create models by means of processing the NL of requirements), our results suggest new research directions to push forward the AMER:

- Especially in the case of attribute extraction, it is necessary to consider new knowledge sources (such as domain ontologies or reference architectures) that can play the role of tacit knowledge about the domain, which is not explicit in the requirements.
- It is necessary to perform specific experiments to evaluate the understanding of the AMER modeling style for the different actors (such as domain experts, engineers or testers), who consume the models in an industrial environment.

Acknowledgements This work has been partially supported by the Ministry of Economy and Competitiveness (MINECO) through the Spanish National R+D+i Plan and ERDF funds under the project Model-Driven Variability Extraction for Software Product Line Adoption (TIN2015-64397-R).

References

1. Pohl, K., Rupp, C.: Requirements Engineering Fundamentals, 1st ed. Rocky Nook (2011)
2. Yue, T., Briand, L.C., Labiche, Y.: A systematic review of transformation approaches between user requirements and analysis models. Requir. Eng. **16**(2), 75–99 (2011)
3. Deeptimahanti, D.K., Sanyal, R.: Semi-automatic generation of UML models from natural language requirements. In: Proceedings of the 4th India Software Engineering Conference, pp. 165–174. ACM, New York, NY, USA (2011)
4. Elbendak, M., Vickers, P., Rossiter, B.N.: Parsed use case descriptions as a basis for object-oriented class model generation. J. Syst. Softw. **84**, 1209–1223 (2011)
5. Ibrahim, M., Ahmad, R.: Class diagram extraction from textual requirements using natural language processing (NLP) techniques. In: 2010 Second International Conference on Computer Research and Development, pp. 200–204, (2010)
6. Popescu, D., Rugaber, S., Medvidovic, N., Berry, D.M.: Reducing ambiguities in requirements specifications via automatically created object-oriented models. In: Monterey Workshop, pp. 103–124 (2007)
7. Sagar, V.B.R.V., Abirami, S.: Conceptual modeling of natural language functional requirements. J. Syst. Softw. **88**, 25–41 (2014)
8. Yue, T., Briand, L.C., Labiche, Y.: aToucan: an automated framework to derive uml analysis models from use case models. ACM Trans. Softw. Eng. Methodol. **24**(3), 13:1–13:52 (2015)
9. Arora, C., Sabetzadeh, M., Briand, L., Zimmer, F.: Automated checking of conformance to requirements templates using natural language processing. IEEE Trans. Softw. Eng. **41**(10), 944–968 (2015)
10. Arora, C., Sabetzadeh, M., Briand, L., Zimmer, F.: Extracting domain models from natural-language requirements: approach and industrial evaluation. In: Proceedings of the ACM/IEEE 19th International Conference on Model Driven Engineering Languages and Systems, pp. 250–260. ACM, New York, NY, USA (2016)
11. Akbik, A., Broß, J.: Wanderlust: Extracting semantic relations from natural language text using dependency grammar patterns. In: WWW Workshop (2009)

12. Rosadini, B., Ferrari, A., Gori, G., Fantechi, A., Gnesi, S., Trotta, I., Bacherini, S.: Using NLP to detect requirements defects: an industrial experience in the railway domain. In: Requirements Engineering: Foundation for Software Quality—23rd International Working Conference, REFSQ 2017, Essen, Germany, Feb 27–Mar 2, 2017, Proceedings, pp. 344–360 (2017)
13. Fanmuy, G., Fraga, A., Lloréns, J.: Requirements verification in the industry. In: Proceedings of the Second International Conference on Complex Systems Design and Management, CSDM 2011, Paris, 7–9 Dec 2011, pp. 145–160 (2011)
14. Lucas, F.J., Molina, F., Toval, A.: A systematic review of UML model consistency management. Inf. Softw. Technol. **51**(12), 1631–1645 (2009)
15. Zave, P.: Classification of research efforts in requirements engineering. ACM Comput. Surv. **29**(4), 315–321 (1997)
16. Capobianco, G., Lucia, A. De, Oliveto, R., Panichella, A., Panichella, S.: On the role of the nouns in IR-based Traceability Recovery. In: Proceedings of the International Conference on Program Comprehension, pp. 148–157. IEEE (2009)
17. Runeson, P., Höst, M.: Guidelines for conducting and reporting case study research in software engineering. Empir. Softw. Eng. **14**(2), 131–164 (2009)
18. Robeer, M., Lucassen, G., v. d. Werf, J.M.E.M., Dalpiaz, F., Brinkkemper, S.: Automated extraction of conceptual models from user stories via NLP. In: 2016 IEEE 24th International Requirements Engineering Conference (RE), pp. 196–205, (2016)
19. Ferrari, A., Dell'Orletta, F., Spagnolo, G.O., Gnesi, S.: Measuring and improving the completeness of natural language requirements. LNCS (including Subser. Lect. Notes Artif. Intell. Lect. Notes Bioinformatics). 8396 LNCS, pp. 23–38 (2014)
20. Ambriola, V., Gervasi, V.: On the systematic analysis of natural language requirements with CIRCE. Autom. Softw. Eng. **13**(1), 107–167 (2006)
21. Ben Abdessalem Karaa, W., Ben Azzouz, Z., Singh, A., Dey, N., S. Ashour, A., Ben Ghazala, H.: Automatic Builder of Class Diagram ABCD: An Application of UML Generation from Functional Requirements. Softw. Pr. Exper. **46**(11), 1443–1458 (2016)
22. Thakur, J.S., Gupta, A.: Identifying domain elements from textual specifications. In: Proceedings of the 31st IEEE/ACM International Conference on Automated Software Engineering, pp. 566–577. ACM, New York, NY, USA (2016)

A Variational Latent Variable Model with Recurrent Temporal Dependencies for Session-Based Recommendation (VLaReT)

Panayiotis Christodoulou, Sotirios P. Chatzis and Andreas S. Andreou

Abstract This paper presents an innovative deep learning model, namely the Variational Latent Variable Model with Recurrent Temporal Dependencies for Session-Based Recommendation (VLaReT). Our method combines a Recurrent Neural Network with Amortized Variational Inference (AVI) to enable increased predictive learning capabilities for sequential data. We use VLaReT to build a session-based Recommender System that can effectively deal with the data sparsity problem. We posit that this capability will allow for producing more accurate recommendations on a real-world sequence-based dataset. We provide extensive experimental results which demonstrate that the proposed model outperforms currently state-of-the-art approaches.

Keywords Recurrent networks · Latent variable models · Deep learning recommender systems

1 Introduction

Recommender Systems (RS) aim to enhance user experience and provide accurate personalized recommendations when used as smart tools in e-commerce applications [1, 2]. Recent studies on RS have been mainly focused on classic collaborative neighborhood techniques or matrix factorization methods. These techniques work

---

A prior version of this paper has been published in the ISD2017 Proceedings (http://aisel.aisnet.org/isd2014/proceedings2017).

P. Christodoulou (✉) · S. P. Chatzis · A. S. Andreou
Cyprus University of Technology, Limassol, Cyprus
e-mail: paa.christodoulou@edu.cut.ac.cy

S. P. Chatzis
e-mail: sotirios.chatzis@cut.ac.cy

A. S. Andreou
e-mail: andreas.andreou@cut.ac.cy

© Springer International Publishing AG, part of Springer Nature 2018
N. Paspallis et al. (eds.), *Advances in Information Systems Development*,
Lecture Notes in Information Systems and Organisation 26,
https://doi.org/10.1007/978-3-319-74817-7_4

well under conditions where a solid user profile is available; this allows for ameliorating the fundamental challenges RS is faced with, such as the cold-start problem and data sparsity [3]. In recent years, researchers have examined the use of RS in a broader range of applications in order to produce accurate suggestions in contexts that have never been introduced in the past, or in complex problems as for example in sequence-based and session-based recommendation.

Session-based recommendation is a newly introduced challenge in the context of RS, firstly presented in the RecSys Challenge, 2015 [4]. In the session-based context, an RS delivers recommendations taking into account only the users' actions in a current session [5]. To achieve this, the RS processes the historical data of users captured in an active session, utilizing at the same time only a slight piece of information that presents the behavior of the current user in order to predict their next move (recommended item).

The success of Deep Neural Networks (DNNs) on image/speech recognition [6] constitutes the main motivation that has inspired use of such models in the context of RS. Moreover, the utilization of Recurrent Neural Networks (RNNs) for modeling variable-length sequence data has gained tremendous attention, and has also been used to deal with the session-based problem [4]. The main difference between feed-forward deep models and RNNs is that RNNs construct a recurrent latent state by leveraging appropriate connections between the units of the network. In a session-based problem, the RS considers as the initial input of the RNN the first item that a user selects when opens a session. Subsequently, each sequential click that follows is used to generate an output that relies upon previous clicks; this is essentially the recommendation the model generates. The main challenges of session-based recommendation are: (i) the large set of available items, that can be in the orders of millions; and (ii) the scalability issues that arise just because the click-stream datasets are vast; thus the time needed to train the model is enormous. In order to tackle the abovementioned challenges, RS use ranking loss functions to train the neural networks and recommend only a set of the top-k items to a user.

This study outlines a model namely Variational Latent Variable Model with Recurrent Temporal Dependencies for Session-Based Recommendation (VLaReT) that utilizes scalable (amortized variational) Bayesian inference [7] to increase the performance of classic RNN session-based RS by allowing for one to deal with data sparsity. Specifically, the proposed approach treats the inferred latent variables of the system as stochastic ones imposed some prior distribution; this helps the RS engine to tackle uncertainty over sparse data, thus producing more accurate results. In addition, the Amortized Variational Inference (AVI) technique, introduced in [8], is used in the proposed model to enable scalability of Bayesian inference to real-world datasets. We provide strong experimental results that demonstrate that the proposed model outperforms modern rival methodologies in terms of accuracy, without suffering from scalability issues.

The remainder of this paper is structured as follows: Sect. 2 presents an overview of current literature while Sect. 3 describes the methodology of the proposed model. Section 4 evaluates the model in a challenging public benchmark dataset, and compares the best performing method with state-of-the-art models. Finally, the last section concludes the paper, summarizing the contributions presenting at the same time future steps.

2 Related Work

Current literature has been mainly focused on neighborhood and matrix factorization models. The work presented in [2] utilizes item-based collaborative filtering approaches to deal with the key challenges of RS. Item-based methods analyze the user-item matrix to identify the relationships that exist between the various items, and then utilize those correlations to produce recommendations. A list of different methodologies for calculating similarities between items are examined in [2, 3, 9], with evaluation outcomes presenting that item-based techniques perform better than the user-based approaches in terms of accuracy.

The study in [9] outlines a series of latent models based on matrix factorization (MF) techniques. These techniques represent both users and items as vectors in the same space, and combine scalability with high accuracy when modeling real-world scenarios. When explicit ratings are not available, RS use MF approaches that provide extra information to facilitate inference of user preferences. According to the literature, MF methods yield better results when compared with neighborhood models; the main reason for this is that MF can combine various kinds of data, such as confidence levels and temporal dynamics.

Shani et al. [10] argues that Markov decision processes (MDPs) can provide an enhanced methodology ready to be utilized in RS and deal with the sequential optimization problem. The proposed MDP model presented in [10] takes into consideration the long-term effects and the estimated value of each suggestion; this has allowed for it to outperform the classic Markov Chain model when implemented on commercial websites.

Nowadays, deep learning approaches have been successfully applied to image and speech recognition [11]. Wang et al. [12] were among the first to present a model that leverages deep learning methods to learn the patterns connecting the content and the ratings matrix, so as to address the data sparsity challenge. Experimental results on a series of real-world scenarios from various contexts have exhibit that the use of the model of [12] performs better than state-of-the-art alternatives.

Salakhutdinov et al. [13] states that most of the current collaborative filtering techniques can't deal with large datasets. To address this problem, they used the Restricted Boltzmann Machine (RBM), which is a two-layer undirected graphical models that can model tabular data. A set of learning and inference methodologies are introduced for the RBM model, which is applied on the Netflix dataset; the results presented in [13] demonstrate its superior performance against mainstream Singular Value Decomposition (SVD) models.

The work in [14] claims that click prediction is one of the main challenges in the World Wide Web, and that most studies in current literature have been focused on dealing with this problem using machine learning techniques. In a real-world commercial website, users' behavior depends on how they acted in the past; thus, the authors in [14] present an innovative model based on a RNN that takes into account users' previous steps. The proposed model was evaluated on click-through logs of a commercial engine, with the results showing advances on click prediction accuracy compared against sequence-independent approaches.

Furthermore, Hidasi et al. [4] outlines an RNN to deal with long sequence-type data that can be obtained from ecommerce websites. As previously mentioned, in such cases of sequential data modeling, the frequently used MF techniques are not accurate enough. The proposed model introduces various alterations on the classic RNN, such as the Gated Recurrent Unit (GRU), and the ranking loss function used for model training. These are designed in a way that also takes into account practical aspects of the session-based recommendation task. For evaluation purposes, the model is executed on two datasets; the first one is the RecSys Challenge 2015 dataset, and the second one is a dataset collected from the OTT video service platform. Experimental results show that the proposed model outperforms item-KNN, which is the best-performing approach from the large corpus of collaborative filtering techniques that are not based on elaborate machine learning models.

Moreover, the work presented in [5] analyzes deeper the RNN-based models for session-based recommendations, and introduces two techniques that improve the model's performance. The proposed work was evaluated on the RecSys Challenge 2015 dataset, and the final outcomes were compared with the results presented in Hidasi et al. [4] indicating that the proposed model performs much better. In addition, Jannach et al. [15] demonstrates how the heuristics-based nearest neighbor (kNN) framework, utilized in session-based recommendation, can lead to better accuracy compared against the classic approach proposed in [4]. Experimental results indicate that the hybrid proposed model that combines the kNN approach with the classic methodology introduced in [4] leads to better results.

Finally, the work in [16] introduces innovative ranking loss functions custom-made for RNNs applied in recommendation frameworks. The proposed model was evaluated on various datasets such as the RecSys 2015 dataset; the final outcomes indicate an increase in the system's accuracy when training the model with novel ranking loss functions compared with the previously mentioned approach presented in [4].

3 Proposed Approach

The leading contribution of this study lies on the development of a novel deep learning model, capable to extract abstract temporal dynamics from sparse user session-based sequence data and then use that information to generate accurate recommendations.

The VLaReT model formulates the session-based recommendation challenge as a sequence-based prediction problem. Let us denote as $\{x_i\}_{i=1}^{n}$ a user session, where x_i is the ith clicked item; then, we formulate the session-based recommendation as the problem of predicting the score vector $y_{i+1} = [y_{i+1,j}]_{j=1}^{m}$ of the available items to users, where $y_{i+1,j} \in R$ is the predicted score of the jth item. We are keen on recommending more than one item at a time; therefore, at each time point we select the *top-k* items to present back to the user. The core inferential engine we develop in this work is a novel deep learning model for predicting the vector y_{i+1}.

3.1 Methodological Background

The proposed approach is motivated by the modern RNN-based method presented in [4], that relies on an RNN structure which utilizes GRU units. The postulated RNN uses as input the current user action at each time step i, and then predicts a score vector for the next user action. The recurrent units' activation vectors of the GRU-based network, h, are updated at time i using the following formula:

$$h_i = (1 - z_i) \cdot h_{i-1} + z_i \cdot \widehat{h}_i \tag{1}$$

where h_{i-1} is the activation vector of the recurrent unit at the previous time point, and $\widehat{h}_i$ is the candidate activation vector of the GRU units:

$$\widehat{h}_i = \tanh(Wx_i + U(r_i \cdot h_{i-1})) \tag{2}$$

In Eq. (1), the z_i is the update gate output, which controls when and to what degree an update to a latent state of the recurrent units should be made; it is given by:

$$z_i = \tau(W_z x_i + U_z h_{i-1}) \tag{3}$$

where τ is the logistic sigmoid function. On the other hand, the r_i, which is given in Eq. (4), is the output of the reset gate of the GRU network; it decides when the internal memory of the GRU units must be reset. We have

$$r_i = \tau W_r(x_i + U_r h_{i-1}) \tag{4}$$

W, U, W_z, U_z, W_r and U_r in the above-mentioned equations are trainable network parameters.

3.2   Model Formulation

The VLaReT model builds upon the concepts discussed in the previous section and introduces a novel methodology that renders the GRU-based model amenable to Bayesian inference. We consider the component recurrent unit activations as stochastic latent variables, and impose a prior distribution over them as show in the formula below:

$$p(h_i) = N(h_i|0, I) \tag{5}$$

where $N(\xi|\mu,\Sigma)$ is a multivariate Gaussian density with mean μ, covariance matrix Σ and identity matrix I.

Moreover, the sought posteriors $q(h)$ take the form of Gaussians with means and isotropic covariance matrices parameterized via GRU networks as follows:

$$q(h_i; \theta) = N\big(h_i|\mu_\theta(x_i), \sigma_\theta^2(x_i)I\big) \tag{6}$$

In Formula (6) the mean vectors $\mu_\theta(x_i)$ and the variance functions $\sigma_\theta^2(x_i)$ are outputs of the GRU network with parameters θ; hence, we now have:

$$\big[\mu_\theta(x_i), \log \sigma_\theta^2(x_{i-1}),\big] = (i - z_i) \cdot \big[\mu_\theta(x_{i-1}) \log \sigma_\theta^2(x_{i-1})\big] + z_i \cdot \widehat{h_i} \tag{7}$$

where

$$z_i = \tau\big(W_z x_i + U_z\big[\mu_\theta(x_{i-1}), \log \sigma_\theta^2(x_{i-1})\big]\big) \tag{8}$$

$$\widehat{h_i} = \tanh\left(W x_i + U\left(r_i \cdot \left[\mu_\theta(x_{i-1}), \log \sigma_{\theta}^2(x_{i-1})\right]\right)\right) \tag{9}$$

$$r_i = \tau\big(W_r x_i + U_r\big[\mu_\theta(x_{i-1}), \log \sigma_\theta^2(x_{i-1})\big]\big) \tag{10}$$

and $[\xi, \zeta]$ denotes the concatenation of vectors ξ and ζ. The values of the hidden variables h_i can be calculated by posterior samples from the inferred posterior density.

Let us continue on the output layer of the proposed model. According to the literature, item ranking [4, 17, 18] can either be pointwise, pairwise or listwise. The proposed approach utilizes various ranking loss functions, such as the matrix factorization method Bayesian Personalized Ranking (BPR) presented in [18], which is a pairwise ranking loss, as well as the cross-entropy loss function and the TOP1 function introduced in [4]. In general, pointwise ranking finds the score of items independently, while pairwise ranking first compares the score of pairs of a positive and a negative item, and then applies the score of the positive item to be higher than the negative one for all the pairs. Listwise ranking uses the scores of all items and compares them to the best ordering.

Finally, this work employs the Multinoulli distribution as the most straightforward conditional likelihood selection for our model; specifically, we postulate:

$$p\left(y_{i+1,j} = 1|h_i\right)\alpha\tau\left(w_y^j \cdot h_i\right) \tag{11}$$

w_y are trainable parameters of the output layer of the model.

3.3 Training Algorithm

The variational inference of the proposed methodology consists in performing inference by resorting to the maximization of a lower-bound to the log-marginal likelihood [19]. Given the formulation of our model, the ELBO expression of VLaReT yields:

$$\log p(D) \geq \sum_i \{-KL[q(h_i; \theta) \parallel p(h_i)] - E[L_S]\} \tag{12}$$

where $KL[q\|p]$ is the KL divergence between the distribution q and the distribution p, as show in formula below:

$$KL[q(h_i; \theta) \parallel p(h_i)] = -\frac{1}{2}\sum_{d=1}^{D}\left[\mu_\theta(x_i)^2\right]_d + \frac{D}{2}\left[1 + \log \sigma_\theta(x_i)^2 - \sigma_\theta(x_i)^2\right] \tag{13}$$

The challenge here is that the posterior expectation $E[L_S]$ cannot be computed analytically. This is due to the non-conjugate formulation of the proposed approach, which stems from its nonlinear assumptions, e.g. the fact we employ nonlinear activation functions. As a result, training the entailed parameter sets θ is not possible. To resolve these problems, one has to resort to approximating this posterior expectation by means of drawing Monte Carlo (MC) [20] samples. However, such a naïve approximation suffers from unacceptably high variance, that would prohibit the learning algorithm from converging to a good solution.

AVI deals with these issues by means of a smart re-parameterization of the MC samples of the postulated Gaussian posterior density [8]. Specifically, the drawn MC samples are now expressed as differentiable functions of the parameters sets θ and some random noise variance ε; thus, the problematic posterior expectation $E[L_S]$ is now sampled over a low-variance random noise variable. Then, to perform inference by means of maximization of the ELBO (12), we can resort to an off-the-shelf stochastic gradient descent algorithm. Specifically, in this work we use Adagrad as the stochastic gradient algorithm of choice, following the suggestions of [21].

4 Experimental Evaluation

4.1 VLaReT Model Configuration

The proposed model was implemented and trained in Theano [22] on an Intel Xeon 2.5 GHz Quad-Core server with 64 GB RAM and an NVIDIA Tesla K40 GPU accelerator. In addition, the model was evaluated using the RecSys Challenge 2015 dataset which it was split into test and training sets following the same procedure as in [4]. The training dataset comprises 7,966,257 sessions of 31,637,239 clicks on 37,483 items and the test dataset contains 15,324 sessions of 71,222 click actions on the equal items.

To experimentally evaluate our model, we utilize a variety of loss functions to perform its training; these include BPR, cross-entropy, and TOP1. Moreover, to implement Adagrad in the context of our approach, we perform session-parallel mini-batch training, and apply a dropout value at each time step in order to reduce over fitting [23]. VLaReT is trained using a specific number of epochs in order to minimize losses, and at the same time to avoid randomizing the order of sessions in each epoch. The latest state is set to zero when a session is completed. We use Adaptive Normalization to transform the time series into data sequences, as suggested in [24]. Finally, during training a Nesterov momentum [25] is applied; parameter initialization is effected using the Glorot uniform technique [26].

According to [4], computing a score for every item in the available list would limit the scalability of the training algorithm of our approach. To alleviate this computational burden, it is essential to sample the output and calculate the score only for a small subset of items. Moreover, for the output, we compute the scores for some negative samples and adjust the weights so that the output is highly ranked; therefore, items are sampled based on their popularity. Our model uses the items from the other training examples of the mini-batch as negative examples. The benefits of this training algorithm setup are that we can reduce the computational time by omitting sampling; hence, matrix operations become quicker and can scale to large datasets. As also pointed out in [4], this approach is essentially reminiscent of popularity-based sampling, since the likelihood of an item being in the other training samples of the mini-batch is proportional to its popularity. Finally, our methodology uses only single-layer recurrent GRUs; this is motivated from the related findings of presented in [4, 5], which show that adding additional layers does not improve the performance of the RNN model in the context of session-based recommendation.

4.2 Performance Metrics

The accuracy of the obtained recommendations was evaluated using the same evaluation metrics as the ones presented in [4]. Recall@20 is the main employed evaluation metric. It expresses the proportion of test cases where the desired item lies between the *top-20* recommended items; it does not take into consideration the projected rank of an item. The second metric used is the MRR@20 (Mean Reciprocal Rank), which describes the average of reciprocal ranks of the desired items; it is set to zero if the rank is above 20. This metric takes into consideration the order of the item, which is crucial in cases where the rank of recommendation matters to the systems users.

4.3 Considering Various Loss Functions

In this section the proposed model is executed utilizing various loss functions such as BPR, cross-entropy and TOP1; the best parameterization settings of each loss function are shown in Table 1.

As it can be observed from Fig. 1, the proposed VLaReT model reaches the best performance on both metrics when using a BPR loss function (VLaReT-BPR).

Further, as we show in Table 2, the VLaReT-BPR model achieves an increase in accuracy that ranges from 22% to 27% on the Recall@20 metric and from an

Table 1 Best parameterization settings

Loss function	BPR	Cross-entropy	TOP1
# Latent units	750	1000	1500
Step size	0.1	0.1	0.05
Momentum	0.3	0	0
Recall@20	0.7971	0.6250	0.6507
MRR@20	0.7845	0.2727	0.3527

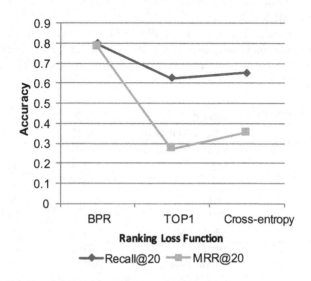

Fig. 1 VLaReT using various loss functions

Table 2 Best performance of VLaReT when utilizing various loss functions

Method	Recall@20	MRR@20
BPR	0.7971	0.7845
TOP1	0.625	0.2727
Cross-entropy	0.6507	0.3527

impressive 222% to 287% on the MRR@20 metric, over the rest of the considered alternatives (loss functions).

4.4 VLaReT-BPR Versus Baselines

In this section, the best performing configuration of our approach, namely the VLaReT-BPR model variant, is compared against the best (baseline) algorithms presented in [4, 5, 15, 16].

We provide the so-obtained results in Table 3; therein, we refer to the best performing model in [4] that achieved the highest accuracy on the Recall@20 metric as "GRU w/BPR Loss". In addition, regarding the same existing work, we refer to the best performing model that outperformed all other approaches on the MRR@20 metric as the "GRU w/TOP1 Loss." M2 and M4 in Table 3 refer to the best performing approaches presented in [5]. WH-1 refers to the best performing method on the Recall@20 metric in [15], and WH-2 refers to the best approach on the MRR@20 metric in the same work. Finally, Table 3 presents also the best performing approaches shown in [16] that utilize GRU with additional samples; we refer to the best method on the Recall@20 metric as GRU-SAMP1, and the best approach on the MRR@20 metric as GRU-SAMP2. As shown in this table, the VLaReT-BPR model outperforms previously reported results on both the Recall@20 and MRR@20 metrics.

Finally, as we show in Fig. 2, the VLaReT-BPR model achieves an increase in accuracy over these previously reported methods that varies between 11 and 28% for the Recall@20 metric, and between 252 and 317% for the MRR@20 metric.

Table 3 Comparison of the VLaReT-BPR model against various baseline algorithms

Method	Recall@20	MRR@20
GRU w/BPR Loss	0.6322	0.2467
GRU w/TOP1 Loss	0.6206	0.2693
M2	0.7129	0.3091
M4	0.6676	0.2847
WH-1	0.6910	0.2650
WH-2	0.6660	0.2760
GRU-SAMP1	0.7112	0.3059
GRU-SAMP2	0.7102	0.3107
VLaReT-BPR	**0.7971**	**0.7845**

The bold presents the best accuracy of the VLaReT-BPR model when compared with the baselines

Fig. 2 VLaReT-BPR accuracy against various baseline algorithms expressed with the Recall and MRR metrics on the top-20 recommended items

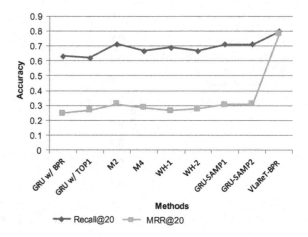

Table 4 Accuracy of the VLaReT-BPR with different hidden units

# of hidden units	Recall@20	MRR@20
100	0.5756	0.2127
500	0.7354	0.6793
750	**0.7971**	**0.7845**
900	0.7801	0.7563
1000	0.7760	0.7443
1250	0.7712	0.7318
1500	0.7629	0.7271
2000	0.7326	0.6737

The bold shows the best accuracy of the VLaReT-BPR model adjusting just its hidden units while having the other settings of the model the same

4.5 Adjusting the Size of Hidden Units

Table 4 outlines how the accuracy of the best performing variant of our model, namely VLaReT-BPR, varies with the number of hidden units while the other settings of the model remain the same as presented in the previous Sect. 4.3. The accuracy on both metrics increases as the number of hidden units reaches 750.

As it can be also observed from Fig. 3 when the value of hidden units passes over 750, there is a minor decrease in accuracy. We believe that this is caused due to overfitting, which becomes stronger as the model grows excessively large.

Fig. 3 Accuracy of the
VLaReT-BPR model for
various hidden units
expressed with the Recall and
MRR metrics on the top-20
recommended items

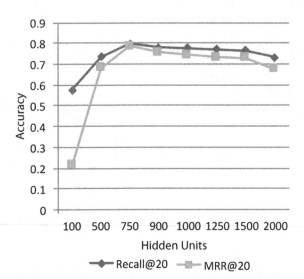

5   Conclusions

This work introduced an innovative model that couples deep learning approaches
with Variational Bayes to tackle the increased complexity that exists in RS when
using session-based datasets and at the same time to deal with data sparsity. The
proposed model, called VLaReT, augments the benefits of RNN-driven
session-based recommendation by utilizing a variational inference notion for
scalable inference under uncertainty. Indeed, as we theoretically explained and
experimentally showed, combining a Bayesian inference technique with RNNs that
use GRU layers provides strengths to analyze temporal patterns that exist in
sequence-based data, and to deal with uncertainty in sparse data when producing
recommendations. Evaluation was performed utilizing various setups on a
real-world benchmark dataset. Final outcomes indicate that proposed model using a
BPR loss function reaches the best ever reported performance, and outperforms the
current state-of-the-art approaches. Future work will be based on validating our
methodology on longer session-based datasets and on using additional samples.

References

1. Konstan, J.A., Riedl, J.: Recommender systems: from algorithms to user experience. User
   Model. User-Adap. Inter. **22**(1–2), 101–123 (2012)
2. Sarwar, B., Karypis, G., Konstan, J., Riedl, J.: Item-based collaborative filtering recommendation algorithms. In: Proceedings of the 10th International Conference on World Wide Web,
   pp. 285–295 (2001)

3. Ning, X., Desrosiers, C., Karypis, G.: A comprehensive survey of neighborhood-based recommendation methods. In: Recommender Systems Handbook, pp. 37–76. Springer US (2015)
4. Hidasi, B., Karatzoglou, A., Baltrunas, L., Tikk, D.: Session-based recommendations with recurrent neural networks. CoRR, abs/1511.06939 (2015)
5. Tan, Y. K., Xu, X., & Liu, Y.: Improved recurrent neural networks for session-based recommendations. In: Proceedings of the 1st Workshop on Deep Learning for Recommender Systems, pp. 17–22 (2016)
6. Russakovsky, O., Deng, J., Su, H., Krause, J., Satheesh, S., Ma, S., Berg, A.C.: Imagenet large scale visual recognition challenge. Int. J. Comput. Vis. **115**(3), 211–252 (2015)
7. Sotirios P., Chatzis: A coupled Indian Buet process model for collaborative filtering. In: Journal of Machine Learning Research: Workshop and Conference Proceedings, vol. 25: ACML 2012, pp. 65–79 (2012)
8. Kingma, D., Welling, M.: Auto-encoding variational Bayes. In: Proceedings of ICLR'14 (2014)
9. Koren, Y., Bell, R.M., Volinsky, C.: Matrix factorization techniques for recommender systems. IEEE Comput. **42**(8), 30–37 (2009)
10. Shani, G., Brafman, R.I., Heckerman, D.: An MDP-based recommender system. In: Proceedings of the Eighteenth Conference on Uncertainty in Artificial Intelligence, pp. 453–460 (2002)
11. Chung, J., Kastner, K., Dinh, L., Goel, K., Courville, A.C., Bengio, Y.: A recurrent latent variable model for sequential data. In: Advances in Neural Information Processing Systems, pp. 2980–2988 (2015)
12. Wang, H., Wang, N., Yeung, D.Y.: Collaborative deep learning for recommender systems. In: Proceedings of the 21th ACM SIGKDD International Conference on Knowledge Discovery and Data Mining, KDD '15, pp. 1235–1244 (2015)
13. Salakhutdinov, R., Mnih, A., Hinton, G.: Restricted Boltzmann machines for collaborative filtering. In: Proceedings of the 24th International Conference on Machine Learning, pp. 791–798 (2007)
14. Zhang, Y., Dai, H., Xu, C., Feng, J., Wang, T., Bian, J., Wang, B., Liu, T.Y.: Sequential click prediction for sponsored search with recurrent neural networks. arXiv preprint arXiv:1404.5772 (2014)
15. Jannach, D., Ludewig, M.: When recurrent neural networks meet the neighborhood for session-based recommendation. In: Proceedings of the RecSys, 17 (2017)
16. Hidasi, B., & Karatzoglou, A. (2017). Recurrent neural networks with Top-k gains for session-based recommendations. arXiv preprint arXiv:1706.03847
17. Steck, H.: Gaussian ranking by matrix factorization. In: Proceedings of the 9th ACM Conference on Recommender Systems, pp. 115–122 (2015)
18. Rendle, S., Freudenthaler, C., Gantner, Z., Schmidt-Thieme, L.: BPR: Bayesian personalized ranking from implicit feedback. In: Proceedings of the Twenty-Fifth Conference on Uncertainty in Artificial Intelligence, pp. 452–461 (2009)
19. Jordan, M.I., Ghahramani, Z., Jaakkola, T.S., and Saul, L.K.: An introduction to variational methods for graphical models. In Learning in Graphical Models, M.I. Jordan (Ed.). Kluwer, Dordrecht, pp. 105–162 (1998)
20. Salakhutdinov, R. and Mnih, A.: Bayesian probabilistic matrix factorization using Markov Chain Monte Carlo. In: Proceedings of ICML'11 (2011)
21. Duchi, J., Hazan, E., Singer, Y.: Adaptive subgradient methods for online learning and stochastic optimization. J. Mach. Learn. Res. 12(July), pp. 2121–2159 (2011)
22. Team, T.T.D., Al-Rfou, R., Alain, G., Almahairi, A., Angermueller, C., Bahdanau, D., ... Belopolsky, A.: Theano: A Python framework for fast computation of mathematical expressions. arXiv preprint arXiv:1605.02688 (2016)
23. Gal, Y., Ghahramani, Z.: A theoretically grounded application of dropout in recurrent neural networks. In: Advances in Neural Information Processing Systems, pp. 1019–1027 (2016)

24. Ogasawara, E., Martinez, L.C., De Oliveira, D., Zimbrão, G., Pappa, G.L., Mattoso, M.: Adaptive normalization: a novel data normalization approach for non-stationary time series. In: The 2010 International Joint Conference on Neural Networks (IJCNN), pp. 1–8 (2010)
25. Qian, N.: On the momentum term in gradient descent learning algorithms. Neural Networks **12**(1), 145–151 (1999)
26. Glorot, X., Bengio, Y.: Understanding the difficulty of training deep feedforward neural networks. In: Proceedings of AISTATS (2010)

Combining Multiple Web Accessibility Evaluation Reports Using Semantic Web Technologies

José R. Hilera, Salvador Otón, Cristian Timbi-Sisalima, Juan Aguado-Delgado, Francisco J. Estrada-Martínez and Héctor R. Amado-Salvatierra

Abstract This work paper describes a process for automatic combination of testing reports for the accessibility of Web applications, obtained by different testing tools and applying different standards on Web accessibility. Interoperability is guaranteed using semantic Web technologies, which allow describing the reports by RDF (Resource Description Framework) triples. The reports refer to elements of a knowledge base consisting of vocabularies, ontologies and rules of inference, in which the conceptual relations between accessibility standards, as WCAG (Web Content Accessibility Guidelines) or Section 508 among others, are formalized. A software prototype that uses the Apache Jena framework for implementing the process is presented.

Keywords Interoperability · Semantic Web · Software testing
Web accessibility

A prior version of this paper has been published in the ISD2017 Proceedings (http://aisel.aisnet.org/isd2014/proceedings2017).

J. R. Hilera (✉) · S. Otón · J. Aguado-Delgado · F. J. Estrada-Martínez
University of Alcalá, Alcalá de Henares, Spain
e-mail: jose.hilera@uah.es

S. Otón
e-mail: salvador.oton@uah.es

J. Aguado-Delgado
e-mail: j.aguado@edu.uah.es

F. J. Estrada-Martínez
e-mail: francisco.estrada@edu.uah.es

C. Timbi-Sisalima
Universidad Politécnica Salesiana, Cuenca, Ecuador
e-mail: ctimbi@ups.edu.ec

H. R. Amado-Salvatierra
Galileo University, Guatemala City, Guatemala
e-mail: hr_amado@galileo.edu

© Springer International Publishing AG, part of Springer Nature 2018   65
N. Paspallis et al. (eds.), *Advances in Information Systems Development*,
Lecture Notes in Information Systems and Organisation 26,
https://doi.org/10.1007/978-3-319-74817-7_5

1 Introduction

The accessibility of a Web application is essential to make it understandable, usable and practical for all users, including disabled people. The evaluation of the accessibility of a website must be done checking the compliance of accessibility requirements established by well-known specifications, standards or laws. The most used standard is WCAG (Web Content Accessibility Guidelines) [1], created by the World Wide Web Consortium (W3C) and adopted as a standard by the International Organization for Standardization (ISO) [2]. Another important set of accessibility requirements are the ones included in the American Law known as Section 508 [3].

When the accessibility of a website is analyzed, the results are collected in an evaluation report, which describes Web pages reviewed, assessment rules applied or automatic evaluation tools used.

It is usual that the results of the assessment depend on the evaluators involved and the testing tools used, obtaining different reports for the same Web page. For instance, an evaluator could use an automated tool that checks that all page images have alternative text, which is necessary so that screen readers can read the text to visually impaired users who cannot see the images, while another evaluator could use a more intelligent tool which also verifies the content of the alternative text makes sense. The first report would appear that everything is correct, while the second could indicate that an image has associated an incorrect alternative text. It might also happen that accessibility standard applied in a report is more demanding than the other one. For example, this occurs with flickering images on the screen, since the requirements of American legislation are more stringent than those of the WCAG standard.

In this context, it is necessary to implement mechanisms that allow interoperability between accessibility assessment tools. The Semantic Web technologies can be very suitable to solve the problem. The term "Semantic Web" refers to W3C's vision of the Web of linked data. Semantic Web technologies enable people to create data stores on the Web, build vocabularies, and write rules for handling data [4].

This paper describes the process shown in Fig. 1 to combine Web accessibility evaluation reports. The starting point are reports of accessibility expressed using Semantic Web vocabularies. It should also have a knowledge base containing information on accessibility standards and relations between them. From this, it uses the open source Semantic Web framework Apache Jena, which allows the application of reasoners to generate new knowledge. Finally, a query language created by the W3C for the Semantic Web is used, in order to obtain the final result of the evaluation.

The following section describes the Semantic Web technologies used. In Sect. 3, the structure of accessibility reports according W3C recommendations is presented. Section 4 describes the steps for combining reports using the Semantic Web technologies. In the final section, some conclusions and other related works are presented.

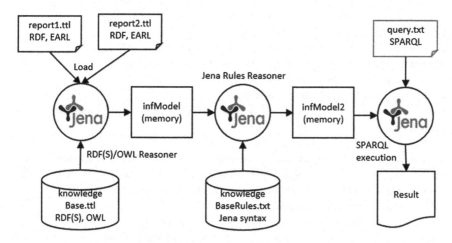

Fig. 1 Process of combining accessibility reports

2 Semantic Web Technologies

In this paper we have used the following technologies that are part of the Semantic Web [5]: RDF(S), OWL, Rules, Reasoners and SPARQL.

RDF is the original core technology of the Semantic Web, named Resource Description Framework, for describing information resources in the form of triples with the following structure, using Turtle notation [6]:

```
Subject Predicate Object.
```

An example of a RDF triple may be the following, extracted from DBPedia. org, which is a RDF representation of the Wikipedia content. It indicates that ACM (Subject) has a headquarter (Predicate) in New York (Object):

```
dbr:Association_for_Computing_Machinery
dbo:headquarter dbr:New_York_City.
```

For simplicity, we have used prefixes for each element of the triple. These prefixes identify the vocabulary in which defined the meaning of each element, which will be associated with an IRI (Internationalized Resource Identifier). Prefix dbo refers to http://dbpedia.org/ontology/, where it is defined what is meant by headquarter.

Coding 1 shows an excerpt of a RDF triples files used in this work. For simplicity, Turtle notation allows combine two or more triples with the same subject (s) in a unique sentence using ";". And triples with the same subject (s) and predicate (p) using ",". Another simplification is the predicate rdf:type, that is expressed only as "a".

```
@prefix owl: <http://www.w3.org/2002/07/owl#>.
@prefix s508: <http://example.org/Sect.508.owl#>.
@prefix wcag2: <http://www.AccessibleOntology.com/WCAG2.owl#>.
#####################################################
# Knowledge about the US Law Section 508
s508:req_1194_22_a a s508:Requirement;
s508:hasDescription "1194.22(a) A text equivalent for every non-text ele-
ment shall be provided"@en.
s508:req_1194_22_j a s508:Requirement;
s508:hasDescription "1194.22(j) Pages shall be designed to avoid causing the
screen to flicker with a frequency greater than 2 Hz and lower than 55 Hz."@en.
#####################################################
# Knowledge about the standard WCAG 2.0
wcag2:SuccessCriterion_111 a wcag2:SuccessCriterion;
wcag2:hasDescription "Non-text Content: All non-text content that is pre-
sented to the user has a text alternative that serves the equivalent purpose,
except for the situations listed below."^^xsd:string.
wcag2:SuccessCriterion_231
    a wcag2:SuccessCriterion;
    wcag2:hasDescription "Three Flashes or Below Threshold: Web pages do
not contain anything that flashes more than three times in any one second
period, or the flash is below the general flash and red flash thresholds."^^xsd:
string.
#####################################################
# Knowledge about relations between WCAG 2.0 and Section 508
s508:req_1194_22_a owl:sameAs wcag2:SuccessCriterion_111.
wcag2:SuccessCriterion_111 owl:sameAs s508:req_1194_22_a.
```

[Coding 1. Extract of the RDF(S)/OWL knowledge base (knowledgeBase.
ttl)]

The ability to reference vocabularies allows a semantic extension of RDF. For
this purpose, other associated technology is RDF Schema (RDFS), a vocabulary for
data modeling [7].

An RDF triple store is a knowledge base. In this context, **OWL (Ontology Web
Language)** can be understood as an RDF vocabulary based on descriptions logics
that can be used in triples. The goal is that a reasoner can subsequently make
inferences about them, generating new triples automatically and obtaining therefore
new knowledge [8]. Coding 1 shows a knowledge base which will be explained in
the next section, where there is a predicate from the OWL vocabulary, it is owl:
sameAs.

When in a knowledge base in the form of RDF triples we want to add **rules** such
as "if / then", it is not sufficient to use OWL, we need a language to express rules.
For this, some languages have been created, as RuleML or SWRL (Semantic Web
Rule Language), still under discussion by the W3C [9]. But there are other

languages defined for this purpose, as the one created by the Apache Jena project [7], which has been used in the example of Coding 2.

Reasoners are programs that can generate new RDF triples in a knowledge base from existing triples described with OWL, and from rules. Some of the best known are Pellet, Racer or FaCT [5].

To consult on an RDF triple store, the **SPARQL** language [10] is used. Coding 10 shows an example of query.

```
@prefix earl: <http://www.w3.org/nss/earl#>.
@prefix s508: <http://example.org/Sect.508.owl#>.
@prefix wcag2: <http://www.AccessibleOntology.com/WCAG2.owl#>.
[rule_epilepsy:
    (?aser earl:test wcag2:SuccessCriterion_231),
    (?aser earl:result ?res),
    (?res   earl:outcome   earl:failed)   ->   (?aser   earl:test   s508:
req_1194_22_j)]
```

[Coding 2. Extract of the rules base (knowledgebaserules.txt)]

2.1 Knowledge Base with OWL and Rules

The process of combining reports of the same website shown in Fig. 1 requires the existence of a knowledge base with the description of the accessibility standards or laws that apply when evaluating the website. Coding 1 shows an extract of the created knowledge base. It contains RDF triples, where it can be distinguished a first part in which the American Law on accessibility (known as Section 508) is described. For simplicity only appears the description of two articles of the law. The first is the one that requires that all images in a page must have alternative text, so that screen readers used by visually impaired people can read the description aloud. The second article included is the one that sets the permissible range of flashing for the contents of a page, to avoid problems of epilepsy.

The second part of the code of Coding 1 shows the description of the WCAG 2.0 accessibility standard created by the W3C, which is the one legally in force in many countries. Only the description of two success criteria established by this standard are shown, the first one refers to the need for alternate text and the second one is about flashing.

The last part of Coding 1 describes the relationship between the two accessibility standards. It only includes the relationship that indicates that the requirement of both standards for alternative text is the same. For this the predicate sameAs defined by OWL [2] is used.

In the case of epilepsy requirement, it is different in both standards, as in the US law the minimum flashing allowed is 2 Hz, while in the WCAG standard is 3 Hz.

So we can say that if a Web page violates the WCAG standard, also violates the American law. Otherwise not be true. This cannot be expressed with OWL, but we can use a rule language to indicate it. In this case we have used the language provided by the Apache Jena [7] framework, and the code of the rule can be seen in Coding 2.

3 Web Accessibility Evaluation Reports Using EARL

When evaluating the accessibility of a page or website, the results are presented in a report. This report may contain information obtained through automatic evaluation tools as described in [11], combined with results achieved by manual testing or with the help of end users, including disabled people. The W3C has created the EARL vocabulary to express this kind of reports using RDF triples [12]. Coding 3 shows an excerpt of an evaluation report of a hypothetical Web page as `http://www.example.org/page.html`, applying the WCAG 2.0 standard and using as support the automatic evaluation tool named `OAW`, whose URL is in the report itself. Some authors of this paper have participated in the development of OAW [13], and for this reason it is used in this example.

```
@prefix earl: <http://www.w3.org/nss/earl#>.
@prefix ptr: <http://www.w3.org/2009/pointers#>.
@prefix doap: <http://usefulinc.com/ns/doap#>.
@prefix a11y: <http://example.org/a11yResources.owl#>.
@prefix wcag2: <http://www.AccessibleOntology.com/WCAG2.owl#>.
@prefix ex: <http://www.example.org#>.
############################################################
# Definition of the accessibility evaluation tool used: OAW
a11y:OAW a earl:Software;
    doap:name "Analizador Web";
    doap:homepage <http://observatorioweb.ups.edu.ec/oaw/>.
############################################################
# Failure 1 about Success Criterion 1.1.1 of ISO WCAG 2.0 in line 37
ex:assertion_OAW_1 a earl:Assertion;
    earl:assertedBy a11y:OAW;
    earl:subject <http://www.example.org/page.html>;
    earl:test wcag2:SuccessCriterion_111;
    earl:result ex:OAWResult_1.
wcag2:SuccessCriterion_111 a earl:TestRequirement.
ex:OAWResult_1 a earl:TestResult;
    earl:outcome earl:failed; earl:pointer ex:ptr_OAWResult_1.
ex:ptr_OAWResult_1 a earl:Pointer, ptr:LineCharPointer;
    ptr:lineNumber "37"; ptr:charNumber "8".
############################################################
```

```
# Failure 2 about Success Criterion 2.3.1 of ISO WCAG 2.0 in line 56
ex:assertion_OAW a earl:Assertion;
    earl:assertedBy a11y:OAW;
    earl:subject <http://www.example.org/page.html>;
    earl:test wcag2:SuccessCriterion_231;
    earl:result ex:OAWResult.
wcag2:SuccessCriterion_231 a earl:TestRequirement.
ex:OAWResult_2 a earl:TestResult;
    earl:outcome earl:failed; earl:pointer ex:ptr_OAWResult_2.
ex:ptr_OAWResult_2 a earl:Pointer, ptr:LineCharPointer;
    ptr:lineNumber "56"; ptr:charNumber "6".
```

[Coding 3. Extract of a first EARL accessibility report]

Coding 4 shows the contents of another evaluation report about the same Web page, but using another tool called AChecker, and applying as accessibility standard the American Law Section 508. This tools is used in this example because is one of the few tools that allow the user to get the report in EARL format [14].

```
@prefix earl: <http://www.w3.org/nss/earl#>.
@prefix ptr: <http://www.w3.org/2009/pointers#>.
@prefix doap: <http://usefulinc.com/ns/doap#>.
@prefix a11y: <http://example.org/a11yResources.owl#>.
@prefix s508: <http://example.org/Sect.508.owl#>.
@prefix ex: <http://www.example.org#>.
############################################################
# Definition of the accessibility evaluation tool used: AChecker
a11y:AChecker a earl:Software;
    doap:name "AChecker: Web Accessibiilty Checker";
    doap:homepage <http://achecker.ca>.
############################################################
# Failure about article 1192.22(a) of US Law "Sect. 508" in line 25
ex:assertion_AChecker a earl:Assertion;
    earl:assertedBy a11y:AChecker;
    earl:subject <http://www.example.org/page.html>;
    earl:test s508:req_1194_22_a;
    earl:result ex:ACheckerResult.
s508:req_1194_22_a a earl:TestRequirement.
ex:ACheckerResult a earl:TestResult;
    earl:outcome earl:failed; earl:pointer ex:ptr1_ACheckerResult.
ex:ptr1_ACheckerResult a earl:Pointer, ptr:LineCharPointer;
ptr:lineNumber "25"; ptr:charNumber "10"
```

[Coding 4. Extract of a second EARL accessibility report]

4 Combining Multiple Reports

We have developed a software prototype for combining multiple accessibility evaluation reports of the same website. Considering that in the reports different assessment tools have been used, and different standards or accessibility laws have been applied. For this, we have used the library Apache Jena for Java, an open source Semantic Web framework that provides an API to extract data from and write to RDF stores (known as graphs); and provides support to execute reasoners on OWL triples and generic rules. In the following sections the operation of the prototype is described, which is based on the scheme in Fig. 1.

4.1 Loading Reports in Memory

As shown in Fig. 1, the first step is to load in memory, in the Jena Model class object called reports, both reports to be combined, available in files with Turtle RDF triples (TTL) format. In Coding 5 the Java code used is shown.

```
import org.apache.jena.rdf.model.Model;
import org.apache.jena.rdf.model.ModelFactory;
...
String report1_file = "report1.ttl";
String report2_file = "report2.ttl";
Model reports = ModelFactory.createDefaultModel();
reports.read(report1_file,"TTL");
reports.read(report2_file,"TTL");
```

[Coding 5. Java code to load the two EARL reports in memory]

4.2 Loading Reports in Memory

The next step is to load in memory the knowledge base described in Coding 1, available as RDF triples in a "TTL" file. Coding 6 shows the Java code for this, creating the object knowledgeBase. It must be also loaded into memory the rules that complete the knowledge base, in this case available in a separate file, with extension txt. The content of this file is in Coding 2. Coding 7 shows the Java code to store the rules in a variable named rules, containing a list of Jena Rule class objects.

```
import org.apache.jena.rdf.model.Model;
import org.apache.jena.rdf.model.ModelFactory;
```

```
String knowledgeBase_file = "knowledgeBase.ttl";
Model knowledgeBase = ModelFactory.createDefaultModel();
knowledgeBase.read(knowledgeBase_file, "TTL");
```

[Coding 6. Java code to load the knowledge base in memory]

```
import java.io.BufferedReader;
import java.io.FileReader;
import java.util.List;
import org.apache.jena.reasoner.rulesys.Rule;
String knowledgeBaseRules_file = "knowledgeBaseRules.txt";
BufferedReader knowledgeBase_rules = new BufferedReader(new FileReader
(knowledgeBaseRules_file));
List     rules     =     Rule.parseRules     (Rule.rulesParserFromReader
(knowledgeBase_rules));
```

[Coding 7. Java code to load rules in memory]

4.3 Using Reasoners to Infer New Knowledge

Once all the knowledge is stored in different objects in memory, it's time to infer new knowledge from the restrictions included in the knowledge base, expressed with OWL and with the rules that complement the base.

First, the internal reasoner that Jena offers to work with OWL is executed. Coding 8 shows the Java code to do this. The reasoner starts from the knowledge base available in memory in the object knowledgeBase, and applies them to the reports stored in the object reports. The final result is the object infModel, which contains all the original RDF triples plus the new ones inferred. In this case, it is evident that new triples have been inferred because of the restriction owl: sameAs, which establishes the equivalence between two accessibility require-ments: the success criteria 1.1.1 of WCAG 2.0 and the article 1194.22(a) from Law Section 508. For every RDF triple in which one of these requirements appears, a new triple is created with the other, as it has been expressed that they are equivalent.

```
import org.apache.jena.reasoner.Reasoner;
import org.apache.jena.reasoner.ReasonerRegistry;
import org.apache.jena.rdf.model.InfModel;
...
Reasoner reasoner = ReasonerRegistry.getOWLReasoner();
reasoner = reasoner.bindSchema(knowledgeBase);
InfModel infModel = ModelFactory.createInfModel(reasoner, reports);
```

[Coding 8. Java code to use reasoner to infer new knowledge]

Then, on the knowledge available in the object infModel (original plus generated), a new reasoner is executed, able to interpret the rules expressed in the Jena rule language, which were loaded into memory in the list rules. Coding 9 shows the Java code to do it, obtaining a final knowledge model in the object infModel2.

```
Reasoner reasoner2 = new GenericRuleReasoner(rules);
InfModel infModel2 = ModelFactory.createInfModel (reasoner2, infModel);
```

[Coding 9. Java code to run the rules reasoner]

In this case, it is also clear that it should have generated new knowledge in the form of new RDF triples, since applying the rule of Coding 2 to the report of Coding 3, it must be inferred that if the website assessed did not meet the requirement on epilepsy according to WCAG 2.0, does not meet the American law on accessibility, which is more restrictive in this regard, as indicates the rule.

4.4 Generating the Final Evaluation Results Using SPARQL

After the steps above, we have in memory, in the object infModel2, a RDF model with all the knowledge associated with the accessibility evaluation of the website, both the included in the two original evaluation reports as new knowledge generated by the two reasoners. It is possible to make queries on the model, which is stored as RDF triples. To do this, we must use the SPARQL language, as stated in Sect. 2. In this case, we will launch a query about the accessibility failures registered in the model, according to American Law Section 508. Coding 10 shows the way to express that query with SPARQL.

```
prefix earl: <http://www.w3.org/nss/earl#>
prefix ptr: <http://www.w3.org/2009/pointers#>
prefix doap: <http://usefulinc.com/ns/doap#>
prefix s508: <http://example.org/Section508.owl#>
SELECT ?tool ?desc ?line
WHERE { ?a a earl:Assertion.
    ?a earl:assertedBy ?tool.
    ?a earl:test ?req.
    ?req a s508:Requirement.
    ?req s508:hasDescription ?desc.
    ?a earl:result ?res.
    ?res earl:outcome earl:failed.
    ?res earl:pointer ?pt.
```

```
?pt ptr:lineNumber ?line.
?pt ptr:charNumber ?char. }
```

[Coding 10. SPARQL sentence to obtain web accessibility evaluation results according US law section 508]

The query with the source code of Coding 10 is stored in a file named query.txt, and it must be loaded into memory and then run it using resources from the Jena framework. In Coding 11 the corresponding Java code is shown.

```
import org.apache.jena.query.Query;
import org.apache.jena.query.QueryExecution;
import org.apache.jena.query.QueryExecutionFactory;
import org.apache.jena.query.QueryFactory;
import org.apache.jena.query.QuerySolution;
import org.apache.jena.query.ResultSet;
String sparql_file = "query.txt";
BufferedReader bf = new BufferedReader(new FileReader(sparql_file));
String line;
String sparql_sentence = "";
while((line = bf.readLine())!=null) {
    sparql_sentence += line;
    }
    bf.close();
Query sparqlQuery = QueryFactory.create(sparql_sentence);
QueryExecution qe =
QueryExecutionFactory.create(sparqlQuery,infModel2);
ResultSet rs = qe.execSelect();
while (rs.hasNext()) {
    QuerySolution sol = rs.next();
    System.out.println(sol.toString());
    }
```

[Coding 11. Java code to load and run the SPARQL sentence]

The query results can be seen in Table 1. The query has been designed to obtain the accessibility requirements unfulfilled by the website evaluated, according to the American legislation. Three columns appear: the first one contains the assessment tool that, according the processed reports, detected the fail. The second column includes the textual description of the unfulfilled requirement. The third column shows the line in the HTML page code where the failure has been found. The importance of the example shown is that it has combined results of both reports, and that some of the results did not explicitly appear in any of the reports, and have appeared thanks to the information inferred by reasoners. Thus, the failure in line 37 appears because of the restriction owl:sameAs on the requirements about

Table 1 Results of the SPARQL query

Tool	Description	Line
AChecker	"1194.22(a) A text equivalent for every non-text ..."	25
OAW	"1194.22(j) Pages shall be designed to avoid ..."	56
OAW	"1194.22(a) A text equivalent for every non-text ..."	37

alternative text. And the failure in line 56 has appeared thanks to the inference rule about the limits of screen flickering.

5   Conclusions

The relationship between Semantic Web technologies and Web accessibility can be treated from different points of view. This relationship is evident in the case of the W3C, because this organization is involved in the development of both fields. Such is the case of EARL language for expressing accessibility test results in the form of semantic RDF triples. It is beginning to appear on the market accessibility evaluation tools that obtain their reports in this format, as is the case of the known AChecker, one of the most used by the evaluators [15]. The advantage of using EARL in reports is that we can apply technologies of the Semantic Web to process these reports, and take advantage of the great possibilities offered, such as those have been shown in this work. EARL 1.0 is a Working Draft since 2011, but it has been reactivated in 2017 mainly due to the creation of the Accessibility Conformance Testing (ACT) Task Force in the W3C, to develop a framework and repository of test rules, to promote a unified interpretation of WCAG 2.0 among different web accessibility test tools, including examples using JSON-LD and EARL [16]. Taking into account that the main developers of evaluation tools are part of this working group, the potential of EARL as a language that they use in the future for evaluation reports is clear.

Semantic Web technologies will facilitate the interoperability between accessibility evaluation tools and will allow the creation of federated evaluation systems to ensure obtaining the best results, as the authors of this paper have proposed in [17].

Other studies have also combined semantic technologies in the context of the evaluation of Web accessibility. In [18, 19] a semantic assessment environment called WaaT (Web Accessibility Assessment Tool) is presented. It uses semantic models, representing the most of main accessibility constrains and terms which are required for the design and development of Web applications, through the use of generic and domain ontologies. This tool evaluates the accessibility status of a Web page according to the WCAG 2.0 and WAI-ARIA [20] guidelines, and generate EARL reports. To do this, it accesses different ontologies to complete the information in reports. One of the ontologies created by the authors of this tool is about the WCAG standard, and has been used in our work as reference vocabulary in the evaluation reports based on this standard (Coding 3). The advantage of ontologies is that it is easy to reuse knowledge, as in this case. Unlike our work, the authors based their work on a single standard as WCAG and a single assessment tool. In our case, we combine several reports obtained from different tools and applying different accessibility standards.

Another relevant work is [21], where a conceptual framework for automatic accessibility evaluation of Rich Internet Applications (RIA) is presented. RIA applications included widgets. In this work, the core semantics of the widgets are represented as OWL ontology. This ontology is used to test the conformance of the application with the WAI-ARIA specification, making use of the taxonomy about WAI-ARIA that has been published by the W3C in RDF format, as an appendix included in the specification itself [12]. Like in the first work, this one also used Semantic Web technologies for the evaluation of accessibility according to a single standard and using a single tool.

In conclusion, we can say that there are no published studies using Semantic Web techniques to combine accessibility reports of different tools and applying different accessibility standards. In general, the published works are aimed at creating assessment tools that use these technologies to generate EARL reports semantically enriched with terms obtained from predefined vocabularies or ontologies.

As future work, we intend to integrate the prototype in a complete service-based system for Web Accessibility Federated Evaluation, whose architecture was presented in [17]. The system will use the federation of RESTful services exposed by different accessibility evaluation tools returning EARL results, and combining the results of evaluations of the same Website by different tools using Semantic Web technologies, applying different criteria or preferences established by the evaluator.

Acknowledgements Thanks to the ESVI-AL Cooperation Network, and to the "Master on Software Engineering for the Web" of the University of Alcalá.

References

1. Caldwell, B., Cooper, M., Guarino, L., Vanderheiden, G.: Web content accessibility guidelines (WCAG) 2.0. World Wide Web Consortium. https://www.w3.org/TR/WCAG20/ (2008)
2. ISO/IEC 40500:2012, Information technology—W3C Web content accessibility guidelines (WCAG) 2.0. International Organization for Standardization (2012)
3. Web-based Intranet and Internet Information and Applications (1194.22). In: Guide to the Section 508 Standards. United States Access Board. https://www.access-board.gov/guidelines-and-standards (2001)
4. Semantic Web. World Wide Web Consortium (2016). https://www.w3.org/standards/semanticweb/
5. Reasoners and rule engines: Jena inference support. Apache Software Foundation. https://jena.apache.org/documentation/inference/ (2017)

6. Beckett, D., Berners-Lee, T., Prud'hommeaux, E., Carothers, G.: RDF 1.1 Turtle. World Wide Web Consortium. https://www.w3.org/TR/turtle/ (2014)
7. Brickley, D., Guha, R.V. (eds.): RDF Schema 1.1. World Wide Web Consortium. https://www.w3.org/TR/rdf-schema/ (2014)
8. Hitzler, P., Krötzsch, M., Parsia, B., Patel-Schneider, P.F., Rudolph, S. (eds.): OWL 2 Web Ontology Language Primer (Second Edition). World Wide Web Consortium. https://www.w3.org/TR/owl2-primer/ (2012)
9. Horrocks, I., Patel-Schneider, P.F., Boley, H., Tabet, S., Grosof, B., Dean, M.: SWRL: A Semantic Web Rule Language Combining OWL and RuleML, W3C Member Submission 21 May 2004. World Wide Web Consortium. https://www.w3.org/Submission/SWRL/ (2004)
10. Harris, S., Seaborne, A. (eds.): SPARQL 1.1 Query Language. World Wide Web Consortium. https://www.w3.org/TR/sparql11-query/ (2013)
11. Web Accessibility Evaluation Tools List. Wide Web Consortium. http://www.w3.org/WAI/ER/tools/ (2016)
12. Abou-Zahra, S. (ed.): Evaluation and Report Language (EARL) 1.0 Schema, W3C Working Group Note 2 February 2017. World Wide Web Consortium. https://www.w3.org/TR/EARL10-Schema/ (2017)
13. Timbi-Sisalima C., Hilera J., Otón S., Ingavelez P.: Developing a RESTful API for a web accessibility evaluation tool. In: 18th International Conference on Enterprise Information Systems (ICEIS'16), pp. 443–450. SCITEPRESS (2016)
14. Timbi-Sisalima C., Martín-Amor, C., Otón, S., Hilera, J.R., Aguado-Delgado, J.: Comparative analysis of online web accessibility evaluation tools. In: 25th International Conference on Information Systems Development (ISD'16), pp. 562–573. University of Economics in Katowice, Poland (2016)
15. AChecker. Inclusive Design Research Centre. http://achecker.ca (2011)
16. Fiers, W., Kraft, M. (eds.): Accessibility Conformance Testing (ACT) Rules Format 1.0 W3C Working Draft, 12 September 2017. World Wide Web Consortium. https://www.w3.org/TR/act-rules-format/ (2017)
17. Hilera, J.R., Otón, S., Martin-Amor, C., Timbi-Sisalima, C.: Towards a service-based architecture for web accessibility federated evaluation. In: 9th International Conference on Advances in Computer-Human Interactions (ACHI'16), pp. 6–10. IARIA (2016)
18. Fernandes, N., Kaklanis, N., Votis, K., Tzovaras, D., Carriço, L.: An analysis of personalized web accessibility. In: 11th Web for All Conference (W4A'14), Article 19, 10 pages. ACM Press, New York (2014)
19. Votis, K., Lopes, R., Tzovaras, D., Carrico, L., Likothanassis, S.: A Semantic accessibility assessment environment for design and development for the web. In: International Conference on Universal Access in Human-Computer Interaction (UAHCI'09), pp. 803–813. Springer, Berlin (2009)
20. Craig, J., Cooper, M. (eds.): Accessible Rich Internet Applications (WAI-ARIA) 1.0. World Wide Web Consortium. https://www.w3.org/TR/wai-aria/ (2014)
21. Doush, I.A., Alkhateeb, F., Al Maghayreh, E., Al-Betar, M.A.: The design of RIA accessibility evaluation tool. Adv. Eng. Softw. **57**, 1–7 (2013)

Employee Security Behaviour: The Importance of Education and Policies in Organisational Settings

Lena Y. Connolly, Michael Lang and Doug J. Tygar

Abstract The growing number of information security breaches in organisations presents a serious risk to the confidentiality of personal and commercially sensitive data. Current research studies indicate that humans are the weakest link in the information security chain and the root cause of numerous security incidents in organisations. Based on literature gaps, this study investigates how procedural security countermeasures tend to affect employee security behaviour. Data for this study was collected in organisations located in the United States and Ireland. Results suggest that procedural security countermeasures are inclined to promote security-cautious behaviour, while their absence tends to lead to non-compliant behaviour.

Keywords Employee security behaviour · Procedural security countermeasures
Information security policy · Security education

1 Introduction

Traditionally, organisations have prioritised a technological approach in order to protect their information assets from potential security attacks. While technical tools are essential, research and practice show that technology is unable to provide

A prior version of this paper has been published in the ISD2017 Proceedings (http://aisel.aisnet.org/isd2014/proceedings2017).

L. Y. Connolly (✉) · M. Lang
National University of Ireland Galway, Galway, Ireland
e-mail: lena.connolly@gmail.com

M. Lang
e-mail: michael.lang@nuigalway.ie

D. J. Tygar
University of California, Berkeley, USA
e-mail: doug.tygar@gmail.com

an adequate solution when it comes to certain illicit human actions such as sharing passwords with colleagues, violation of a clear desk policy, or inappropriate disposal of confidential documents [1]. Compliance with such rules entirely depends on employees' motivation to conform, while various sources refer to humans as the weakest link in the security chain [2].

Research and Crossler et al. [2, p. 90] have drawn attention to a notable gap in the literature which has arisen because much of the focus of extant security research is on technical issues, "although a predominant weakness in properly securing information assets is the individual user within an organisation". Behavioural InfoSec research focuses on the mitigation of threats to information assets by identifying factors that promote security cautious behaviour or trigger illicit acts of individuals. These studies enhance our understanding of employee security behaviour by drawing on perspectives such as criminology [3], psychology [4], and organisational control [5]. Additionally, IS researchers have suggested various security countermeasures that can be employed to combat non-compliant behaviour of employees [6]. Based on the predictions of the general deterrence theory (GDT), security countermeasures can serve as deterrent mechanisms to prevent information systems IS misuse [7].

This paper introduces an extended GDT model, indicating that in addition to their negative deterrent effect, security countermeasures also have a positive impact upon employee security behaviour. The results advance our understanding of the underlying process through which security countermeasures affect employee security actions and highlight the important role of employee information security awareness in this process. Our findings also have important implications for the practice of IS security management.

2   Literature Review

Organisational strategies for reducing IS misuse generally fall into four stages—*deterrence, prevention, detection*, and *recovery*. These four stages are collectively referred as the Security Action Cycle [8]. Based on this model, effective IS security management should aim to maximise the number of deterred and prevented incidents of non-compliant behaviour and minimise those that are detected and punished. The focus of this paper is on the stage of *deterrence*. This phase refers to the use of deterrent security countermeasures such as information security policies and security education with the aim to reduce IS misuse. Following Hovav and D'Arcy [9], we use the term "procedural security countermeasures" to collectively describe these controls.

An *information security policy* is defined in this research as a "written statement that defines the requirements for the organisational security management, the employees' responsibility and obligations, sanctions and countermeasures for non-compliance" [10, p. 448]. In line with a deterrence perspective, security policies rely on the same fundamental mechanisms as societal laws,—that is, outlining knowledge of what constitutes illicit behaviour increases the perceived threat of punishment for unacceptable actions [6].

Security education is defined in this study as "instructions that provide users with general knowledge of the information security environment, along with the skills necessary to perform any required security procedures" [6, p. 5]. Security education has a similar deterrent effect through an ongoing security training. The ultimate purpose of education is to enable users to make good decisions by reminding them of the guidelines regarding an acceptable usage of information systems and the potential outcomes in the event that users circumvent the outlined rules.

Several IS researchers have empirically assessed the effectiveness of procedural security countermeasures. The majority of these studies have employed GDT (or some variation of GDT) as a theoretical foundation, assuming that procedural security countermeasures operate as deterrent mechanisms by increasing perceptions of some form of penalty for unacceptable behaviour and hence, reducing IS misuse. Despite this solid theoretical basis, a comprehensive literature review conducted in the course of this study has demonstrated that the findings of deterrent-based research are inconclusive. Although some studies provide evidence that information security policies reduce IS misuse [11], others contradict these inferences [12]. Similarly, Barlow et al. [13] reported that security education is an important predictor of security-compliant behaviour, but Lee et al. [12] concluded that security awareness programmes do not reduce IS misuse. Furthermore, under the presumption that a simple presence of security policies in organisations has no impact on employee actions, additional studies reported that user awareness about information security policy [6] and policy visibility [11] encourages compliance with security policies.

Although these previous studies are highly informative, they investigated the direct effect of procedural security countermeasures on employee security behaviour, overlooking the important role of the users' information security awareness. In particular, a simple presence of the information security policy may not have a desired effect on employee security behaviour [1]. The purpose of the information security policy, as is that of security education, is to increase information security awareness, which, in turn, will promote security-cautious behaviour [2]. However, within the established literature territory, we have not found any empirical studies confirming that security policies and security education affect security actions in organisations indirectly through information security awareness. Additionally, various IS studies emphasised that information security awareness plays an important role in encouraging security-cautious behaviour [1], while empirical findings appeared to be contradictory. For example, although Bulgurcu et al. [1] reported that users' general awareness about information security has a positive effect on their behaviour, Lee et al. [12] asserted that a degree of awareness has no impact on employee security actions. Moreover, there are calls in the literature to "identify factors that lead to information security awareness as it would be an important contribution to academics, since there is a gap in the literature in this direction" [1, p. 543].

Hence, despite the growing body of knowledge in the area of Behavioural InfoSec in recent years, which offers practical solutions on how to encourage security-cautious behaviour and prevent non-compliant actions of employees, there are still several avenues of research that have only barely been explored. In particular, in comparison to other areas of Behavioural InfoSec research, the impact of security countermeasures on security-related behaviour has received relatively little attention. Moreover, the empirical findings are contradictory and therefore inconclusive. Hence, taking in consideration the aforementioned literature gaps, the objective of this study is to answer the following research question:

- How do procedural security countermeasures affect security behaviour in organisational settings?

3   Theoretical Context

Our proposed theoretical model, shown in Fig. 1, integrates *procedural security countermeasures*, *information security awareness*, and *employee security behaviour*. The model expands on GDT by including procedural security countermeasures as factors that tend to increase employees' information security awareness. In turn, employees' awareness about organisational information security requirements, security threats and consequences of illicit actions is inclined to lead to compliant behaviour. That is, procedural security countermeasures influence employee security behaviour indirectly through employee security awareness.

3.1   General Deterrence Theory

The theory of deterrence relies on three individual components: severity, certainty, and celerity of sanctions. Based on the rational choice view of human behaviour, GDT is based upon the central proposition that illicit behaviour can be controlled by the threat of sanctions. Therefore, GDT focuses on disincentives against committing a criminal act and the effect of these disincentives on deterring others from committing deviant acts [14]. The original theory assumes that if a punishment is severe, certain and swift, a rationally calculating human being will measure the

Fig. 1 Conceptual framework

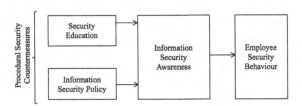

gains and losses before engaging in crime and will desist from a criminal act if the loss is greater than the gain. Therefore, GDT posits that "people respond to policing and the punishment that is associated with the effective policing" [7, p. 258].

Classic GDT has been widely employed in the IS security context under the presumption that employees choose to engage in inappropriate behaviour and therefore that organisational sanctions will prevent deviant actions of employees and deter computer abuse [9]. GDT was further extended and policing is being associated with security countermeasures, including information security policies [12], security education [13], and technical controls [1], assuming that these controls also deter illicit actions of individuals. Therefore, in line with GDT, scholars assume that organisations can reduce IS misuse by implementing anti-virus software, using password protection systems, and implementing procedural security measures.

3.2 Employee Security Behaviour

In this research, *employee security behaviour* is defined as "the behaviour of employees in using organisational information systems (including hardware, software, and network systems etc.), and such behaviour may have security implications" [15, p. 243]. Examples of employee security behaviour include how members of staff handle their passwords, how they deal with organisational data, and how they use network resources [15]. This behaviour may pose or moderate IS security threats. This study does not focus on any specific type of behaviour but at the same time aims to distinguish between positive and negative behaviours because factors that influence these actions may vary. Subsequently, the behaviours of interest include *compliant behaviour* (i.e. adhering to the policies, procedures, and norms of an organisation in relation to information security) and *non-compliant behaviour* (i.e. intentional but non-malicious behaviours of employees that may put organisational information systems at risk and entail non-compliance to the policies, procedures, and norms of an organisation in relation to information security).

3.3 The Role of Information Security Awareness

Bulgurcu et al. [1, p. 532] defined *information security awareness* as "an employee's overall knowledge and understanding of potential information security-related issues and their ramifications, and what needs to be done in order to deal with security-related issues". Security-aware employees are familiar with the security practices and rules of an organisation as well as their responsibilities regarding organisational information resources and the consequences of abusing them, including loss of reputation, substantial financial losses, and even complete disruption of business. When employees understand the purpose of organisational security requirements, they tend to conform with organisational security rules [1]. Prior research confirmed that public awareness can reduce certain illicit acts like shoplifting [16] and workplace drug use [17]. Furthermore, Bulgurcu et al. [1] and D'Arcy et al. [8] emphasised the important role of user security awareness in encouraging compliant behaviour. Procedural security countermeasures are important organisational artifacts that raise employees' awareness regarding potential security threats and consequences of devious behaviour [8]. In turn, the increased awareness has a positive impact upon security-related behaviours because employees tend to understand the importance of following organisational information security rules [1].

4   Research Approach

The endeavour of our research is to understand social interactions between security countermeasures and employee behaviour from the perspective of study participants. Rich qualitative findings within a given context as opposed to broad generalisations are essential for this purpose and therefore, a qualitative approach was adapted in this study. The methodology employed in this research draws on the analytical grounded theory approach [18] and employs the constant comparative method [19].

Data collection was carried out using semi-structured in-person interviews. In total, 19 individuals were selected for interviews, drawn from organisations across a range of industry sectors. Nine interviews were conducted in California and ten were conducted in Ireland. Details about the interviewees and their organisations are given in Table 1. The interview guide was constructed following a thorough analysis of the literature. The guide included questions about procedural security countermeasures, information security awareness and the impact of these factors on employee security behaviour.

Organisations and participants were purposefully selected. In this particular study, it was important to interview organisations from a broad range of industries in order to capture data from organisations with various levels of security with the aim to grasp a holistic view of the research problem. The initial intent was to interview one person in a managerial position and one regular employee in each organisation in order to understand views of both an experienced user and someone with little (if any) experience in the area of information security. Although this proved to be difficult due to the access issues, overall out of nineteen interviewees, eight had expert knowledge on the topic of information security, six had very good knowledge, and the remaining five had basic knowledge regarding information security.

The principle of theoretical sampling was employed in order to guide data collection. Data collection was divided into four stages. In the opening stage (Stage 1), four US organisations of various sizes and with different levels of security were selected, particularly RetCoUS, FinCoUS, PublCoUS, and CivEngCoUS. Four interviews—one in each organisation—were conducted. This data was analysed

Table 1 Facts about interviews of Californian and Irish organisations

Name (aliases)	Organisations' facts	Interviewees' facts
CloudSerUS	IT; 1998; large	1 person: Software Developer
RetCoUS	Finance; 1932; large	1 person: Security Executive
CivEngCoUS	Civil Engineering; 1945; SME	1 person: Civil Engineer
TechCorpUS	IT; 1968; large	2 people: Security Researchers
EducInstUS	Education; 1868; large	2 people: Clerk and Professor
FinCoUS	Finance; 1982; large	1 person: Security Consultant
PublCoUS	Publishing; 2005; SME	1 person: Business Owner
TechCorpIRL	IT; 1968; large	2 people: Manager and IT Exec.
CharOrgIRL	Charity; 1883; large	1 person: Data Protection Officer
BevCorpIRL	Beverage Manuf.; 1944; large	1 person: IT Executive
PublOrgIRL	Publishing; 2000; SME	1 person: Chief Editor
EducOrgIRL	Education; 1845; large	2 people: Clerk and Lecturer
TelCommCorpIRL	IT; 1984; large	1 person: Software Developer
ResRegIRL	Energy Regulation; 1999; SME	1 person: Policy Analyst
BankOrgIRL	Finance; 1982; large	1 person: Security Executive

Table 2 Results of phases 1 and 2 in Ireland and California

Emerged associations
Information Security Policy **and** Increased Information Security Awareness
Lack of Information Security Policy **and** Lack of Information Security Awareness
Security Education **and** Increased Information Security Awareness
Lack of Security Education **and** Lack of Information Security Awareness
Increased Information Security Awareness **and** Compliant Behaviour
Lack of Information Security Awareness **and** Non-compliant Behaviour

(Phases 1 and 2 of data analysis) in order to guide further data collection. Phase 1 of data analysis involved the segmentation of the body of data into discrete 'incidents' [19]. In Phase 2, a set of first-round provisional categories was generated, to which the segmented data would be coded. These categories took two forms: participant-driven and researcher-driven. Having segmented and labelled the body of data and generated a set of first-round provisional categories, one-third of incidents or units were examined and placed into one or more of these categories, and, analysis of their content gave rise to the formation of additional provisional categories. As the process unfolded, connections between emerged categories started to arise (Table 2).

Following the emerged associations between the aforementioned concepts, the next step of data collection (Stage 2) was to interview organisations where procedural security countermeasures were either present or absent in order to find out how these controls tend to influence security behaviour. Furthermore, selecting interviewees with different levels of knowledge in the area of information security was vital to discover the role of information security awareness. To select suitable organisations, a short questionnaire was conducted over the telephone with potential participants. Subsequently, five interviews were conducted in CloudSerUS, TechCorpUS, and EducInstUS. The body of data was analysed again (Phases 1 and 2 of data analysis, see Fig. 1) and provisional results have confirmed the associations emerged in Stage 1.

Furthermore, the same process was repeated in Ireland. In particular, Stage 3 involved selecting comparable organisations in terms of the size and level of security, including BankOrgIRL, CharOrgIRL, ResRegIRL, BevCorpIRL, and PublOrgIRL. Five interviews were conducted in these organisations (one in each organisation) and subsequently analysed (Phases 1 and 2 of data analysis). Concepts and associations between these concepts started to emerge and were similar to the provisional findings discovered in the US organisations interviewed in Stage 1 of data collection (Table 2). Therefore, the selection criteria for Stage 4 was similar to the criteria used to choose organisations in California for Stage 2. Three organisations located in Ireland (TechCorpIRL, TelCommCorpIRL, and EducOrgIRL) and comparable with the US organisations selected in Stage 2 in terms of the size and level of security, were chosen for further interviewing. Five more interviews were conducted in these organisations. The interviews were transcribed and analysed (Phases 1 and 2 of data analysis) and results have confirmed the associations emerged in Stages 1 and 3 (Table 2). It is important to note that the study's findings are based on the data combined from both data sets.

The next phase of data analysis (Phase 3—Coding on) involved merging both data sets and further breaking down of incidents of data identified in the first phase in order to offer a more in-depth understanding of the highly qualitative aspects and offer clearer insights into the meaning embedded therein. In Phase 4, the provisional categories identified in the second phase were analysed for their characteristics and properties so as to develop a 'rule for inclusion' in the form of a propositional statement, coupled with sample data. As a 'rule of inclusion' was developed for each category, the remaining two thirds of the data segments were analysed, compared and coded. As the constant comparative procedure progressed, data incidents that fitted with a 'rule for inclusion', validated that category and emerging theoretical insights. Furthermore, data incidents that failed to fit with existing categories, generated leads to the formation of additional categories. Over the course of this analytical process, categories underwent various changes: while some of them were substantiated quickly, others were eliminated as irrelevant to the focus of inquiry; some were merged due to overlaps or needed to be redefined, and new categories emerged. Subsequently, data reduction (Phase 5) was performed in order to emphasise findings relevant to the objectives of this study. Finally, Phase 6 involved writing analytical memos and validating the proposed findings by seeking evidence in data. Eisenhardt [20] argued that theoretical saturation is reached when a researcher is observing phenomena that have been seen before and therefore, incremental learning becomes minimal. In this study, it was determined that the point of theoretical saturation has been reached once 19 interviews were conducted.

5 Research Findings and Discussion

Our findings indicate that *procedural security countermeasures* tend to increase *information security awareness*, which, in turn, has a tendency to encourage *compliant behaviour*.

5.1 Security Education and Information Security Awareness

Study participants from CloudSerUS, TechCorpUS, TechCorpIRL, and CharOrgIRL reveal that security education tends to increase employee information security awareness. An IT Executive from TechCorpIRL comments:

> When a new member of staff starts, they have to do a generic training to increase their understanding [about security], so that they do not compromise the company...

In contrast, study participants from organisations such as BankOrgIRL, EducOrgIRL, TelCommCorpIRL, and CivEngCoUS share that the lack of security education tends to lead to the lack of information security awareness. For example, a Security Executive of TechCorpIRL notes:

> A lot of security issues are associated with human ignorance. I think there is an aspect of what people do not know. If they do not know, it then causes the gaps and exposures.

However, interviewees from CloudSerUS, RetCoUS, CivEngCoUS, EducInstUS, TechCorpUS, TechCorpIRL, and BevCorpIRL emphasise that in order for security education to be *effective*, it must meet certain requirements. For example, an IT Executive from BevCorpIRL believes that *effective* security training should include *clear examples with consequences* and an *explanation why certain rules are implemented*:

> ...I would give some very clear examples. I would probably try and get some examples from all around BevCorpIRL, where people have done something to bypass the system and there has been a huge impact to the business. So [people would understand the reason behind rules] rather than dictating the rules and policies. I think people need to be educated a little bit more on that. And then have regular, proper security audits where people are held accountable.

A Software Developer shares that CloudSerUS offers *continuous education* in the event policies or rules change:

If any of the policies have been updated or any norms have changed or if anything has changed, we have to do the training again.

Furthermore, a Software Developer from CloudSerUS explains that *security education is mandatory for everyone*, including senior management:

Everybody has to do it. We have mandatory training across every employee right from the CEO down...

Overall, out of 19 interviewees participated in this research project, seven (from six organisations) report an *absence of security training*, while nine (from seven organisations) report its *presence*. Two organisations, PublCoUS and PublOrgIRL, are not included in this analysis because they are too small to have security education in place. PublCoUS has four employees (including Business Owner), two of which are working on a part-time basis. The Business Owner reports that the only confidential information PublCoUS possesses is credit card details of their clients, which are paper-based and stored in a physical safe in the office. The office administrator is the only employee who has access to the safe and she is aware that it has to be locked at all times.

PublOrgIRL is a small voluntary organisation within an educational institution and is responsible for issuing a local newspaper for students. Five journalists, who are writing for the newspaper, are students of the same educational institution and are managed by the Chief Editor. Additionally, the Chief Editor reports that only one journalist has an access to confidential information. She explains that clear instructions on how to keep this information safe were given to this student. It is unnecessary to implement formal security education in this organisation.

Out of seven organisations that provide security education, six consider information security as their top priority and offer *effective* security training. Although security training is implemented in TelCommCorpIRL, a Software Developer shares that the training is rather a 'token' and information security is not taken seriously in TelCommCorpIRL.

Further, data analysis revealed that in organisations, where *effective* security education is implemented, employees have high information security awareness, while in organisations where security training is lacking or present but is inadequate as is the case with TelCommCorpIRL, employees have low information security awareness (Table 3).

Overall, our results demonstrate that *security education* tends to increase employee *information security awareness*. The purpose of security training is to educate employees on how to protect vital organisational assets and why a certain set of rules has to be in place. The 'why' is particularly important because if employees underestimate the significance of a certain rule, they may not be able to justify the extra effort they need to make in order to follow the rule, and, consequently, violate information security requirements. Additionally, when employees fail to understand the reason behind security rules, they may give inaccurate interpretation of their presence and, consequently, misjudge the importance of

Table 3 Link between security education and information security awareness

Organisation	Security training assessment	Information security awareness level
CloudSerUS	Effective	High
RetCoUS	Effective	High
TechCorpUS	Effective	High
FinCoUS	Effective	High
TechCorpIRL	Effective	High
CharOrgIRL	Effective	High
CivEngCoUS	Not present	Low
EducInstUS	Not present	Low
BevCorpIRL	Not present	Low
EducOrgIRL	Not present	Low
ResRegIRL	Not present	Low
BankOrgIRL	Not present	Low
TelCommCorpIRL	Present but inadequate	Low

security requirements. It is also very important to repeat security education due to any changes in rules and/or policies.

Security education appeals to employee conscience by providing details of dreadful consequences that an organisation may experience in the event of a security breach. Fear appeals are induced when consequences for the offender are outlined during security education sessions. Once all these aspects are covered through security education (e.g. how to protect sensitive information, why there is a need to follow rules, consequences of non-conformity for both the organisation and the offender), employees become information security conscious and therefore, are inclined to follow rules. Furnell et al. [21] argued that user information security knowledge is critical to ensure compliance and can be delivered to end-users through education and training. While studies by Barlow et al. [13], Siponen et al. [11] and Straub [7] indicated that security education has a direct effect on employee security actions, it must be noted that information security awareness is an outcome of security education and therefore, security education tends to lead to compliant behaviour indirectly, through security awareness.

5.2 Information Security Policy and Information Security Awareness

Study informants from CloudSerUS, TechCorpIRL, TechCorpUS, and RetCoUS suggest that a policy is inclined to increase employee security awareness. A Product Manager reveals that information security is a top priority in TechCorpIRL. There is a detailed information security policy in place that outlines organisational information security requirements and instructs employees in terms of appropriate and inappropriate actions. The Product Manager asserts:

> I think [when policy is present], people are very conscious of what is appropriate and what is not appropriate because the policy dictates what they can do and what they cannot do...

Although the information security policy is an important information security measure, its simple presence in an organisation may not have the desired effect. Study participants from CloudSerUS, RetCoUS, EducInstUS, CharOrgIRL, BevCorpIRL, and EducOrgIRL propose that for the information security policy to be *effective*, it has to have certain qualities. In particular, for the policy to have a desired effect, it must be *visible*. For example, an IT Manager from BevCorpIRL reveals:

> I have definitely seen rules being broken just to get stuff done. Employees do not understand the implications of why the rule is in place... There are information security policies but they are hidden away on some website someplace.

Furthermore, study participants assert that security policies must be *up-to-date*. For example, a Security Executive from RetCoUS suggests that information security policies have to be *updated* regularly because information security is constantly evolving, such as threats are changing and therefore, security controls have to change accordingly:

> ...Information security is always changing, the threats are always changing, the environment is always changing, and so we have to keep policies up to date.

As it stands today, cybercrime is a fully commercialised enterprise with functions identical to legitimate businesses. The fundamental goal of online fraud is to generate profit, although some cyber attacks have a different purpose. Therefore, cybercriminals continuously develop new types of malware in order to deceive computer users, steal valuable information, or pocket funds. As a result, organisational security policies must be updated as regards to new threats and solutions to defeat these threats.

Next, interviewees suggest that *employee feedback* has to be taken in consideration for the information security policy to function properly. In particular, employees have to apply rules outlined in the information security policy in practice and if a certain rule is hard or impossible to utilise, employees will circumvent it. A Security Executive from RetCoUS stresses:

> Having this open dialogue, employees can change the rules by bringing things up. I have seen it happen in the past. So the policies have been changed based upon the use of the users and them providing that feedback. RetCoUS wants to make sure that information security is implemented to augment the business and not prevent the business from moving forward and so that feedback is really important.

Typically, policy makers lack first-hand experience of applying the very same rules they outline in the policies. In particular, policy implementers take in consideration data protection laws and organisation's priorities in terms of the value of information assets, but rarely the applicability of the rules. Consequently, employees repeatedly hit the wall of overly bureaucratic rules and often break rules.

Moreover, employees point out that policies must be *enforced*. In particular, regular audits have to be in place to check if policies are adhered to. Additionally, employees who break the rules as well as managers on duty must be held accountable. An IT Executive from BevCorpIRL suggests:

> We have a clean desk policy but it is not adhered at all. It would take a simple check by a manager in the evenings to enforce it but it is not done... It is important to have regular, proper security audits, where people and their managers are held accountable.

Crime occurs despite the rewards and punishments that have been devised to encourage compliance. Although crime is a type of behaviour that is condemned by society, human beings still engage in criminal activities for various reasons. Merriam-Webster dictionary defines crime as "an activity that is against the law". Since security policies can be considered as organisational laws, breaking organisational information security rules is a type of crime. Because crime is inevitable, organisations must have measures in place to control wrongful activities of employees. For example, security policies must be enforced through various mechanisms, including audit checks.

In total, out of 19 interviewees participated in this research project, two (from two organisations) report that they are not aware if the information security policy is present in their organisations, while twelve study participants (from 11 organisations) inform that the information security policy is present. Two organisations, PublCoUS and PublOrgIRL, are not included in this analysis because they are too small to have the information security policy in place (see detailed explanation in Sect. 5.1). Out of twelve study informants that report the presence of the information security policy, eight (from six organisations) share that their organisations consider information security as the top priority and offer *effective* information security policies (Table 4). An *effective* policy has a desired effect on information security awareness and therefore, on employee security behaviour, as opposed to *inadequate* policy that exists to rather 'tick a box'.

Further data analysis revealed that in organisations where the information security policy not only exists but is also *effective*, employees are inclined to have a high level of *information security awareness*, while in organisations where the information security policy is either *not present* or present but *inadequate*, employees tend to have a low level of *information security awareness*.

Our findings demonstrate that a security policy tends to increase employee awareness about information security. Typically, a security policy aims to outline organisational information security requirements and the rules that derive from these requirements. Furthermore, security policies provide information on sanctions in the event of non-compliant behaviour, and rewards to encourage compliant behaviour. Although Chan et al. [22] and Straub [7] confirmed that the establishment of information security policies in organisations is vital to encourage security compliant behaviour, these studies do not specify that security policies affect employee actions indirectly through information security awareness. However, Lee

Table 4 Link between information security policy and information security awareness

Organisation	Security policy assessment	Information security awareness level
CloudSerUS	Effective	High
RetCoUS	Effective	High
TechCorpUS	Effective	High
FinCoUS	Effective	High
TechCorpIRL	Effective	High
CharOrgIRL	Effective	High
CivEngCoUS	Unaware if policy is present	Low
EducInstUS (Clerk)	Unaware if policy is present	Low
BevCorpIRL	Present but inadequate	Low
EducOrgIRL	Present but inadequate	Low
EducInstUS (Prof)	Present but inadequate	Low
BankOrgIRL	Present but inadequate	Low
ResRegIRL	Not present	Low
TelCommCorpIRL	Not present	Low

et al. [12] found that the information security policy has no impact on IS misuse behaviour. This contradicting finding could be explained by the employees' lack of awareness of the security policies existence.

Bulgurcu et al. [23] asserted that the mere presence of the information security policy in an organisation does not lead to desirable actions. Employees must be aware of the document and its content and must understand why certain security measures are in place. The most common way to inform employees about security policies is through security education. Data findings of this study are in accordance with these claims.

5.3 Information Security Awareness and Employee Security Behaviour

Study participants from CloudSerUS, CharOrgIRL, TechCorpUS, and EducInstUS share that employee awareness as regards information security tends to lead to compliant behaviour. In particular, a Software Developer from CloudSerUS reports the following:

> When [employees] generally know that there is a good reason for not doing something, they tend to adhere to the information security policy… But if [employees] do not know, then it is bad…

On the other hand, study informants from BevCorpIRL, EducOrgIRL, and EducInstUS report that the lack of information security awareness prompts employees to circumvent information security rules or exercise poor practices. An IT Executive from BevCorpIRL shares:

> Information security rules are useful... But I can see why people circumvent them. Employees are not seeing the implications of why the rule is in place. So they just see it as a challenge to bypass a system...

The above statements confirm that employee information security awareness tends to lead to compliant behaviour. In particular, study participants reveal that when employees understand that there is a good reason behind a certain rule, they exercise safe practices. Knowledge about consequences of non-compliant behaviour is vital. On the other hand, when employees do not understand why a certain rule is in place, they try to bypass it as they perceive it as a barrier to perform their main duties. Bulgurcu et al. [1] and D'Arcy et al. [6] confirmed the important role of information security awareness, suggesting that when users are aware that security policies exist, they are less likely to engage in IS policies misuse. Our findings are in accord with these studies. Although Lee et al. [12] reported that degree of security awareness has no impact on employees' actions, our results show the opposite.

6   Conclusion

Our study builds on general deterrence theory to make an empirical contribution, which takes its place amongst the very few studies in Behavioural InfoSec research that investigate how procedural security countermeasures affect employee security behaviour. Further, prior studies that investigated the impact of procedural security countermeasures on employee security behaviour report contradictory and therefore, inconclusive results. This research provides empirical evidence that procedural security countermeasures, including information security policies and security education, tend to lead to compliant behaviour.

Moreover, prior research projects that focused on procedural security countermeasures, investigated the direct effect of these measures on employee security behaviour. Therefore, the role of information security awareness has been neglected in the extant literature. While IS scholars argued that the ultimate purpose of procedural security countermeasures is to increase information security awareness [13], empirical evidence that supports these claims is lacking. Also, there are calls in the IS literature for studies that investigate factors that lead to information security awareness since information security awareness plays the key role in employees' compliance behaviour [1]. Finally, IS scholars reported contradictory results in terms of the effect of information security awareness on employee security behaviour (e.g. Bulgurcu et al. [1] vs. Lee et al. [12]). The findings of this research project fill the aforementioned gaps and demonstrate that procedural security countermeasures tend to lead to compliant behaviour indirectly, through information security awareness. These insights extend general deterrence theory in a novel way. In particular, the deterrent effect of procedural security countermeasures tends to increase information security awareness. This awareness, in turn, tends to deter malicious actions of employees and encourage security-cautious behaviour. Furthermore, general deterrence theory is typically used to study negative behaviours, while there are calls in the literature to apply the theory across the variety of behaviours, including negative and positive [24]. The focus of this study is on both negative and positive behaviours, which further extends general deterrence theory.

Our findings confirm that a simple presence of security policies and security education in organisations may not have the desired effect. For an information security policy to be *effective*, it must retain certain characteristics. In particular, security policies must be *up to date* and *visible*. The most common way to introduce employees to security policies is through security education. Additionally, policies must be *enforced*, such as employees have to be checked if they follow the rules and held accountable if not. Furthermore, managers on duty have to be held accountable if rules are not adhered to. Moreover, *employee feedback* is important when designing and implementing information security policies since employees have the practical experience of applying information security rules. If a certain rule prevents employees from completing other tasks, they may try to circumvent it. With regards to security education, it must be *mandatory for everyone*, including senior management. *Clear examples* of past security breaches or breaches that took place in other organisations are essential, including consequences that follow after the incident for both the organisation and the offender. Such content will offer employees an *explanation why certain rules are implemented and important to follow*. Additionally, *continuous education* must be enforced; that is if any change takes place in policies, rules, norms or procedures, it must be channeled to the employees through additional training.

Our results also make an important practical contribution. First, this study highlights the vital role of procedural security countermeasures in managing illicit actions in organisations. Security practitioners must realise that focusing on technical measures alone puts organisations at higher risk of security breaches occurring due to "human error". Second, since information security awareness is the key factor in encouraging compliant behaviour, IS security managers must design security education and policies with the aim to increase awareness about security threats and consequences of information security breaches. In particular, real life incidents should be part of security education. Employee awareness that a security breach may lead to organisation's bankruptcy and complete shutdown and consequently, their job loss, would be a strong drive to comply with organisational information security requirements. Third, security practitioners must take in consideration the important characteristics procedural security countermeasures must retain to properly function and fulfil their purpose.

In terms of study limitations, qualitative data is prone to subjective interpretations. Although various techniques were employed to avoid research bias (e.g. member checks, peer debriefing), there is still a possibility that data interpretations had some element of subjectivity. One of the main concerns with qualitative studies is the generalisability of research findings. As this study is exploratory in nature, it is not attempting to generalise the findings but rather to present the uniqueness within study's context. Furthermore, our research would benefit from a secondary data source. However, the access to organisational documents was not possible as it is often the case with studies that investigate sensitive issues. Nevertheless, our study provides some interesting insights on how procedural security countermeasures tend to affect employee security behaviour in organisational settings and answer the research question.

References

1. Bulgurcu, B., Cavusoglu, H., Benbasat, I.: Information security policy compliance: an empirical study of rationally-based beliefs and information security awareness. MIS Q. 34(3), 523–548 (2010)
2. Crossler, R.E., Johnston, A.C., Lowry, P.B., Hu, Q., Warkentin, M., Baskerville, R.: Future directions for behavioral information security research. Comput. Secur. 32, 90–101 (2013)
3. D'Arcy, J., Hovav, A.: Deterring internal information systems misuse. Commun. ACM 50 (10), 113–117 (2007)
4. Lee, Y., Larsen, K.R.: Threat or coping appraisal: determinants of SMB executives' decision to adopt anti-malware software. Eur. J. Inform. Syst. 18(2), 177–187 (2009)
5. Boss, S.R., Kirsch, L.J., Angermeier, I., Shingler, R.A., Ross, R.W.: If someone is watching, I'll do what I'm asked: mandatoriness, control, and information security. Eur. J. Inform. Syst. 18(2), 151–164 (2009)
6. D'Arcy, J., Hovav, A., Galletta, D.: User awareness of security countermeasures and its impact on information systems misuse: a deterrence approach. Inform. Syst. Res. 20(1), 1–20 (2009)
7. Straub, D.W.: Effective IS security: an empirical study. Inform. Syst. Res. 1(3), 255–276 (1990)
8. Straub, D.W., Welke, R.J.: Coping with systems risk: security planning models for management decision making. MIS Q. 22(4), 441–469 (1998)
9. Hovav, A., D'Arcy, J.: Applying an extended model of deterrence across cultures: an investigation of information systems misuse in the U.S. and South Korea. Inf. Manag. 49(2), 99–110 (2012)
10. Cheng, L., Ying, L., Wenli, L., Holm, E., Zhai, Q.: Understanding the violation of IS security policy in organizations: an integrated model based on social control and deterrence theory. Comput. Secur. 39, 447–459 (2013)
11. Siponen, M., Mahmood, M.A., Pahnila, S.: Are employees putting your company at risk by not following information security policies? Commun. ACM 52(12), 145–147 (2009)
12. Lee, S.M., Lee, S.G., Yoo, S.: An integrative model of computer abuse based on social control and general deterrence theories. Inf. Manag. 41(6), 707–718 (2004)
13. Barlow, J.B., Warkentin, M., Ormond, D., Dennis, A.R.: Don't make excuses! Discouraging neutralization to reduce IT policy violation. Comput. Secur. 39 (Part B), 145–159 (2013)
14. Blumstein, A., Cohen, J., Nagin, D.: Deterrence and incapacitation: Estimating the effects of criminal sanctions on crime rates. In: Bridges, G., Crutchfield, R., Weis, R.L. (eds.) Crime and Society: Reading in Criminal Justice, vol. 3, pp. 96–100. Pine Forge Press, Thousand Oaks (1996)
15. Guo, K.H.: Security-related behavior in using information systems in the workplace: a review and synthesis. Comput. Secur. 32, 242–251 (2013)
16. Sacco, V.F.: Shoplifting prevention: the role of communication-based intervention strategies. Can. J. Criminol. 27(1), 15–29 (1985)

17. Quazi, M.M.: Effective drug-free workplace plan uses worker testing as deterrent. Occup. Health Saf. **62**(6), 26–31 (1993)
18. Matavire, R., Brown, I.: Profiling grounded theory approaches in information systems research. Eur. J. Inform. Syst. **22**(1), 119–129 (2013)
19. Maykut, P., Morehouse, R.: Beginning Qualitative Research: A Philosophic and Practical Guide. The Falmer Press, London (1994)
20. Eisenhardt, K.M.: Building theories from case study research. Acad. Manag. Rev. **14**(4), 532–550 (1989)
21. Furnell, S.M., Gennatou, M., Dowland, P.S.: A prototype tool for IS security awareness and training. Int. J. Logistics Inform. Manag. **15**(5), 352–357 (2002)
22. Chan, M., Woon, I., Kankanhalli, A.: Perceptions of information security at the workplace: linking information security climate to compliant behaviour. J. Inform. Priv. Secur. **1**(3), 18–41 (2005)
23. Bulgurcu, B., Cavusoglu, H., Benbasat, I.: Quality and fairness of an information security policy as antecedents of employees' security engagement in the workplace: an empirical investigation. In: 43rd Annual Hawaii International Conference on System Sciences, pp. 1–7. IEEE Press (2010)
24. D'Arcy, J., Herath, T.: A review and analysis of deterrence theory in the IS security literature: making sense of the disparate findings. Eur. J. Inform. Syst. **20**(6), 643–658 (2011)

Exploring How Environmental and Personal Factors Influence Knowledge Sharing Behavior Leads to Innovative Work Behavior

Van Dong Phung, Igor Hawryszkiewycz and Muhammad Binsawad

Abstract Many governments have been struggling to build a higher education system that is innovative to the requests of national knowledge-based development. It is essential to explore knowledge sharing behavior (KSB) from environmental and individual perspectives. It can help to contribute to innovative work behavior (IWB) towards knowledge-based development initiatives, in particular regarding the phenomenon of knowledge sharing (KS) in higher education institutions (HEIs). The aim of this research is to propose a research model based on social cognitive theory (SCT) that comprises environmental factors (subjective norms, trust), personal factors (knowledge self-efficacy, enjoyment in helping others, organizational rewards, reciprocal benefits, and psychological ownership of knowledge), KSB and IWB. We advance to conduct a survey to examine our proposed conceptual model. It is expected that this research will contribute to deeper understanding of the effects of personal and environmental factors and KSB on IBW within HEIs. Implications and future work in this area are also proposed.

Keywords Knowledge sharing · Knowledge sharing behavior · Innovative work behavior · Social cognitive theory

A prior version of this paper has been published in the ISD2017 Proceedings (http://aisel.aisnet.org/isd2014/proceedings2017).

V. D. Phung (✉) · I. Hawryszkiewycz
University of Technology, Sydney, Australia
e-mail: dongpv@gmail.com

I. Hawryszkiewycz
e-mail: Igor.Hawryszkiewycz@uts.edu.au

M. Binsawad
King Abdulaziz University, Jeddah, Saudi Arabia
e-mail: Mbinsawad@kau.edu.sa

© Springer International Publishing AG, part of Springer Nature 2018   97
N. Paspallis et al. (eds.), *Advances in Information Systems Development*,
Lecture Notes in Information Systems and Organisation 26,
https://doi.org/10.1007/978-3-319-74817-7_7

1 Introduction

The aim of this paper is to investigate how environmental and personal factors influence knowledge sharing (KS) can facilitate or impede innovative work behavior (IWB) by using social cognitive theory (SCT)-based model. By studying the relationships between critical KS factors, knowledge sharing behavior (KSB) and IWB, this research is help to examines how higher education institutions can foster a KS culture that will support their employees' IWB.

IWB can be defined as "the intentional creation, introduction and application of new ideas (within a work role, group or organization)" to meet new challenges in complex environments [1–3]. It is widely stated to be vital for the productive functioning and long-lived sustainable development of organizations [1, 4] which depend on their employees' capability to innovate methods, goods, services and operations [5]. Furthermore, IWB helps to find a better way to do or make something new that others want to use or ways to organise resources better [6]. Thus, it is essential to create a culture where IWB is practiced throughout the organization and every person generates, promotes, and uses knowledge in imaginative ways [7].

An organization can successfully promote IWBs by directly integrating knowledge in its business plan, and promoting individuals' attitudes and behaviours consistent with KS as well [8]. Nevertheless, KS has not met many organizations' expectation. It has been argued that individuals believe that their knowledge is power and valuable, therefore, sharing knowledge is generally unusual [9]; hoarding knowledge is the real propensity [10, 11]. Moreover, knowledge management (KM) has only highlighted on the technology aspect in many organizations, in particular technology infrastructures [10, 12]. It is not surprisingly, KS is problem for organizations with the existing of information systems [13–15]. Finally, several studies have indicated that KM often fails in encouraging KS practices because of it ignores the importance of the willingness of KS [15]. Undoubtedly, the biggest challenge in promoting IWB is the individual willingness to share knowledge with others. There have been two issues are involved in this respect [10, 16]. One is personal perceptions, which are based on self-efficacy and outcome expectations [10, 16]. The other is social influences based on trust and subjective norms [10, 16, 17]. Investigating the personal perceptions [17, 18] and the influence of the social environment on KSB lead to IWB [17, 19, 20] would help both and practitioners get insights into how to encourage KS in teams, groups or the organization in order to facilitate IWB. In order to achieve this goal, this paper will propose an integrated research model based on social cognitive theory (SCT).

SCT has been widely used in the literature of information systems for identifying the individual behavior [10, 21]. SCT states that an action that has personal perception in a social environment would be taken by a person. A personal perception to behave in a certain way has some cognitive factors. One is self-efficacy or the belief is a potential significant factor impacting the decision of sharing knowledge [22]. Other important factor has significant influence on individual KS decisions is outcome expectations that are related to rewards systems and reciprocal benefits [10, 16, 23]. Furthermore, subjective norm shows individual's feeling about the social pressure they feel about a given behaviour surrounding them. Employees having positive subjective norms towards given behaviours than the concerned behaviour intentions are more likely to be positive in KS. Finally, trust has also been identified as an important factor influencing KS [10, 16].

To sum up, then, it is an imperative need to take into account the influences of environmental and personal factors on KSB in order to improve IWB in the context of higher education institutions. This paper will contribute to the literature of KS by investigating and answering the two main research questions as follows: (1) How do environmental and personal factors impact on KSB? (2) How does the KSB impact individuals' IWB?

The organization of this paper is as follows. The next section present the literature review, followed by describing the research model development. Then, the sample and data collection methods, questionnaire design and data analysis are described in the proposed research method section. Finally, the conclusion is presented.

2 Literature Review

2.1 Innovative Work Behavior

In this current study, we intend to examine the relationships between environmental and individual factors and KSB lead to IWB in the higher education institutions context, using a model including IWB factor derived from Janssen [1]. IWB comprises three components: idea creation, idea promotion, and idea implementation. The first step of the individual innovation is to create idea that is generation of new and valuable ideas in any field [1, 4, 24]. Second, potential colleagues or partners will be promoted the idea which occurs when an individual has created an idea and engages in social activities to get supporter surrounding an idea [1]. Finally, the innovation process involves idea application by developing a model or innovative prototype that is likely to be tried and utilized in teams, groups or the whole organization [24]. Basic innovations are usually accomplished by individuals; whilst the completion of more complicated innovations often needs teamwork relies upon a diversity of knowledge, ability, and work roles [1, 24]. With the belief that individual IWB have positively effects on work outcomes, several researchers have dedicated increasing attention to factors that potentially foster IWB such as KS, organizational climate and IWB [20], KS and IWB [18], KS determinants, behaviors, and IWB [19], and organizational climate for innovation and organizational performance and IWB [25]. However, the relationship between KSP and IWB is still largely unexamined, especially in non-Western countries [25] in higher education institutions.

2.2 Knowledge Sharing Behavior

Knowledge is a significant organizational resource. KS contributes to developing competitive advantages for organizations in complex environments, such as the improvement of intellectual capital, by encouraging the exchange and creation of knowledge within an organization. This is because knowledge is the key factor for achieving continuous innovation at both individual and organizational levels. It is also examined a closely related factor for the progress of any individual or organization, hence it is an essential indicator to be studied in the KS on individual IWB in higher education institutions. KSB can be defined as the process involving the exchange of knowledge between individuals and groups of people [9]. The authors develop the measurement of KSB by the frequency of knowledge dissemination (giving or presenting knowledge to potential receivers) that can also be beneficial for an organization in general, a higher education institution in particular. In turn, KS is relied upon knowledge management, which is a necessary activity in all businesses. Any KS practice occurring within organizations between its employees will always be based on both knowledge-giving and knowledge-receiving. Knowledge management is a broader term that caters to a wide range of topics, while KS is a specific focus area of knowledge management [26]. KS, when performed in conjunction with other aspects of the step-by-step process of knowledge management (creation, storage, sharing, and application) can fulfil a strategic necessity for organizations that wish to improve their capabilities and performance [27].

3 Theoretical Background and Research Model

KSB is related to the employees' willingness of sharing their knowledge with the others in the organization [10]. Previous studies have emphasized several factors that impact personal willingness of KS including subjective norm, trust, psychological ownership, and motivation (e.g., Hsu et al. [10]; Lin [23]). Thus, the study could rationally suppose that employee' behavior for KS would be leaded by individual perceptions and social influences. We are examining the influence of environmental and personal factors on KSB, using the proposed model based on Bandura's SCT [28] (see Fig. 1). In SCT model, environmental influences, personal

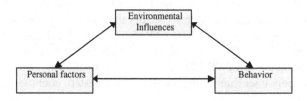

Fig. 1 The interactions between environment, person and behavior (Bandura's SCT [28])

factors, and behavior act as interactive relationships [29]. Bandura [30] explains the main concepts of SCT by the "triadic reciprocal causation" as follows:

1. Environmental influences that influence the personal capacity to successfully fulfill the behavior;
2. Personal factors determine whether a person has low or high knowledge self-efficacy leads to his/her behavior;
3. Behavior is the response which a person gains after his/her performing a certain behavior.

This research focuses on the exploration of the role of the environmental and personal factors on individual behaviors. The literature available on previous studies is limited to the similar study context that could provide a theoretical foundation for this study will be cited. Table 1 presents the summary of the prior research models.

The proposed conceptual model consists of four main constructs, including environmental factors, personal factors, KSB and IWB (Fig. 2). Each of these constructs and their sub-constructs will be described below.

Environmental factors: The factors from the social environment dimension.

- Subjective norms (SN): The extent to which an individual perceives whether social pressure will influence the performance of KS behavior [31].
- Trust (TRU): Refers to "The extent of belief in good behaviors, competence, and reliability of members with respect to sharing knowledge in the organization" [15, 32].

Table 1 Dimensions of environmental and individual factors, KS and IWB across studies

Related literature	SN	TRU	KSE	EHO	REW	RB	POK	KS	IWB
Hsu et al. [10]		✓	✓		✓			✓	
Han et al. [35]						✓			
Lin et al. [15]		✓	✓					✓	
Lin [23]				✓					
Tsai and Cheng [53]			✓		✓			✓	
Janssen [1]					✓				✓
Dong et al. [54]	✓	✓			✓			✓	
Lin [8]			✓		✓			✓	
Othman [33]		✓			✓			✓	
Yu et al. [20]								✓	✓
Radaelli et al. [18]						✓		✓	✓
Akhavan et al. [19]	✓							✓	✓

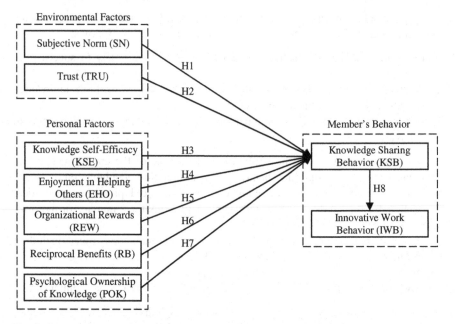

Fig. 2 The proposed research model showing factors based on SCT

Personal factors: The factors from the individual dimension.

- Knowledge self-efficacy (KSE): The extent of confidence in employees' ability to sharing knowledge that is important to the organization [15].
- Enjoyment in helping others (EHO): Refers to "Knowledge workers who derive enjoyment from helping others may be more favorable oriented toward KS and more inclined to share knowledge" [8].
- Organizational rewards (REW): Refers to "The degree to which a reward system to share any new and creative ideas and effectiveness KS" [33].
- Reciprocal benefits (RB): "Reciprocal benefit is a form of conditional benefit; that is, individual expect future benefits from his or her present actions" [34].
- Psychological ownership of knowledge (POK): "The extent to which individuals believe on the possession and are responsible towards the knowledge they possess" [35].

Knowledge sharing behavior (KSB): The extent to which a person performs KS activities in the organization [9, 15].

Innovative work behavior (IWB): "The extent to which employees behave to create, promote, and implement new ideas in an group or organization" [1].

3.1 Environmental Dimensions

• Subjective norm and knowledge sharing behavior

According to Ajzen [31], the subjective norm is a social factor which can be defined as the degree to which one perceives social pressure to carry out or not to carry out a certain behavior. Subjective norm has acquired significant empirical support as an import antecedent to behavioral [17, 36]. Hee [37] emphasized the impact of others who are important to the employee such as "close friends, relatives, colleagues, or business partners". Subjective norm shows personal emotion regarding the social pressure they perceive about given behaviors surrounding them. Also, employees having positive subjective norms lead to given behaviors than the concerned behavior intentions are more likely to be positive in KS. Therefore, we hypothesize that.

H1: Subjective norm has a positive effect on KSB.

• Trust and knowledge sharing behaviour

Trust can be defined as "maintaining reciprocal faith in each other in terms of intention and behaviors" [32, 38]. It may encourage the exchange of knowledge to be substantive, influential, and open [32, 39, 40]. Trust affects KS decisions and with trust, a person becomes less willing to share knowledge with others [9, 15]. According to Nonaka [41] interpersonal trust is a key factor in teams, groups and organizations to establishing an environment for KS. Employees are more willing to engage into KS when they have a high level of trust in their relationships [32]. Thus, interpersonal trust increases individuals' tendency to participate in KS practices [42]. Therefore, we hypothesize that:

H2: Trust has a positive effect on KSB.

3.2 Individual Dimensions

• Knowledge self-efficacy and knowledge sharing behaviour

Knowledge self-efficacy is an individual's judgment of his or her ability to organize and execute successful performance in everyday tasks [15]. The individual's sense of self-efficacy is affected by the tendency of individuals to take actions such as level of problems, expressed interest, persistence and task effort [10]. Lin's study shows that knowledge sharing contributions improve an organization's performance if staff increase their willingness to donate and collect knowledge [8]. Accordingly:

H3: Knowledge self-efficacy has a positive effect on KSB.

• Enjoyment in helping others and knowledge sharing behaviour

Prior research shows that employees are inherently interested in giving knowledge because of the enjoyment acquired from helping others [43]. Thus, employees are likely more favorably oriented toward sharing their knowledge in terms of both giving and receiving [23]. Therefore, we hypothesize that:

H4: Enjoyment in helping others has a positive impact on KSB.

- Organizational rewards and knowledge sharing behavior

According to Lin [23], from an extrinsic motivational aspect, a person's behavior is driven by its perceived benefits and the values of the behaviour. Receiving organizational rewards or beneficial reciprocity are the main purposes of motived behaviors [23, 44]. Providing incentives and rewards to motivate staff to contribute in knowledge sharing adoption are recommended [45]. Individuals who share their knowledge may improve team performance and consecutively increase the personal rewards received [46]. Incentives and rewards encourage staff to share knowledge [17]. Organizational rewards point out what the organizational values form individual behaviors [8]. Organizational rewards can vary according to the organization policies from monetary incentives (e.g. increased salary and bonuses) to non-monetary awards (e.g. promotion incentives and job security) [8, 9]. Therefore, we hypothesise that:

H5: Organizational rewards has a positive effect on KSB.

- Reciprocal benefits and knowledge sharing behavior

Reciprocal benefit is a form of conditional benefit; that is, the individual expects future benefits from his or her present actions. It means that an action is done in response to prior friendly behaviors [34]. Many researchers have conducted detailed analyses of reciprocity and indicated that it can be valuable to knowledge contributors as they anticipate future help from others [34]. Also, studies have investigated that reciprocity can yield an effective motivation to encourage KS and consequently establish long-term mutual cooperation [23]. Thus, people who expect reciprocity from other members through sharing their knowledge will share more useful and creative ideas and their satisfaction with the meeting will be higher KS intentions [23, 34]. Therefore, we hypothesize that:

H6: Reciprocal benefits has a positive effect on KSB.

- Psychological ownership of knowledge (POK) and knowledge sharing behavior

POK can be described as the degree to which people believe on the possession and are responsible towards the knowledge they possess [47]. That is, POK explains the feeling of possession linking to knowledge in a psychological sense that makes persons regard intangible/tangible objectives as an addition of themselves [35]. Van Dyne and Pierce [48] found that the POK can stimulate an altruistic spirit, supporting to extra-role behaviour such as KSB and individuals who have a sense of POK may display a sense of belonging which impacts altruistic spirit and which influences KSB. Thereby, POK is conductive to KSB on the part of individuals. Therefore, we hypothesize that:

H7: Psychological ownership of knowledge has a positive impact on KSB.

3.3 Knowledge Sharing and Innovative Work Behavior

It is clear that an employee's ability to transfer and utilise knowledge may encourage his or her level of individual innovation, for example, faster problem-solving capacity and improved rapid reaction to new challenges. Many academics highlighted the importance of KS to improve individual IWB [18–20]. Effective knowledge processes can create important organizational intellectual capital and intangible resources to improve performance [49]. For example, when the employee transfer tacit knowledge into explicit knowledge, the entire organization will benefit from it [35]. This shows that when organizations manage their knowledge assets better, the organization will then have a greater chance of better performance in both organizational and individual levels [35, 44]. This research expects that individual willingness to share knowledge with each other is likely to sustain IWB and thus contribute to better position the organization with regard to long-term competitive advantage in complex environments. Therefore, we hypothesize that.

H8: Knowledge sharing behavior positively impacts innovative work behaviour.

4 Proposed Research Method

The sequential mixed-methods, including quantitative and qualitative methods, will be used to accomplish the research goal with the sample of academic staff in higher education institutions in Vietnam, an Asian developing country. The questionnaires will be conducted in stage one to collect the data from the study sample about their influencing factors that will then be used in the research framework. Based on that stage two will be undertaken by interviews to validate the quantitative results.

4.1 Sample and Data Collection

After being developed from the reviewed literature, the comparability of the English and Vietnamese versions of the questionnaire will be double checked by two language experts (NAATI—the National Accreditation Authority for Translators and Interpreters). A total of 4 universities will be randomly selected from the list of 37 public universities in the north of Vietnam published by the

Ministry of Education and Training. This study chooses to use a sample size of 800 which is well above the recommended thumb-rule of sample size of the 200–400 range with 10–15 indicators to conduct the structure equation modelling [50]. Then, the questionnaire with a cover letter will be delivered to and collected from a total of 800 academic staff (volunteers) by the administrative staff of respective departments before being returned in sealed envelopes to ensure voluntary participation and the anonymity of the participants.

4.2 Measures

In this study, the existing measures from prior studies will be used for the questionnaire. All items used to operationalise constructs will be mainly adapted for use in the KS context in Vietnam. All items will be measured using a five-point Likert-type scale (ranging from 1 = never to 5 = awlays or 1 = strongly disagree to 5 = strongly agree). Subjective norm will be measured through three items adapted from Bock et al. [17] and Ajzen [31]. A six-item scale adapted from Lee and Choi [32] will be used to measure trust. A four-item scale was adapted to measure knowledge self-efficacy based on Lin [23]. Organizational rewards will be measured by four items adapted from Lin [23]. Moreover, reciprocal benefits will be measured using three items adapted from Lin [23]. A four-item scale adapted from Lin [23] will be used to measure enjoyment in helping others. Additionally, a five-item scale measuring psychological ownership of knowledge was adapted from Dyne and Pierce [48] and Han [35]. Furthermore, KSB will be measured by five items adapted from an examination Davenport and Prusak [9] and Hsu et al. [10]. Finally, nine items adapted from Janssen [1] will be used to measure IWB. Table 2 summarizes the measurement scales for the constructs of the proposed model.

4.3 Data Analysis

We intend to analyse our data in two phases. For phase 1 (Quantitative data analysis), a multivariate statistical approach will be implemented to quantitatively analyse data collected from the questionnaires including descriptive data analysis to find if the data is ready to continue to the multivariate data analyses step (participants' profiles and data screening by studying normality, means, standard deviations and standard error of the mean), measurement scale analysis to capture the meaning of each model construct through an assessment of reliability and validity (Cronbach's alpha) addition to this, item-total correlations will be used to assess the extent to which a particular item belonged to its scale, the validity of the measurement by using Explanatory Factor Analysis (EFA) and Confirmatory Factor Analysis (CFA) and Structural Equation Modelling (SEM) to examine the causal relationships of the model [51].

Table 2 The summarization of the measurement scales for each construct

Measures/items	Sources
Subjective norm: 3 items • My president thinks that I should share my knowledge with other members in the organization • My department's leader thinks that I should share my knowledge with other members in the organization • My colleagues think that I should share my knowledge with other members in the organization	Bock et al. [17], Ajzen [31]
Trust: 6 items Our organization members ... • Are generally trustworthy • Have reciprocal faith in other members' behaviors • Have reciprocal faith in others' ability • Have reciprocal faith in others' behaviors to work toward organizational goals • Have reciprocal faith in others' decision toward organizational interests than individual interests • Have relationships based on reciprocal faith	Lee and Choi [32]
Knowledge self-efficacy: 4 items • I am confident that I possess knowledge that others in my organization would consider valuable • I have the expertise required to provide valuable knowledge for my organization • Most other employees can provide more valuable knowledge than I can. (Reverse coded) • It does not really make any difference whether I share my knowledge with colleagues	Lin [23]
Enjoyment in helping others (EHO): 4 items • I enjoy sharing my knowledge with colleagues • I enjoy helping colleagues by sharing my knowledge • It makes me feel good by helping someone by sharing my knowledge • Sharing my knowledge with colleagues is pleasurable	Lin [23]
Rewards: 4 items • I will receive a higher salary in return for my knowledge sharing • I will receive a higher bonus in return for my knowledge sharing • I will receive increased promotion opportunities in return for my knowledge sharing • I will receive increased job security in return for my knowledge sharing	Lin [23]
Reciprocal benefits: 3 items When I share my knowledge with colleagues ... • I strengthen ties between existing members of the organization and myself • I expand the scope of my association with other organization members • Expect to receive knowledge in return when necessary	Lin [23]

(continued)

Table 2 (continued)

Measures/items	Sources
Psychological ownership of knowledge: 5 items • I feel that the knowledge I have is mine • I am willing to treat my own knowledge as if it belongs to everybody in the organization • I feel a very high degree of personal ownership for the knowledge that I possess • I believe that the knowledge I have acquired during the course of my job is my personal intellectual property • Most of the people that work for this organization feel as though they own the company	Han [35], Dyne and Pierce [48]
Knowledge sharing behavior: 5 items • I frequently participate in knowledge sharing activities in my department or/and the company • I usually spend a lot of time conducting knowledge sharing activities in my department or/and the company • When participating in my department or/and the university, I usually actively share my knowledge with others • When discussing a complicated issue, I am usually involved in the subsequent interactions • I usually involve myself in discussions of various topics rather than specific topics	Davenport and Prusak [9], Hsu et al. [10]
Innovative work behavior: second-order factor *Idea generation: 3 items* • I create new ideas for difficult issues • I search out new working methods, techniques, or instruments • I generate original solutions for problems *Idea promotion: 3 items* • I mobilize support for my new ideas • I make important organizational members enthusiastic for my new ideas • I acquire approval for my new ideas *Idea implementation: 3 items* • I transform my new ideas into useful applications • I introduce my new ideas into the work environment in a systematic way • I evaluate the utility of my new ideas	Janssen [1]

The study chooses to employ EFA prior to do SEM (including CFA) because of three main reasons below:

1. All items of the current research instrument have been adapted from prior studies and an extensive literature review into the knowledge-sharing behavior context. In this context of study, the current sample substantially differs from that previous research as well as these measured variables had not been operated extensively. Thus, EFA is considered essential for this study.
2. Although the proposed research model was developed based on previously tested empirical research, but it has not been tested [52].

3. Using EFA that helps the researcher can be assured that the measures are valid and reliable prior to do SEM. Otherwise the researcher do not know if it can be relied on the findings from SEM. In general, an EFA prepares the data set to be used for cleaner SEM.

We will use the Statistical Package for the Social Sciences (SPSS) (22.0) and Amos 22. For Phase 2 (Qualitative data analysis), data collected from interviews will be interpreted to validate the quantitative results as it provides a rich and in-depth investigation of the organizational context where KS happens [16].

5 Conclusion and Future Work

This work has explained the study in exploring influence of knowledge sharing (KS) practices on innovative work behavior (IWB) in the higher education institutions context. The significant contributions will yield to both theory and practice. The contributions to the literature of knowledge management are as follows: (1) to deeper understand the impact of environmental (subjective norms, trust) and personal factors (knowledge self-efficacy, enjoyment in helping others, organizational rewards, reciprocal benefits, and psychological ownership of knowledge) on knowledge sharing behavior (KSB) and (2) explore and explain what are the effects of KSB in facilitating or impeding IWB. It will contribute to practitioners as two following aspects: (1) to help university leaders and managers understand how environmental and personal factors can help facilitate or impede the KSB that occurs during the exchange of knowledge between individuals within teams, groups and/or the whole organization and (2) to guide university leaders and managers in building the appropriate policies in promoting KS environment in their organization in order to improve IWB in higher education institutions which contributes to knowledge-based development initiatives.

Future work can test this proposed model empirically by using the questionnaire, followed by the validation of this model that described in Sect. 4. Our model is expected to be tested in any organizations in which future researchers or practitioners wish to test this model.

References

1. Janssen, O.: Job demands, perceptions of effort-reward fairness and innovative work behavior. J. Occup. Organ. Psychol. **73**, 287–302 (2000). https://doi.org/10.1348/096317900167038
2. Javed, B., Naqvi, S., Khan, A., Arjoon, S., Tayyeb, H.: Impact of inclusive leadership on innovative work behavior: the role of psychological safety. J. Manag. Organ., 1–20 (2017). https://doi.org/10.1017/jmo.2017.3
3. Scott, S.G., Bruce, R.A.: Determinants of innovative behavior: a path model of individual innovation in the workplace. Acad. Manag. J. **37**, 580–607 (1994)

4. Amabile, T.M., Conti, R., Coon, H., Lazenby, J., Herron, M.: Assessing the work environment for creativity. Acad Emy Manag. J. **39**, 1154–1184 (1996)
5. Afsar, B., Badir Y.: The impacts of person-organization fit and perceived organizational support on innovative work behaviour: the mediating effects of knowledge sharing behavior. Int. J. Inform. Syst. Change Manag. (IJISCM) **7**(4) (2015)
6. Hawryszkiewycz, I.T.: Knowledge Management: Organizing Knowledge Based Enterprises, First. Palgrave Macmillan, Basingstoke, England (2010)
7. Hawryszkiewycz, I.T.: Designing Creative Organizations: Tools, Processes and Practice, 1. Emerald Books, Bingley, UK (2017)
8. Lin, H.F.: Knowledge sharing and firm innovation capability: an empirical study. Int. J. Manpower **28**(3/4), 315–332 (2007)
9. Davenport, T.H., Prusak, L.: Working Knowledge: How Organizations Manage What They Know. Harvard Business School Press, Boston (1998)
10. Hsu, M.H., Ju, T.L., Yen, C.H., Chang, C.M.: Knowledge sharing behavior in virtual communities: the relationship between trust, self-efficacy, and outcome expectations. Int. J. Hum.-Comput. Stud. **65**(2), 153–169 (2007)
11. Webster, J., Brown, G., Zweig, D., Connelly, C.E., Brodt, S., Sitkin, S.: Beyond knowledge sharing: knowledge withholding at work. In: Martocchio, J.J. (ed.) Research in Personnel and Human Resources Management, vol. 27, pp. 1–37. Emerald Group Publishing, Bradford (2008)
12. Pfeffer, J., Sutton, R.: Knowledge "What" to do is not enough: turning knowledge into action. Calif. Manag. Rev. **42**(1), 83–108 (1999)
13. Bakker, M., Leenders, R.T.A.J., Garray, S.M., Kratzer, J., Van Engelen, J.M.L.: Is trust really social capital? Knowledge sharing in product development projects. Learn. Organ. **13**(6), 594–607 (2006)
14. Argote, L., Ingram, P., Levin, J.M., Moreland, R.L.: Organizational Learning: Creating, Retaining, and Transferring Knowledge. Kluwer Academic Publishers, Boston, MA (2000)
15. Lin, M.J., Hung, S.W., Chen, C.J: Fostering the determinants of knowledge sharing in professional virtual communities. Comput. Hum. Behav. **25**(4), 929–939, ISSN 0747-5632 (2009)
16. Wang, S., Noe, R.A.: Knowledge sharing: A review and directions for future research. Hum. Resour. Manag. Rev. **20**(2), 115–131, ISSN 1053-4822 (2010)
17. Bock, G.W., Zmud, R.W., Kim, Y., Lee, J.: Behavioral intention formation in knowledge sharing: examining the roles of extrinsic motivators, social psychological forces, and organizational climate. MIS Q. **29**(1), 87–111 (2005)
18. Radaelli, G., Lettieri, E., Mura, M., Spiller, N.: Knowledge sharing and innovative work behaviour in healthcare: a micro-level investigation of direct and indirect effects. Creativity Innov. Manag. **23**, 400–414 (2014). https://doi.org/10.1111/caim.12084
19. Akhavan, P., Hosseini, S.M., Abbasi, M., Manteghi, M.: Knowledge-sharing determinants, behaviors, and innovative work behaviors: an integrated theoretical view and empirical examination. Aslib J. Inform. Manag. **67**(5), 562–591 (2015)
20. Yu, C., Yu, T., Yu, C.: Knowledge sharing, organizational climate, and innovative behavior: a cross-level analysis of effects. Soc. Behav. Pers. Int. J. **41**, 143–156 (2013)
21. Compeau, D.R., Higgins, C.A.: Computer self-efficacy development of a measure and initial test. MIS Q. **19**(2), 189–211 (1995)
22. Bock, G.W., Kim, Y.G.: Breaking the myths of rewards: an exploratory study of attitudes about knowledge sharing. Inform. Res. Manag. J. **15**(2), 14–21 (2002)
23. Lin, H.F.: Effects of extrinsic and intrinsic motivation on employee knowledge sharing intentions. J. Inform. Sci. **33**(2), 135–149 (2007)
24. Kanter, R.: When a thousand owners bloom: structural, collective, and social conditions for innovation in organizations. In: Staw, B.M., Cummings, L.L. (eds.) Research in Organizational Behavior, vol. 10, pp. 169–211. JAI Press, Greenwich, CT (1988)

25. Shanker, R., Bhanugopan, R., Beatrice, I.J.M., Van Der Farrell, F.: Organizational climate for innovation and organizational performance: the mediating effect of innovative work behavior. J. Vocat. Behav. **100**, 67–77 (2017)
26. Hendriks, P.: Why share knowledge? The influence of ICT on the motivation for knowledge sharing. Knowl. Proc. Manag. **6**(2), 91–100 (1999)
27. Lee, S.M., Hong, S.: An enterprise-wide knowledge management system infrastructure. Ind. Manag. Data Syst. **102**(1), 17–25 (2002)
28. Bandura, A.: Social foundations of thought and action: a social cognitive theory. Prentice-Hall, Englewood Cliffs, NJ (1986)
29. Wood, R., Bandura, A.: Social cognitive theory of organizational management. Academy of management. Acad. Manag. Rev. **14**(3), 361–384 (1989)
30. Bandura, A.: Social cognitive theory of mass communication. In: Bryant, J., Oliver, M.B. (eds.) Media Effects: Advances in Theory and Research, pp. 94–124. Routledge, New York, NY (2002)
31. Ajzen, I.: The theory of planned behavior. Organ. Behav. Hum. Decis. Process. **50**(2), 179–211 (1991)
32. Lee, H., Choi, B.: Knowledge management enablers, processes, and organizational performance: an integrative view and empirical examination. J. Manag. Inform. Syst. **20**(1), 179–228 (2003)
33. Othman, F., Hawryszkiewycz, I., Kang, K.: The influence of socio-technical factors on knowledge-based innovation in Saudi Arabia Firms. In: Proceedings of the 25th Australasian Conference on Information Systems, Australian Conference on Information Systems, ACIS, Auckland, New Zealand, pp. 1–10 (2014)
34. Hung, S.Y., Durcikova, A., Lai, H.M, Lin, W.M.: The influence of intrinsic and extrinsic motivation on individuals' knowledge sharing behavior. Int. J. Hum.-Comput. Stud. **69**(6), 415–427, ISSN 1071-5819 (2011)
35. Han, T.S., Chiang, H.H., Chang, A.: Employee participation in decision making, psychological ownership and knowledge sharing: Mediating role of organizational commitment in Taiwanese high-tech organizations. Int. J. Hum. Resour. Manag. **21**(12), 2218–2233 (2010)
36. Mathieson, K.: Predicting user intentions: comparing the technology acceptance model with the theory of planned behavior. Inform. Syst. Res. **2**(3), 173–191 (1991)
37. Hee, S.P.: Relationships among attitudes and subjective norm: testing the theory of reasoned action across cultures. Commun. Stud. **51**(2), 162–175 (2000)
38. Kreitner, R., Kinicki, A.: Organizational Behavior. Richard D. Irwin, Homewood, IL (1992)
39. Nelson, K.M., Cooprider, J.G.: The contribution of shared knowledge to IS group performance. MIS Q. **20**(4), 409–429 (1996)
40. O'Dell, C., Grayson, J.: Knowledge transfer: discover your value proposition. Strategy Leadersh. **27**(2), 10–15 (1999)
41. Nonaka, I.: A dynamic theory of organizational knowledge creation. Organ. Sci. **5**, 14–37 (1994)
42. Fukuyama, F.: Trust: The Social Virtues and the Creation of Prosperity. The Free Press, New York (1995)
43. Wasko, M.M., Faraj, S.: Why should I share? Examining social capital and knowledge contribution in electronic networks of practices. MIS Q. **29**(1), 35 (2005)
44. Kowal, J., Fortier, M.S.: Motivational determinants of flow: contributions from self-determination theory. J. Soc. Psychol. **139**(3), 355–368 (1999)
45. Wong, K.Y.: Critical success factors for implementing knowledge management in small and medium enterprises. Ind. Manag. Data Syst. **105**(3/4), 261–279 (2005)
46. Bartol, K., Srivastava, A.: Encouraging knowledge sharing: the role of organizational reward systems. J. Leadersh. Organ. Stud. **9**(1), 64–76 (2002)
47. Pierce, J.L., Kostova, T., Dirks, K.T.: Toward a theory of psychological ownership in organizations. Acad. Manag. Rev. **26**, 298–310 (2001)

48. Van Dyne, L., Pierce, J.L.: Psychological ownership and feelings of possession: three field studies predicting employee attitudes and organizational citizenship behavior. J. Organiz. Behav. **25**, 439–459 (2004)
49. Nold III, H.A.: Linking knowledge processes with firm performance: organizational culture. J. Intellect. Capital **13**(1), 16–38 (2012)
50. Hair Jr., J.F., Black, W.C., Babin, B.J., Anderson, R.E., Tatham, R.L.: Multivariate data analysis, 6th edn. Pearson-Prentice Hall, Upper Saddle River, NJ (2006)
51. Hair, J.F., Black, W.C., Babin, B.J., Anderson, R.E.: Multivariate Data Analysis. Pearson Education Limited (2013)
52. Bates, R., Kauffeld, S., Holton III, E.F.: Examining the factor structure and predictive ability of the German-version of the learning transfer systems inventory. J. Eur. Ind. Training **31**(3), 195–211 (2007)
53. Tsai, M.T, Cheng, N.C.: Programmer perceptions of knowledge-sharing behavior under social cognitive theory. Expert Syst. Appl. **37**(12), 8479–8485, ISSN 0957-4174 (2010)
54. Dong, G., Liem, C.G., Grossman, M.: Knowledge-sharing intention in Vietnamese organizations. VINE **40**(3/4), 262–276 (2010). https://doi.org/10.1108/03055721011071395

FABIOLA: Towards the Resolution of Constraint Optimization Problems in Big Data Environment

Luisa Parody, Ángel Jesús Varela Vaca, Mª Teresa Gómez López
and Rafael M. Gasca

Abstract The optimization problems can be found in several examples within companies, such as the minimization of the production costs, the faults produced, or the maximization of customer loyalty. The resolution of them is a challenge that entails an extra effort. In addition, many of today's enterprises are encountering the Big Data problems added to these optimization problems. Unfortunately, to tackle this challenge by medium and small companies is extremely difficult or even impossible. In this paper, we propose a framework that isolates companies from how the optimization problems are solved. More specifically, we solve optimization problems where the data is heterogeneous, distributed and of a huge volume. FABIOLA (FAst BIg cOstraint LAb) framework enables to describe the distributed and structured data used in optimization problems that can be parallelized (the variables are not shared between the various optimization problems), and obtains a solution using Constraint Programming Techniques.

Keywords Big data · Optimization problem · Constraint programming
Data structure

A prior version of this paper has been published in the ISD2017 Proceedings (http://aisel.aisnet.org/isd2014/proceedings2017).

L. Parody (✉) · Á. J. Varela Vaca · M. T. Gómez López · R. M. Gasca
Universidad de Sevilla, Seville, Spain
e-mail: lparody@us.es

Á. J. Varela Vaca
e-mail: ajvarela@us.es

M. T. Gómez López
e-mail: maytegomez@us.es

R. M. Gasca
e-mail: gasca@us.es

© Springer International Publishing AG, part of Springer Nature 2018
N. Paspallis et al. (eds.), *Advances in Information Systems Development*,
Lecture Notes in Information Systems and Organisation 26,
https://doi.org/10.1007/978-3-319-74817-7_8

113

1 Introduction

Nowadays, huge volumes of data are generated by running services for organization's information systems. The concept of Big Data has been defined as data that exceeds the capability of commonly used hardware environments and software tools to capture, manage, and process it within a tolerable elapsed time for its user population [1]. This concept is being increasingly defined by the four V's, which are: (1) Volume, which represents the size of the data; (2) Velocity, that represents the speed at which data is created, stored, analysed, processed, and visualized in real-time; (3) Variety, which distinguishes the forms of data by considering two aspects: syntax and semantics; and (4) Value, that is especially linked to the commercial value that any new sources and forms of data can add to the business.

Software technologies have been evolving to facilitate the management of the Big Data. Hadoop [2, 3] is a popular open-source map-reduce implementation which is being used as an alternative to store and process extremely large data sets on commodity hardware. However, the map-reduce programming model is very low level and requires developers to write custom programs which are hard to maintain and reuse. For this reason, more abstract solutions have been developed to elevate the abstract level, such as Spark. Spark [4] is nowadays the most active Big Data project in the open source community, and it is already used by more than a thousand organizations. Spark is a cluster computing engine that is optimized for an in-memory processing, and it unifies support for a variety of workloads, including batch, interactive querying, streaming, and iterative computations.

One of the challenge of the Big Data solution is the isolation of the users from the heterogeneous use and location of data. For this reason, several components have been developed in the ecosystem of Hadoop. Unfortunately, the optimization of problems using the Constraint Programming techniques is still a problem to be solved.

In this paper, we present FABIOLA (FAst BIg cOstraint LAb) framework, an open-source data problem optimization solution built on top of Hadoop. FABIOLA supports the distribution of the Constraint Optimization Problems in order to obtain the optimal solutions for independent subsets of distributed data. Constraint Optimization Problems are compiled into map-reduce jobs executed on Hadoop that can be combined with Hive [5] in order to infer more information after founding the optimized values.

The rest of the paper is organized as follows. Section 2 introduces previous and related works. Section 3 describes FABIOLA data model, the Constraint Optimization problem, and the parameters that can be included to obtain the evaluation of the optimization. Section 4 describes the architecture and an overview of the query life-cycle. Section 5 provides various real examples where and how FABIOLA is used. Finally, conclusions are drawn and future work is proposed in Sect. 6.

2   Related Work

Big Data faces up new challenges [6, 7] in how to carry out optimization problems with heterogeneous, incomplete, and uncertainty data in addition to immediately responses for some types of questions.

The Apache Hadoop project [2] actively supports multiple projects with the aim of extending Hadoop's capabilities and make it easier to use. There are several top-level projects to helping in the creation of development tools as well as for managing Hadoop data flow and processing. Many commercial third-party solutions build on their developed technologies within the Apache Hadoop ecosystem.

Spark [4], Pig [8], and Hive [5] are three of the best-known Apache Hadoop projects. All of them are used to create applications to process Hadoop data. While there are a lot of articles and discussions about which is the best one, in practice, many organizations use various of them since each one is optimized for a specific functionality. Although FABIOLA is not a new Big Data solution, it aims to be part of the Hadoop ecosystem. FABIOLA provides the necessary components to drive the solution of constraint optimization problems with distributed data on a Hadoop-based architecture.

Constraint Programming (CP) presents a challenge in the scalability by solving some type of hard problems. However, CP has been successfully applied in different domains for solving optimization problems, such as scheduling and planning. Although there exist several CP tools, such as IBM-ILOG CPLEX Optimization [9] and Choco Solver [10], none of them provides a Big Data solution. Big Data provides to CP a new perspective with regard to the size and volume of data, and it is a great opportunity to exploit its possibilities to gain efficiency and optimization in operational processes [11]. Additionally, Big Data tackles new challenges [12] dealing with automation of decision-making that involves several (millions) decision variables in optimization of resource consumption, sustainability services, and finance. Nevertheless, the optimization problems in CP need more flexibility and adaptability since the exploration of heterogeneous, enormous and dynamic generation of data requires a quick adaptation of optimization problem in order to provide more holistic solutions.

Although there is an initiative to create a new language to adapt CP languages for Big Data applications [13], it is currently a very immature approach with no continued development.

3   Formalization of the Problem

The elements that conform FABIOLA framework are: The Constraint Optimization Problem, Data Model (Input data, Output data, Other data), and a set of parameters to delimit the search. The search consists on to find the optimal solution described in the Constraint Optimization Problem for each set of input data and in different nodes. Then, several optimizations are executed in parallel.

3.1 Constraint Optimization Problem

FABIOLA enables to find the optimal solution for several data input. In other words, FABIOLA solves the same type of problem but with different input data, thereby founding its corresponding and different optimal solutions. A Constraint Optimization Problem (COP) is created in order to find these solutions. To introduce COPs, it is firstly necessary to explain what is a Constraint Satisfaction Problem (CSP).

A CSP [14] represents a reasoning framework consisting of variables, domains and constraints $\prec V, D, C \succ$, where V is a set of n variables $v_1, v_2 \ldots v_n$ whose values are taken from finite domains $D_{v_1}, D_{v_2} \ldots D_{v_n}$ respectively, and C is a set of constraints on their values. The constraint $c_k(x_{k_1}, x_{k_2}, \ldots, x_{k_n})$ is a predicate that is defined on the Cartesian product $D_{k_1} \times \cdots \times D_{k_j}$. This predicate is true iff the value assignment of these variables satisfies the constraint c_k. If only the solution that optimize (minimize or maximize) a function f wants to be obtained, it is called a Constraint Optimization Problem (COP).

Since the aim of FABIOLA is the resolution of the COP, the building of the constraints is essential and inevitable. However, these constraints can be automatically and dynamically codified with respect to the set of data.

Some of the variables V can be matched with the input and output variables defined in the Data Model (defined in next subsection). As a consequence, some input variables fix their values to a subdomain and modify the possible optimal solutions found for each tuple. It seems a meta-COP which is partially instantiated for each tuple. In order to understand it better, the following subsection sells out an example.

3.2 Data Model: Input, Output and Other Data

FABIOLA works with tables, analogous to tables in relational databases. It does not mean that the information is stored in a relational database, but there exists a view where the data is structured in tuples and with the same set of attributes. This data might be stored in HDFS, NFS or local directories in different nodes. Each table can have one or more partitions which determine the distribution of data in the various nodes.

Being $\{A_1, A_2 \ldots A_n\}$ attributes for the domains $\{D_1, D_2 \ldots D_n\}$, where the set $\{A_1 : D_1, A_2 : D_2 \ldots A_n : D_n\}$ is a relational-schema. Each tuple is $\{A_1 : d_1, A_2 : d_2 \ldots A_n : d_n\}$ where $\{d_1 \in D_1, d_2 \in D_2, \ldots, d_n \in D_n\}$. FABIOLA supports primitive column types (Integers, Floating point numbers, Strings, Dates and Booleans).

This set of attributes is divided into three disjoined groups: Input (*IN*), Output (*OUT*) and Others (*OT*), where $IN \cap OUT = \emptyset$, $IN \cap OT = \emptyset$ and $OT \cap OUT = \emptyset$. The descriptions are:

- *IN* describes the input variables used in the optimization problem.
- *OUT* describes the variables of the optimization problem obtained after the search.
- *OT* describes other variables of the table that can be used to make further queries combining the outputs and these variables. They are not related to the optimization problem since they do not influence in its resolution.

3.2.1 Example of a COP Evaluated with Multiple Tuples

A clear example to understand how the input affects the obtained outputs is a model-based diagnosis problem [15]. The example represents a component composed of 5 elements (two summations and three multipliers). The component obtains two outputs (*f* and *g*) according to the inputs (*a, b, c,* and *d*). Each element is associated to a Boolean variable (C_1, C_2, C_3, C_4, C_5) that describes if its behavior is correct or incorrect (a *true* or *false* value). To know if the component *i* is working correctly, it is necessary to know if every C_i can take the value *true*, thereby the value of the variable *sum* is 5. The Constraint Optimization Problem is shown in Table 1.

Table 2 shows some possible scenarios, where the output data is obtained according to each input data (per tuple). Every input data can be instantiated (*tuples #1* and *#2*), and the output is obtained describing that every element is working correctly (*sum* is equal to 5), or not (*sum* is equal to 4). Also, it is possible that some input values are unknown, and the COP tries to find values for them to optimize the variable sum (*tuples #3, #4* and *#5*).

Other attributes, such as *Man* (*Manufacturer*), are not part of and do not influence over the resolution of the optimization problem. However, they can be of

Table 1 Constraint satisfaction problem example	//Variables and domains

	$a, b, c, d, f, g, x, y, x$: FLOAT;
	 C_1, C_2, C_3, C_4, C_5: Boolean;
	 sum: Integer;
	 //Constraints
	 $C_1 = (a * c = x) \wedge C_2 = (b * d = y) \wedge C_3 = (c * e = z) \wedge$
	 $C_4 = (x + y = f) \wedge$
	 $C_5 = (y + z = g)$
	 //Optimization Function
	 $sum = C_1 + C_2 + C_3 + C_4 + C_5$

Table 2 Example of tuples in model-based diagnosis

#TupleID	Inputs							Outputs	Others	
	a	b	c	d	e	f	g	Sum	Test ID	Man
#1	2	3	3	2	2	10	12	4	Test1	Telco
#2	1	3	5	7	2	26	31	5	Test2	IBM
#3	2	3	3	2	2	12	12	5	Test3	Telco
#4	null	3	null	null	2	10	12	5	Test4	IBM
#5	5	null	2	2	1	9	18	3	Test5	Sony

help to answer queries, such as: Which is the manufacturer with more failed components?

3.3 Configuration of Outputs

Since the data is evaluated in different nodes, and the values of this data are also different according to each tuple, the optimization time and the obtained outputs can be extremely different. For this reason, FABIOLA enables to indicate some parameters to adequate the search to each case:

- **Maximum Time (t)**: In order to avoid the delay of evaluating a set of tuples, it is possible to delimit the maximum time to solve each COP. If t is reached, it can obtain a solution since a local optimal solution can be found during the search. But if the search has not finished, we cannot ensure that the solution found is the global optimal.
- **Optimal found?** (*optimal*): If the solution obtained cannot be ensured as the optimal, it would be possible to determine whether the best solution found in t is included in the outputs or not. If the parameter takes the value *true*, a new column is automatically added to the output variables (called *optimal*) and it describes the nature of the optimal: global or partial. The column *optimal* can take *true* or *false* value.
- **Output Type** (*any* or *range*): The output that is optimized can be achieved with fixed values in other variables, or with a set of different values (*range*). To determine if *any* value might be obtained or the possible *range* wants to be known, the output data can be attributed with the parameter *any* or *range*, being *any* by default.

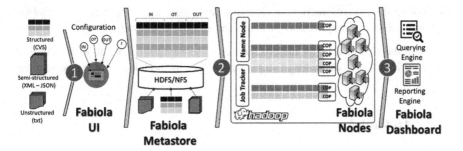

Fig. 1 Architecture of FABIOLA

4 FABIOLA's Architecture and Methodology

4.1 Architecture

Figure 1 shows the main components of FABIOLA architecture and its integration with a Big Data infrastructure based on Hadoop.

FABIOLA is composed of four components:

1. **FABIOLA UI** is a client side (web application) which enables to upload and load data from heterogeneous external resources. Currently, the supported data sources are: (1) structured data from databases; (2) semi-structured data, such as XML or JSON files; and (3) unstructured data from text files or similar. FABIOLA UI also enables users to point out attributes from imported data as input data of the COP (cf. *IN* in Fig. 1), the establishment of output data (cf. *OUT*), other types of attributes necessary for the problem (cf. *OT*), and finally the specific values for the configuration variables, such as t (cf. *t* at Fig. 1).

2. **FABIOLA Metastore** is provided as a system catalogue where data is organized in the form of tables and schemes, such as in Hive [5]. These tables and schemes are only a virtual representation or view of the data since it is internally organized in the original format of a distributed file system, for example, HDFS, NFS or AFS.

3. **FABIOLA Nodes** are solver nodes on top of Hadoop that enables to compute COPs. Thus, each row (tuple) instantiates a COP which is uniformly allotted among the available nodes in order to be solved. The possible solutions of those COPs feed the *OUT* column of each tuple in the Metastore.

4. **FABIOLA Dashboard** is a reporting and querying component that enables users an easy-querying and visualization of data and results.

With the aim of a better understanding of the application of the architecture to any problem, a systematic list of steps is given as a methodology in the next section.

4.2   Methodology

The necessary steps to fully execute and take all the advantages of FABIOLA framework are:

1. **Data Load and pre-processing**. The user is in charge of identifying the data to be processed by FABIOLA. More specifically, he must create table/schemes in FABIOLA Metastore as explained below:

    (a) Load data from external resources through FABIOLA UI.
    (b) Establish which attributes from loaded data are *IN* and point out them in FABIOLA Metastore.
    (c) Establish which attributes are *OUT* and point out them in FABIOLA Metastore[1].
    (d) Specify the values of the configuration parameters if they are necessary. Such as, the values of maximum time (t), *optimal* and output type (*any| range*).

2. **Data Processing**. FABIOLA components are the responsible of automatically processing the data:

    (a) FABIOLA takes a meta-COP (explained in Sect. 3.1) and instantiates a COP model for each row of data in FABIOLA Metastore. To do that, *IN* and *OUT* values of each row are aligned with the variables of the COP.
    (b) The instantiated COPs are sent in parallel to FABIOLA Nodes in order to be computed.
    (c) Each FABIOLA Node is executed to solve each COP.
    (d) Afterwards, the process finishes and *OUT* attributes are fulfilled (if a solution has been found in t and according to the configuration parameters explained in Sect. 3.3).

3. **Results** are visualized in a configurable dashboard, where the user can even submit queries by combining every attribute of the FABIOLA Metastore.

Figure 2 shows two snapshots of FABIOLA tool: (a) the form to load and pre-processing the data (step 1), and (b) the presentation of results in FABIOLA Dashboard (step 3). As it is shown, the interface is user-friendly, and supports user

---

[1]All the attributes that are not categorized as *IN* or *OUT* are grouped in *OT* in FABIOLA Metastore.

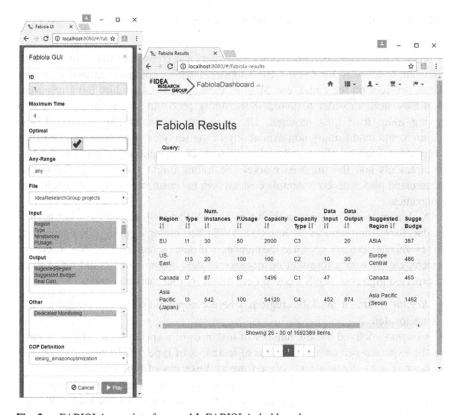

Fig. 2 **a** FABIOLA user interface, and **b** FABIOLA dashboard

throughout the application of the methodology, either explaining each step or suggesting specific configurations. Furthermore, although the description of the set of constraints can be a hard task, it is done once and applied to every set of data. FABIOLA also provides an easy language to define the constraints based on the query language of Constraint Databases [16–18].

5 Example of Application Scenarios

FABIOLA can be applied to different types of contexts and we have used it in several real scenarios, as explained in the following subsections.

5.1   Contract and Use of Supply Services

In order to success in their operations, customers and companies must contract third companies' services for some basic supplies, such as communications, light and water, services on the cloud, etc. Most of the time, customers hire more resources than they need in order to avoid shortcoming problems. However, it turns into paying more than it is required. On the contrary, contracting services below requirements might imply non-availability of the services or even an extra cost for overused resources. The study of resources consumption for each individual requirements and the imposed market constraints might result in an elastic and customized plan with considerable cost savings for customers and high benefits for companies.

A clear example is Amazon Web Services (AWS) [19], one of the most leading product for hosting services on the cloud. AWS offers multiple pricing plans depending on several characteristics, such as the number of instances, region of location, operative system, etc. A wrong foresight on resource or data consumption could range in an unexpected high cost. AWS's cost is determined by four main categories:

- *Region*: fourteen available regions where computational instances and storage are located.
- *Compute*: defined by: the number of instances of a specific type i (*NInstances*); the expected percentage of usage of instances of type i (*%Usage*); the cost per hour $(Cost - Region(i, r))$ of performing instances of type i in region r.
- *Storage*: defined by various parameters: capacity of storage (*StorageCapacity*), type of storage (*StorageType*), and cost of the capacity c for the type of storage st $(Cost - Storage(c, st))$.

Data Transfer: gigabyte of input data per month (*DataInput*), gigabyte of output data per month (*DataOutput*), and the cost of transfer data into/outside the services in a region r (*CostDataTransfer(r)*).

There are several optional parameters that can be used to customize the services but they do not increase the final price of the service, such as monitoring options. The objective is to determine the minimum cost in any region when the percentage of usage in computational instances is greater than 0%. For example, which is the minimum cost for an expected hardware whose requirements are n instances of type $t1$, a pool of storage of at least 1000 GB, 20 GB/Month of input/output data, and a maximum workload of 50% for each $t1$.

- **Data Model**:
    - IN: *Region, InstanceType, NumberOfIntances, %Usage, StorageCapacity, StorageType, DataInput, DataOutput.*
    - OUT: *Region, EstimatedCost*
    - OT: *Description, DedicatedMonitoring, ELB, OperativeSystem.*

- **Constraint Optimization Problem**:
  - *{Region, InstanceType, ..., DataOutput} Integer;*
  - $\forall i \in \{0...\text{NumberIfInstances}\}$ *%Usage$_i \geq 1$ & %Usage$_i \leq 50 \rightarrow$*
    *CostCompute = %Usage$_i$ * CostRegion(InstanceType, Region);*
  - *CostStorage =*
    *CostStorage(StorageType, Region) * StorageCapacity;*
  - *CostData = CostDataTransfer(Region) * DataOutput;*
  - *Minimize(CostCompute + CostStorage + CostData);*

- **Example of Queries**: Which is the region where the estimated cost is minimum, or less than 100 per month, with a specific configuration? Which are the instances with more than one hundred of extra elastic IPs?

5.2 *Diagnosis Problem for Heat Exchangers*

The diagnosis problem in a set of reading sensors is an important challenge that manages a huge number of systems that can be diagnosed in parallel. Model-based diagnosis can be described as an optimization problem, where the minimal explanation of a malfunction can be found [20, 21]. A set of constraints describes the relation that each part of the system must follow. The objective is to describe the relations between them and to detect and diagnose the possible errors that occur in the system.

Each system, shown in Fig. 3, is composed by: six heat exchangers, called $E_1, E_2, E_3, E_4, E_5, E_6$, and eight nodes, called $N_{11}, N_{12}, N_{13}, N_{14}, N_{21}, N_{22}, N_{23}, N_{24}$. Each connection (tube) between an exchanger and a node is defined by two parameters: a flow (f_i) and a temperature (t_i) (where i is the enumerated name of the connection). For example, the three input arrows of the system in Fig. 3, enumerated as *11, 21,* and *31,* defines three input flows, called $f_{11}, f_{21},$ and $f_{31},$ and three temperatures, called $t_{11}, t_{21},$ and $t_{31}.$ This nomenclature is applied to the rest of

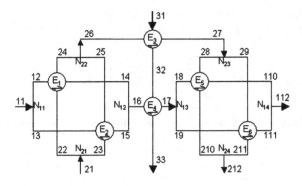

Fig. 3 Heat exchanger

connections between exchangers and nodes. The correctness of a system is defined by a set of constraints that relates the flow and temperature of each connection that the exchangers and nodes manage [15]. More specifically, there are a set of polynomial constraints that defines three different kinds of balances that the exchangers and nodes must satisfy:

- $\sum_i f_i = 0$: mass balance at each node.
- $\sum_i f_i \dots t_i = 0$: thermal balance at each node.
- $\sum_{IN} f_i \dots t_i - \sum_{OUT} f_i \dots t_i = 0$: enthalpy balance for each heat exchanger.

A component works correctly if it satisfies its corresponding balances constraints. Thus, in order to diagnoses the minimum malfunction components, the objective is to maximize the number of correct components. Following the defined parts of FABIOLA, the components are:

- **Data Model**:
  - **IN**: $t_{11}, t_{12}, t_{13}, t_{16}, t_{17}, t_{18}, t_{19}, t_{112}, t_{21}, t_{26}, t_{27}, t_{212}, t_{31}, t_{33},$
    $f_{11}, f_{12}, f_{13}, f_{16}, f_{17}, f_{18}, f_{19}, f_{112}, f_{21}, f_{26}, f_{27}, f_{212}, f_{31}, f_{33}$
  - **OUT**: $N_{11}, N_{12}, N_{13}, N_{14}, N_{21}, N_{22}, N_{23}, N_{24}, E_1, E_2, E_3, E_4, E_5, E_6$
  - **OT**: Name, Location.

- **Constraint Optimization Problem**:
  - $\{t_{11}, t_{12}, \dots, t_{31}, t_{33}, f_{11}, f_{12}, \dots, f_{33}\}$ Integer;
  - $N_{12}^a, N_{12}^b, N_{21}^a, N_{22}^b, E_1^a, E_1^b, E_1^c, E_2^a, E_2^b, E_2^c$ Boolean;
  - $N_{12}^a = f_{14} + f_{15} - f_{16} = 0$
  - $N_{12}^b = f_{14} * t_{14} + f_{15} * t_{15} - f_{16} * t_{16} = 0$
  - $N_{21}^a = f_{21} - f_{22} - f_{23} = 0$
  - $N_{21}^b = f_{21} * t_{21} - f_{22} * t_{22} - f_{23} * t_{23} = 0$
  - $N_{22}^a = f_{24} - f_{25} - f_{26} = 0$
  - $N_{22}^b = f_{24} * t_{24} - f_{25} * t_{25} - f_{26} * t_{26} = 0$
  - $E_1^a = f_{12} - f_{14} = 0$
  - $E_1^b = f_{22} - f_{24} = 0$
  - $E_1^c = f_{12} * t_{12} - f_{14} * t_{14} + f_{22} * t_{22} - f_{24} * t_{24} = 0$
  - $E_2^a = f_{13} - f_{15} = 0$
  - $E_2^b = f_{23} - f_{25} = 0$
  - $E_2^c = f_{13} * t_{13} - f_{15} * t_{15} + f_{23} * t_{23} - f_{25} * t_{25} = 0$
  - $Maximize(N_{12}^a + N_{12}^b + N_{21}^a + N_{22}^b + E_1^a + E_1^b + E_1^c + E_2^a + E_2^b + E_2^c)$

- **Example of Queries**: Which are the locations where N_{12}^a is failing (N_{12}^a or N_{12}^b is *false*)? Which is the *Name* of the systems that are working correctly?

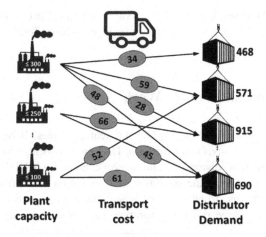

Fig. 4 Automobile supply chain model

5.3 Automotive Supply Chain Problem for a Demand-Driven Distribution

In the area of automotive industry, and any other kind of industry where production and delivery are necessary, it is necessary to transport the products from production centres (n Plants) to distribution centres (m Dist), where $n \ll m$ (see Fig. 4). Different demands on these last centres determine the different solutions, that are represented in a bidimensional array, called *Assign[n,m]*.

The objective is to obtain the minimal transport cost in order to maintain a competitive advantage. The constraints of this problem are defined according to the characteristics of the different logistic enterprises of the market. Following the defined parts of FABIOLA, where each tuple represents the distribution per day, the components are:

- **Data Model**:
    - IN: *Capacity: Array[NFact] of Integer, Demand: Array[MDist] of Integer, Cost: Array[NFact,MDist] of Integer.*
    - OUT: *TotCost: Integer, Assign: Array[NFact,MDist] of Integer.*
    - OT: *Name of the Logistic Enterprise.*

- **Constraint Optimization Problem**:
    - *Assign[NFact, MDist]* : *Integer*; *TotalCost* : *Integer*;
    - $\forall p \in \{0, \ldots, n\} \sum_{c=1}^{m} Assign[p,c] \leq capacity[p]$;
    - $\forall c \in \{0, \ldots, m\} \sum_{p=1}^{m} Assign[p,c] \leq demand[c]$;
    - $TotalCost = \sum_{p=1}^{n} \sum_{c=1}^{m} Assign[p,c] * cost[p,c]$
    - $Minimize(TotalCost)$;

- **Example of Queries**: Which are the Assign and *TotalCost* for the DHL logistic enterprise? Which are the logistic enterprises whose *TotalCost* is less than 50,000?

6 Conclusions and Future Work

Optimization problems are found in several real examples. It becomes a higher problem when the data involved is in a Big Data environment, which implies huge quantity of information, distributed and heterogeneous. FABIOLA framework has been formalized to support the definition and resolution of distributed Constraint Optimization Problems, isolating from where the data is, and how the optimal outputs are found. Three different examples have been introduced to show the flexibility of the proposal. An interface has also been developed to approach the solution to final users.

As future work, it would be interesting to extend the type of elements included in the input and output variables, such as nestable collection types-array and map. These types imply the management of semi-structure and non-structured information. The possibility of giving users the opportunity to define their own types programmatically could be also helpful.

Acknowledgements This work has been partially funded by the Ministry of Science and Technology of Spain (TIN2015-63502-C3-2-R) and the European Regional Development Fund (ERDF/FEDER).

References

1. Chattopadhyay, B., Lin, L., Liu, W., Mittal, S., Aragonda, P., Lychagina, V., Kwon, Y., Wong, M.: Tenzing a SQL implementation on the mapreduce framework. In: Proceedings of VLDB, pp. 1318–1327 (2011)
2. Apache Hadoop. http://wiki.apache.org/hadoop. Accessed 15 Apr 2017
3. White, T.: Hadoop: The Definitive Guide. O'Reilly Media, Inc., 1st edition (2009)
4. Zaharia, M., Xin, R.S., Wendell, P., Das, T., Armbrust, M., Dave, A., Meng, X., Rosen, J., Venkataraman, S., Franklin, M.J., Ghodsi, A., Gonzalez, J., Shenker, S., Stoica, I.: Apache spark: a unified engine for big data processing. Commun. ACM **59**(11), 56–65 (2016)
5. Thusoo, A., Sarma, J.S., Jain, N., Shao, Z., Chakka, P., Anthony, S., Liu, H., Wyckoff, P., Murthy, R.: Hive: a warehousing solution over a map-reduce framework. Proc. VLDB Endow. **2**(2), 1626–1629 (2009)
6. Labrinidis, A., Jagadish, H.V.: Challenges and opportunities with big data. Proc. VLDB Endow. **5**(12), 2032–2033 (2012)
7. Nasser, T., Tariq, R.S.: Big data challenges. Comput. Eng. Inform. Technol. **4**(3), 1–10 (2015)
8. Olston, C., Reed, B., Silberstein, A., Srivastava, U.: Automatic optimization of parallel dataflow programs. In: USENIX 2008 Annual Technical Conference, ATC'08, pp. 267–273. Berkeley, CA, USA (2008)

9. IBM-ILOG CPLEX Studio. http://www-03.ibm.com/software/products/es/ibmilogcpleoptistud. Accessed 15 Apr 2017
10. Choco Solver. http://www.choco-solver.org/. Accessed 15 Apr 2017
11. O'Sullivan, B.: Opportunities and challenges for constraint programming. In: Proceedings of the Twenty-Sixth AAAI Conference on Artificial Intelligence, AAAI'12, pp. 2148–2152. AAAI Press (2012)
12. Freuder, E.F., O'Sullivan, B.: Grand challenges for constraint programming. Constraints **19**(2), 150–162 (2014)
13. Rossi, F., Saraswat, V.: Constraint programming languages for big data applications
14. Rossi, F., van Beek, P., Walsh, T. Handbook of Constraint Programming. Elsevier (2006)
15. Ceballos, R., Gómez-López, M.T., Gasca, R.M., Del Valle Sevillano, C.: A compiled model for faults diagnosis based on different techniques. AI Commun. **20**(1), 7–16 (2007)
16. Gómez-López, M.T., Ceballos, R., Gasca, R.M., Del Valle Sevillano, C.: Developing a labelled object-relational constraint database architecture for the projection operator. Data Knowl. Eng. **68**(1), 146–172 (2009)
17. Gómez-López, M.T., Gasca, R.M.: Using constraint programming in selection operators for constraint databases. Expert Syst. Appl. **41**(15), 6773–6785 (2014)
18. Gómez-López, M.T., Gasca, R.M.: Object Relational Constraint Databases for GIS. Encyclopedia of GIS 2017, pp. 1449–1457 (2017)
19. Amazon-Web Services. http://aws.amazon.com/whitepapers/. Accessed 15 Apr 2017
20. Gasca, R.M., Del Valle Sevillano, C., Gómez-López, M.T., Ceballos, R.: NMUS: structural analysis for improving the derivation of all muses in overconstrained numeric CSPs, pp. 160–169. CAEPIA 2007 (2007)
21. Gómez-López, M.T., Ceballos, R., Gasca, R.M., Del Valle Sevillano, C.: Applying constraint databases in the determination of potential minimal conflicts to polynomial model-based diagnosispp, pp. 75–89. CDB 2004 (2004)

Gaps Between Theory and Practice on IT Governance Capabilities

Oscar González-Rojas, Juan E. Gómez-Morantes
and Guillermo Beltrán

Abstract Nowadays, Information Technology (IT) governance is a core activity either adopted or at least expected by most organizations, to control the behavior of IT assets. However, this discipline faces a growing gap between the views, priorities and practices of academics and practitioners. This paper presents a consolidated view of capabilities for implementing IT governance within an organization. We evaluated such capabilities in the practice of Colombian companies within the logistics industry. The main gaps that arise when adopting IT governance capabilities are discussed, and research insights are provided for aligning theory and practice.

Keywords IT management · ICT governance · Capability model
Business-ICT alignment · Risk management

1 Introduction

Initially considered as a sub-set of corporate governance, IT Governance (ITG) has emerged as its own discipline since the 90s [1]. Even though the term ITG did not gain traction in literature until the late 90s, similar concepts were used as early as 1963 [2]. Later, in the mid-2000s, evidence about the link between ITG and

---

A prior version of this paper has been published in the ISD2017 Proceedings (http://aisel.aisnet.org/isd2014/proceedings2017).

O. González-Rojas (✉) · G. Beltrán
Systems and Computing Engineering Department, Universidad de los Andes,
Bogotá, Colombia
e-mail: o-gonza1@uniandes.edu.co

G. Beltrán
e-mail: ga.beltran66@uniandes.edu.co

J. E. Gómez-Morantes
Systems Engineering Department, Pontificia Universidad Javeriana, Bogotá, Colombia
e-mail: je.gomezm@javeriana.edu.co

© Springer International Publishing AG, part of Springer Nature 2018
N. Paspallis et al. (eds.), *Advances in Information Systems Development*,
Lecture Notes in Information Systems and Organisation 26,
https://doi.org/10.1007/978-3-319-74817-7_9

performance in large organizations [3] generated great interest from both academics and practitioners. Since then, an ample body of literature has been published regarding different aspects of ITG.[1] However, most of this literature is focused on the definition of ITG and its dimensions, the benefits of proper ITG schemes, contingency research looking for the most appropriate ITG model in a given scenario [4], and prescriptive models of ITG implementations [5, 6].

While this stream of research has achieved important milestones in the field, it is becoming evident that there is a growing gap between the views, priorities and practices of academics and industry practitioners (see Sect. 2.2). In order to understand the roots and impacts of this gap, it is important to increase the empirical base of ITG research as a way to build stronger bridges between these communities and to allow for ITG research to be better informed by actual ITG practice; something essential to close the theory-practice gap discussed in this paper.

The remainder of this paper is as follows. In Sect. 2, we discuss current issues on ITG research by emphasizing on related work on ITG gaps between research and practice. Section 3 discusses the methodological approach we followed to identify the gap between the ITG practices proposed in the literature and those used by practitioners. Section 4 describes a capabilities model created to consolidate ITG literature. Section 5 presents the ITG practices of four Colombian companies of the logistics sector and compares them with the capabilities model. As a result, we present the identified gaps and a characterization of the capabilities of this industry. Finally, conclusions and future work are presented in Sect. 6.

2   IT Governance: Context, Issues, and Gaps

Multiple definitions of ITG have been proposed from different perspectives and with different focuses and objectives [1, 7]. From a more practice-focused perspective, plenty of literature exists covering ITG frameworks, implementation processes, and good practices. This is a difficult issue because the lack of consensus within the academic community about the very definition of the concept hinders any advancement in the field. Furthermore, the lack of consensus between academics and practitioners about this definition affects the communication between these groups, and reduces the chances of collaboration between them [8].

The issue of multiple ITG definitions has been debated in recent literature [1, 2]. It is now commonly accepted that the core of ITG is composed by four dimensions: (a) the allocation of IT decision making rights, (b) the management of IT risks, (c) the mechanism to align IT decisions and business strategy, and (d) organizational structures to monitor and control IT decisions. As suggested by Weill, "IT Governance is not about what specific decisions are made, that is management" [3].

---

[1]More than 30,000 publications found in Google Scholar using the query "IT Governance".

This means that ITG is about the specification and implementation of organizational structures and processes that are in charge of making and monitoring IT decisions.

2.1 Current Issues on IT Governance Research

Parting from the definition of ITG presented earlier, it is now time to examine some of the limitations of the concept and current research issues in the field. One of the main gaps in ITG research is its dynamic nature. New literature is required to analyze the conditions that will result in a change in ITG over time, as well as the transition process from one model to another. This issue is relevant not only because the current business climate is one of constant change and disruption, but also because advancements in the IT field (e.g. cloud computing) are challenging our current knowledge about ITG and how it is performed [9].

Another issue regarding ITG research is the limitations of the rational theories used so far to study this phenomenon. According to Jacobson, ITG scholars have relied too much on what he calls rational theories of the organization; theories that "are based in economics and assume managers' ability to systematically be aware of, rank, and then choose best alternatives based on certain criteria (e.g. costs and benefits) to achieve a desired outcome (e.g. improved efficiency)" [5]. The biggest issue with the over-reliance on these rational theories is that they are not well equipped to understand some of the social aspects of ITG such as change, improvisation, external influences, politics, etc. Finally, there is the issue of gaps between theory and practice in ITG. Since this issue is the focus of this paper, it is discussed in more detail below.

2.2 Gaps Between Theory and Practice

Since IT issues include multiple actors (e.g. IT producers, consultants, client organizations, regulators, users, academics, etc.), it is easy to find disconnections between them. In ITG literature, the theory-practice gaps are one of the most relevant gaps. These particular kinds of gaps can be defined as a disconnection between practitioners and the main body of literature in the discipline (i.e. academic publications, standards, frameworks). It is important to note, however, that a disconnection between theory and practice should not be confused with a lack of knowledge from practitioners, as practitioners, despite being fairly familiar with the literature, can choose to depart from it. This distinction is important because the objective of researching theory-practice gaps is to highlight the areas in which practitioners can inform the literature and open new research avenues.

These gaps between ITG definitions and representations have been discussed by multiple authors. Keyes-Pearce [8] compares practitioners' motivations in the implementation of IT models or processes in their organizations, against the managerial drivers expressed in academic publications on ITG. The author found that the motivations for the adoption of ITG models diverge from the "IT as a source of competitive advantage" discourse encountered in the literature and are closer to a more pragmatic "IT as a competitive necessity" discourse. Additionally, the author noticed that practitioners are often unable to articulate what ITG means for them. Ko and Fink [10] studied gaps in three dimensions of ITG: structures, people, and processes. Even though they do not provide any explicit definition of gap, a reader could infer that they understand gaps as any ITG decision that deviates from the literature. This approach, however, can be criticized for being slightly pro-literature because it assumes that the positions of the ITG literature are superior to those of practitioners, without much discussion.

Simonsson and Ekstedt [7] studied the ways in which industry and literature assigned priorities to different components of the ITG definition. Using a survey-based methodology, the authors concluded that even though there are no major differences in the priorities of these groups, there are some differences in the priorities assigned by them. Regarding the decision making process, practitioners tend to give more priority to the understanding phase of the process, while the literature gives more importance to the monitoring phase of the process. Also, practitioners assign less importance to tactical issues than the literature. Willson and Pollar [6] present an in-depth study of ITG practices in a large Australian organization. In this case, the authors found practices not currently covered in the ITG literature like performance measuring as a tool in ITG. Furthermore, the authors found factors like organizational history and nature that have a significant impact on ITG models and practices. This case is instrumental in arguing that the academic literature can learn a lot from studying actual ITG practices. Finally, Winkler et al. [11] focused on the structural elements of ITG to explore the impacts of new technology models, like the Software as a Service (SaaS), on current ITG practices.

In summary, the current literature on ITG theory-practice gaps can be classified into three categories: ontological gaps, ITG antecedents' gaps, and dynamic gaps. Ontological gaps refer to the differences concerning what an ITG is, how it is performed, and which factors are important in its practice. Antecedents gaps refer to the importance of ITG, the business imperative of ITG efforts, and the priorities on ITG practices vs those expressed by the literature. Finally, dynamic gaps refer to the lack of literature on the change and evolution of governance practices.

3   Research Methodology

In order to contribute to a better understanding of theory-practice gaps in ITG, the main research question (RQ) of this paper is as follows: What are the differences between the ITG practices proposed in the literature and those actually used in practice?

Because of the complexity of ITG practices and the importance of gathering detailed information to measure theory-practice gaps in ITG, this paper adopts a qualitative approach based on the case study method. The case studies follow a multiple-case design with embedded units of analysis [12] to introduce an element of triangulation at the empirical level, thus improving the veracity of the findings.

The main four companies within the logistics and transportation industry in Colombia were selected as case studies. Two of them have presence exclusively in Colombia while the other two are multinational companies; we only analyzed the Colombian subsidiary of the latter. The companies' sizes range from 800 to 3000 employees. Between one and three in-depth interviews with high ranking managers (e.g. CIO, CEO) were performed for each case. The interviews followed a semi-structured model based on a survey of 49 questions. The questionnaire was designed around four embedded units of analysis (i.e. the four ITG dimensions that were identified in Sect. 2) by covering ITG concerns such as vision, current practices, undesired IT behaviors, decision-making archetypes among business units, strategic and operational mechanisms, among others.

The data analysis is based on an ITG capabilities model (see Sect. 4) that represents expected ITG actions (what to do) and specific ITG capabilities to perform those actions (how to do it) based on different frameworks and academic literature. This model decomposes actions and capabilities within three levels: strategic, tactical, and operational. This decomposition aims to highlight important areas for the evaluation and research of existing ITG theory-practice gaps. The data gathered in the interviews was used to build an ITG practices profile for each company. These profiles were then compared to the capabilities model and a gap analysis was performed. This allows for the measurement of the gap between theory (represented in the capabilities model) and practice (represented in the profiles).

This research has two main limitations. On the one hand, it only includes Colombian companies from the logistics industry and, since ITG issues are highly contingent (i.e. they depend on the context), the data and conclusions presented in this research could differ from those obtained in other regions or industries. The second limitation is related to the methodology used in this research. Since only four cases were selected, this research does not present any statistically significant results that could be generalized to other populations. However, it is important to note that this research does not intend to achieve generalizability to populations but to theoretical elements. This means that the value of this research does not lie in any predictive or prescriptive statement, but in the ITG capability model presented in Sect. 4 as a tool to evaluate ITG theory-practice gaps.

4 Core Capabilities on IT Governance

A Capability is a particular ability that an organization or system has in order to achieve a specific goal [13]. These abilities are enabled by a combination of resources (e.g. people, processes, IT) and by how those resources are managed [14].

Therefore, the application of ITG capabilities and their continuous improvement and evolution over time can differentiate the companies within an industry.

We created a capabilities model by aggregating different sources of information regarding ITG. These capabilities were grouped into four dimensions (decision-making, risk management [15], value delivery and alignment, and performance management [15]) and then characterized into three levels (strategic, tactical and operational capabilities).

Strategic capabilities refer to high-level decision-making grants and guidelines defined to control IT assets. Tactical capabilities refer to the coordination of activities and resources to enforce a given decision or guideline. Finally, operational capabilities refer to concrete day to day actions to automate and control ITG activities. These capabilities do not pretend to guide how ITG must be performed; they are a summary of the expected actions presented in the literature. Thus, multiple and contrasting capabilities can be performed to achieve a desired ITG state.

Table 1 summarizes the core actions and capabilities identified regarding decision-making rights and responsibilities on ITG [3].

Table 2 describes the actions and capabilities identified for the value delivery and alignment dimension. This dimension focuses on using IT investments as linkages between company-wide ITG, business unit levels and the project team level, both for the business and IT. Such linkages represent value to the organization as a whole [20].

Table 3 describes the core actions and capabilities identified in regards to risk management on ITG. Risk management covers the unplanned events that may represent an IT failure, which could threaten enterprise goals due to IT pervasiveness [17].

Table 1 Actions and capabilities to support the decision-making dimension

	Action (What)	Capabilities (How)
Strategic	1. Establish desired IT behavior [3] 2. Establish decision accountability on IT Principles, Enterprise Architecture, Business Application Needs, IT Infrastructure, IT Investment and prioritization [3] 3. Establish input rights on decisions [3] 4. Identify archetypes per decision type (e.g. Monarchy, Federal, IT Duopoly, Feudal) [3]	**Structures** 1. Committees (Executive Committee, IT Leaders Committee, Process Team, Account Managers) [3] **Information/Artefacts/Resources** 2. Decision maps per delegation of authority (accountabilities) and archetype [3] 3. Politics for exception handling [3] 4. Internal communication mechanisms (e.g. web portals) [3]

(continued)

Table 1 (continued)

	Action (What)	Capabilities (How)
Tactical	1. Evaluate conflicts on decision-making 2. Evaluate impact on decision-making (risks, profit, asset utilization, growth) 3. Coordinate decision-making according to the desired IT behavior 4. Prioritize the IT processes to be designed and implemented (an implementation roadmap) [16]	**Processes** 1. Coaching stakeholders that are not following decision rules [3] **Information/Artefacts/Resources** 2. Agreement definition (SLA, OLA, UC) [3] 3. Definition of target decision maps [16] 4. Coaching stakeholders not following decision rules [3] **Communication** 5. Managerial alerts [3]
Operational	1. Define control on decision making [3] 2. Specialize generic decisions within the five strategic decision categories	**Processes** 1. Audit procedures [17] 2. Measuring asset utilization—COBIT EDM04 ensure resource optimization [18] 3. Monitoring of agreements—COBIT APO09 manage service agreements [18] 4. Processes on IT frameworks (e.g. COBIT [18], ITIL [19]) **Information/Artefacts/Resources** 5. IT Metrics regarding decision rights [3]

Table 2 Actions and capabilities to support the value delivery and alignment dimension

	Action (What)	Capabilities (How)
Strategic	1. Establish guidelines for value delivery measurement [18] 2. Prioritize investment initiatives based on clearly defined criteria (e.g. higher benefits, less risk) [3, 18]	**Structures** 1. Board of directors [18] 2. Management Committee [18] 3. Project Management Office (PMO) [18] 4. IT executives with deep understanding of business environment [21] **Processes** 5. Project management [18]
Tactical	1. Manage IT value generation and delivery [18] 2. Identify opportunities for IT portfolio improvement [18] 3. Prioritize new IT investments and projects [18]	**Structures** 1. Project Management Office (PMO) [18] **Processes** 2. Definition of metrics with non-financial value [18]

(continued)

Table 2 (continued)

	Action (What)	Capabilities (How)
	4. Evaluate IT portfolio distribution after organizational changes [18]	3. Quantification of non-financial metrics [22] 4. Processes of IT investment portfolio management—COBIT process BAI01 Manage Programmes and projects [18] **Information/Artefacts/Resources** 5. Financial value metrics (e.g. ROA, ROI, ROE, NPV) [3] 6. Ratio between IT operation costs and obtained benefits [18]
Operational	1. Evaluate benefits generated by IT services, assets and investments defined on the IT portfolio [18] 2. Implement new IT investments and projects following a project management methodology [18] 3. Quantify the business value delivery from IT services 4. Measure the value generated between architectures 5. Calculate the value flow between architectures 6. Project the value of IT services	**Processes** 1. Calculation of benefits generated by IT services and investments defined on the IT portfolio [18] 2. Calculation of the financial value delivered to the business, regarding IT services behavior (risks, service agreements, costs, income, and alignment) [28] **Information/Artefacts/Resources** 3. Metrics by asset [18] 4. Project management methodology [18] 5. Value flow measurement techniques

Table 3 Actions and capabilities to support the risk management dimension

	Action (What)	Capabilities (How)
Strategic	1. Plan and direct risk management [23] 2. Align IT risk policy with corporate risk policy [18] 3. Build a risk-aware culture [17] 4. Define and implement a risk governance process [17]	**Structures** 1. Executive level (Board of directors, management committee) [17, 18] **Information/Artefacts/Resources** 2. Risks map 3. Risk appetite and tolerance [18] **Processes** 4. COBIT Process EDM03—Ensure Risk Optimization [18] 5. List of breaches that executives could be accountable for [24]

(continued)

Table 3 (continued)

	Action (What)	Capabilities (How)
		6. Segmented audiences based on their role towards risk awareness [17]
Tactical	1. Assess IT-related risks that may affect the organization [18] 2. Create and maintain an IT risk management portfolio [25] 3. Align IT risk management with corporate risk management	**Structures** 1. Management committee [3] 2. IT specialized committees [3] **Processes** 3. OCTAVE (Operationally Critical Threat, Asset and Vulnerability Evaluation) processes for assessing risks on Information Security [26] 4. Risk policies and standards [23] 5. COBIT process APO12—manage risks (create and maintain a formal document with the identified risks) [18] **Communication** 6. COBIT process EDM03.02 (channels to deliver the campaigns to all the employees) [18]
Operational	1. Collect and analyze information regarding IT risks [17] 2. Perform a cost-benefit analysis on risks [17] 3. Design and prove a business continuity plan [17] 4. Identify and close vulnerabilities in the IT assets base [17] 5. Implement controls and industry best practices [18] 6. Simulate solution scenarios to control risks 7. Report risks materialization [18]	**Structures** 1. Service manager [18] 2. Business-IT Council [3] 3. IT specialized committees [3] 4. IT Audit [3, 17, 27] **Processes** 5. COBIT process APO12.01—Manage Risks [18] 6. Risk quantification of operational assets (processes, IT services) [28, 29] 7. Business Impact Analysis (BIA) [17] 8. Business continuity plan with responsible and expected quality of service levels [17] 9. IT audits [27] 10. COBIT process APO12.02 (Cost-benefit analysis on risks treatment) [18] **Information/Artefacts/Resources** 10. List of critical IT assets and their vulnerabilities [26] 11. Test environments [18] **Communication** 12. Channels to notify materialization of a risk to whomever is responsible

Table 4 describes the actions and capabilities identified for the performance management dimension. This dimension covers the definition, monitoring and evaluation of business and IT goals and metrics against expected performance goals [18].

Table 4 Actions and capabilities to support the performance management dimension

	Action (What)	Capabilities (How)
Strategic	1. Identify agreements with the stakeholders regarding the expected performance of IT investments [18] 2. Manage the use of IT resources	**Structures** 1. Executive committee [3, 18] 2. IT specialized committees [3] **Processes** 3. Models of IT agreements or contracts [18] 4. Measurement of resources use (time, costs) [18]
Tactical	1. Specify agreements with the stakeholders regarding the performance goals and metrics expected from IT [18] 2. Rationalize asset use 3. Evaluate IT performance on profit, asset utilization, growth [3]	**Structures** 1. Management committee [3] **Processes** 2. IT performance on profit (executive committee, architecture process, capital approval, tracking of business value) 3. IT performance on asset utilization (Business/IT relationship manager, Process teams with IT members, SLA and Chargeback, IT leadership decision making body) 4. IT performance on growth (budget approval, risk management, local accountability, portals)
Operational	1. Monitor performance of IT services, assets and investments so as to identify improvement opportunities 2. Manage IT assets [18] 3. Manage utilization of human resources among multiple business processes 4. Collect information on the performance of the IT services and assets defined in the IT portfolio [18]	**Processes** 1. COBIT process MEA01-Monitor and evaluate performance and conformance [18] 2. COBIT process BAI09-Manage Assets [18] 3. COBIT process APO07-Manage human resources [18] **Information/Artefacts/Resources** 4. Map of IT assets and corporate processes supported by those assets [18] 5. IT portfolio [18]

5   Measuring Gaps on IT Governance Capabilities

5.1   Assessment Criteria

Table 5 describes how the capabilities defined in Sect. 4 can be evaluated in terms of two elements: existence and function. This means that an organization has capabilities not just because it has an ITG structure but because this structure performs certain tasks as well.

Table 5 Expected evidence on IT governance capabilities

	Strategic	Tactical	Operational
Decision-making support	DS1. Decisions are explicit DS2. Decision-making structures are defined DS3. Decisions made among different structures are aligned DS4. Decision-making responsibilities are clearly defined DS5. The decision-making archetype is known and aligned with expected IT behavior	DT1. Decision-making archetypes are defined and recognized for each type of decision DT2. The agreements on decisions are formally defined DT3. Framework implementation initiatives consider stakeholders to create an implementation plan DT4. Decisions are made only by those formally defined to make them	DO1. All decisions are clearly identified and classified into one of five decision types DO2. Governance model is based on proactive mechanisms over reactive ones DO3. Defined agreements are periodically monitored using technical tools
Risk management	RS1. There is an organizational risk awareness culture RS2. Risk appetite and tolerance are formally defined RS3. There is a formally defined IT risk policy, aligned with the corporate risk policy RS4. Risk awareness programs are implemented within the organization	RT1. IT risks that may affect the organization are clearly identified and assessed RT2. There is a formal definition of owners and managers that are responsible for IT risk RT3. There is an IT risk management portfolio that collects information on the identified risks	RO1. Cost-benefit analyses of IT risks are performed periodically RO2. A business continuity plan is defined and tested periodically RO3. Controls over IT risks are implemented based on cost-benefit analysis and industry best practices RO4. IT risks are quantified RO5. IT audits are performed regularly to identify and close vulnerabilities over IT assets
Value delivery and alignment	VS1. There are clearly defined guidelines to measure value delivery VS2. IT investments are prioritized based on specific criteria (e.g. higher benefits, lesser risk)	VT1. IT portfolio is constantly monitored to assure the transfer of benefits VT2. Organization is constantly looking for investment opportunities to improve the IT portfolio	VO1. There is an IT portfolio that contains information on IT services, assets and investments VO2. IT investment and projects follow project management methodologies VO3. The business value delivery from IT services is quantified

(continued)

Table 5 (continued)

	Strategic	Tactical	Operational
		VT3. New IT investment initiatives are prioritized according to organizational criteria VT4. IT portfolio is periodically reviewed to keep it updated with organizational changes	
Performance Management	PS1. There is a formal definition of expected performance of IT services, from the stakeholders PS2. There is an understanding of the business value delivered by IT	PT1. Formal agreements of expected performance are defined with stakeholders PT2. Formal evaluations are executed to measure IT performance	PO1. IT services are evaluated against stakeholders' expectations PO2. IT assets are periodically evaluated to guarantee that they are used effectively to support business requirements PO3. Human resources are used effectively to support multiple business processes

5.2   Gap Analysis for the Logistics Industry

Based on the previous criteria, this section presents the most significant theory-practice gaps that we identified after evaluating the ITG capabilities of the four companies mentioned in Sect. 3. After performing this analysis, we identified an approach that can be taken as a characterization of the sector.

Since decision-making is important for most companies at the strategic level, the three analyzed companies had clearly defined decision-making structures and critical decisions to control. However, there was a lack of mechanisms (e.g. decision maps) to align decisions made from different structures. At the tactical level, only one company had formally defined service level agreements and controlled decisions, which could only be made by the defined structures. The lack of agreements in the remaining three companies generated conflicting decisions. All companies lacked the capabilities to prioritize ITG mechanisms (i.e. IT processes) to be designed and implemented. This entailed the creation of informal implementation plans with low controllability. At the operational level, the governance model for all companies was based on reactive mechanisms (e.g. committees). Therefore, there was a lack of mechanisms to control the impact of decisions (monitoring, auditing, process execution).

Risk management, even when considered one of the most important dimensions both for researchers and practitioners, was commonly being ignored, or not considered as critical from a strategic perspective. The lack of business-IT alignment regarding risk management may have created different risk mitigation strategies that do not respond to the business' requirements. A formal and corporate risk aware culture was missing in all four companies. At the tactical level, the two local companies had identified IT risks and controls. The two multinational companies were missing a formally defined IT-RM portfolio. At the operational level, none companies had implemented control mechanisms to analyze cost-benefits on IT risks, to provide continuity plans, or to quantify IT risks and their propagation on business and IT assets.

We also found that value delivery was the most important dimension for all companies. Each of the companies had structures (i.e. committees) specifically dedicated to measuring the business value delivered by IT investments. Through periodical meetings and a formal process, the analyzed organizations monitored value delivery to achieve business-IT alignment and identify new IT investment opportunities. This is very important at the tactical level because it settles the foundation on how IT will support the business requirements and strategy. This can then be used by the IT department to identify critical IT services and assets, and to define controls that help mitigate risks over those IT resources. Even though the development of strategic level capabilities was expected to follow a top-down approach, some companies were capable to include those strategic capabilities leveraged by the already existing tactical and operational capabilities (on a bottom-up approach). All four companies would improve their value delivery at the operational level by incorporating capabilities to quantify non-financial value, to measure the value flow among IT architectures, and to forecast the value of IT assets.

Performance management was supported in all companies at the strategic level. This became evident through their clear definition of IT to support business strategy and through their periodical reports to the executive board regarding the performance of IT projects. However, at the tactical level, there were no agreements with the business units regarding the expected performance of IT nor was this performance measured. None of the companies performed periodic evaluations to determine if the utilization of IT assets (e.g. ROA), the rationalization of assets, or IT performance (profit, assets utilization, growth) were appropriate. At the operational level, all companies lacked the capabilities to control the utilization of inter-project or inter-process human resources and to monitor process performance.

5.3   Gap Analysis by Company

Gap analysis for the first multinational company (MC1)

Decisions were made by the International Headquarters (HQ) and then transmitted to the corresponding regional offices, where such decisions were adapted to a particular reality. Each regional office transmitted these decisions to the local subsidiaries in each country. As a result, the Colombian subsidiary had to comply with the global decisions.

Decision-making in this company was therefore constrained by the unified operational model of the organization (high standardization and integration of processes [3]). The organization had clearly defined decision-making structures and critical decisions to control. However, the interview data showed that the information was not as standardized as expected. This evidences the need for greater ITG efforts at the operational level in order to achieve more control. At a tactical level, the decision-making archetypes were not clearly identified for all decision types, especially because decisions were made by global or regional structures. There were formally defined service level agreements and the decisions were made only by the defined structures. However, this does not mean that the decisions were made by the right structure.

Risk management support at the strategic level was defined by the global HQ. Risk management in the Colombian subsidiary was focused on supporting project management but was not considered a mechanism to relate IT and corporate governance. Thus, risk management could be misdirected into different directions, causing misalignment between the business and IT. We noticed that risk management was a top priority for IT, but it was not considered important by the business. This explains the lack of a risk awareness culture in the Colombian subsidiary. To close this gap, the organization started implementing COBIT to identify the business impact on risk materialization. At the tactical level, there was not a formally defined IT risk management portfolio with detailed information of identified risks, IT assets and their vulnerabilities, nor was there any risk accountability. Finally, at the operational level, since no formal procedure of risk treatment was defined, the controls to treat the identified risk were implemented without a detailed cost-benefit analysis, and no IT audits were performed periodically to detect new vulnerabilities.

Value delivery was the most important dimension for this organization as declared by both the IT and business units. This was supported at the strategic level by a formal process to periodically measure and follow the business value delivered by IT, a regional committee to prioritize investments, and a budget approval committee for evaluating IT initiatives based on their Return On Investment (ROI). At a tactical level, the IT portfolio was periodically monitored to assure that the expected benefits were being transferred to the business, and periodic meetings were arranged to identify new IT investment. Finally, at the operational level, the organization had an IT portfolio with information regarding IT services, assets and investments. IT investments were implemented using project management methodologies. However, some business units considered that IT initiatives were not delivering as much business value as they could. This can be improved by incorporating communication mechanisms and by quantifying the non-financial value delivered by IT investments.

Performance management at the strategic level was well supported through a clear definition of IT for supporting business strategy while keeping the operation running. The executive board received periodical reports regarding the performance of IT projects. However, these expectations were no longer defined at the tactical and operational levels; there were no agreements with the business units regarding the expected IT performance, nor was this performance measured. Moreover, there were no periodic evaluations to determine if the utilization of IT assets was appropriate. Project metrics, such as the expected delivery time and the budget of IT projects, were missing resource utilization metrics to keep the project within the expected boundaries.

Gap analysis for the first local company (LC1)
This company behaved similarly to MC1 due to its clearly defined structures to make decisions. However, this organization did not define nor monitor agreements, something that generated conflicting decisions.

Even though this company had a risk awareness culture (risk management is critical for IT and the business), risk management was not considered as a mechanism to relate IT and corporate governance. As a result, risk management could be misdirected into different directions, causing misalignment between the business and IT. Risk appetite and tolerance were not formally defined. At the tactical level, IT risks on processes, controls, and initiatives were identified to improve the risk awareness culture. According to the data from the interviews, the performance of these initiatives was favorable throughout the entire organization. Consequently, the existing initiatives should leverage the formalization of risk management at a strategic level.

The capabilities of the value delivery dimension were not supported in this company. The prioritization of IT investments was performed by the board of directors and the budget was approved by the CEO and the CFO. Based on the data from the interviews, we identified a misalignment between the business and IT areas regarding value delivery. For example, IT did not consider it crucial that all IT initiatives delivered business value, despite this being a non-negotiable requirement for the business. The lack of a strategic support for value delivery may have caused this misalignment. A strategic approach regarding the measurement of business value delivered by IT is necessary in order to guarantee that all IT investments have a return.

Performance management at the strategic level evidenced a clear understanding of the expectations this business had concerning IT. The role of IT was exclusively operational (e.g. keeping the IT platform working, customer support). Therefore, the capabilities at tactical and operational levels were limited and no formal agreements or monitoring processes were defined. Moreover, despite the performance of IT services being measured in terms of platform availability and the organization not using standard project management methodologies, less than one project per year was delivered out of time or budget.

Gap analysis for the second multinational company (MC2)

Much like MC1, decision-making in MC2 was mainly supported by the international HQ and then transferred to a regional office and local subsidiaries, which lacked decision-making structures. The decision making archetypes at the corporate level were known throughout the organization as well as the conformation of the different committees making the decisions.

IT risk management evidenced the lack of a risk awareness culture from both, IT and the business, within the subsidiary (cf. risk awareness on IT in MC1). There was no alignment between the IT risk policy and the corporate risk policy. At the tactical level, there was no formally defined IT risk management. At the operational level, since no formal procedure of risk treatment was defined, the controls implemented to treat the identified risk were implemented without a detailed cost-benefit analysis, and no IT audits were performed periodically to detect new vulnerabilities.

Value delivery at the subsidiary had a formally established process to measure the business value delivered by IT, as well as a regional committee coordinated by the subsidiary to perform the prioritization of the investments. Furthermore, a budget approval committee, including the CEO and the CFO, ensured that all the approved IT initiatives had an associated ROI. At tactical and operational levels, the IT portfolio was periodically monitored to ensure that the expected benefits were being transferred to the business, and that periodic meetings were arranged to identify new IT investment opportunities that could better support the operation of the company. However, one of the findings that stems from analyzing this company is that value delivery from IT initiatives is not a priority for the business nor for IT. This could cause the company to spend resources on IT investments that do not deliver a return for the business.

Performance management at the strategic level constraints the IT role to keep the standards defined by HQ and to provide a good service for internal and external customers. At the tactical and operational levels, there were agreements with the business units regarding the expected performance and benefits of IT, but there were no formal evaluations of IT performance. There were no periodic evaluations to determine that the utilization of IT assets was appropriate either. Similarly to company LC1, performance of IT services was measured in terms of platform availability and customer satisfaction. Regarding customer satisfaction, the organization had results that indicated a score of 4 out of 5 in customer satisfaction concerning the IT services, which shows a good service level with opportunity for improvement.

Gap analysis for the second local company (LC2)
Despite the organization having defined structures to make decisions, decision-making responsibilities were not clearly defined. Moreover, at the tactical level, the decision making archetypes were not clearly identified because there was no detailed approach on who participated in each decision-making structure and, specifically, if there was any IT presence in the structures. The company had formally defined service level agreements and the decisions were made only by the defined structures.

Risk management was considered a mechanism that related IT and corporate governance, which helped to align the IT risk policy to the corporate risk policy, as well as to improve the risk-aware culture in the organization. This can be proved by reviewing the relative importance of risk management for both IT and the business. The company started working on the implementation of COBIT, and has focused on identifying the business impact of the materialization of an IT risk. At the tactical level, IT risk identification in the organization and prevention of risk materialization over business core processes had been implemented and monitored. At the operational level, there were no periodic IT audits to detect new vulnerabilities. Since there is a relation between IT and corporate risk policies, controls were defined based on a cost-benefit analysis.

The company had a formal process to measure the business value delivered by IT, which was carried out by the board of c-level executives. It also had a process to prioritize IT investments and a budget approval mechanism. Contrary to the other cases where the budget approval included either the CEO or the CFO, the person responsible for this approval was the purchase leader. This decision could be explained when considering that the purchase leader can get better prices from suppliers. At tactical and operational levels, the IT portfolio was periodically monitored to ensure that the expected benefits were being transferred to the business, and that periodic meetings were arranged to identify new IT investment opportunities that can better support the operation of the company. However, one of the metrics commonly used to identify value delivery, customer satisfaction with IT services, was not considered as critical for the business nor for IT. This induced the organization to spend resources on IT while disregarding the requirements and considerations of the customers, both internal and external.

Performance management included the IT role to provide technical solutions to business requirements and to comply with the guidelines defined by the organization. Customer satisfaction, peer review, and business process improvements were the critical metrics required to evaluate IT performance. As we mentioned before, at tactical and operational levels, customer satisfaction performance in this company was deficient for internal and external customers.

6 Conclusion

In this paper, we presented a set of capabilities for ITG practice at different levels (strategic, tactic, operational), according to the ITG academic literature, and classified them around the four dimensions of ITG. A similar exercise was then performed, but this time based on the ITG capabilities identified in four Colombian organizations of the logistics industry. The comparison between these two exercises allows us to conclude that there are indeed considerable gaps regarding the risk management dimension of ITG, as well as when considering the priorities assigned to the value delivery dimension. The bigger gaps are evident at an operational level.

One interesting finding is that even companies that used commercial frameworks like COBIT had significant gaps in their risk management dimension, something that could be read in one of two ways: (a) the importance of the IT risk management dimension is over-emphasized in the literature, or (b) practitioners see the recommendations of the ITG literature regarding IT risk management as an overkill and prefer a more relaxed approach. It is important to note, however, that this research does not intend to comment on the convenience of a robust and structured approach to IT risk management nor on the relaxed approaches assumed by the organizations in this research.

Finally, this research also supports the importance of considering the social aspects of ITG practices because, even though the interviewees talked very highly about the commercial frameworks used in their companies, most of them did not apply them fully and even went against the recommendations of such frameworks. This questions if the source of legitimacy of these frameworks is truly based on their technical value (a value that this research does not put into question) or if it is the result of political, social or marketing processes. These questions should be studied more carefully in future works about ITG.

References

1. Webb, P., Pollard, C., Ridley, G.: Attempting to define IT governance: wisdom or folly? In: Proceedings of the 39th Hawaii International Conference on System Sciences, pp. 1–10. IEEE (2006)
2. Brown, A., Grant, G.: Framing the frameworks: a review of IT governance research. Commun. Assoc. Inform. Sys. **15**, 696–712 (2005)
3. Weill, P.: Don't just lead, Govern: how top-performing firms govern IT. MIS Q. Exec. **3**(1), 1–17 (2004)

4. Giraldo O.L., Herrera, A., Gómez, J. E.: IT Governance State of Art at enterprises in the Colombian Pharmaceutical Industry. In: Quintela Varajão J.E., Cruz-Cunha M.M., Putnik G. D., Trigo A. (eds) ENTERprise Information Systems. CENTERIS 2010. CCIS, vol. 109. Springer, Berlin, Heidelberg
5. Jacobson, D.D.: Revisiting IT governance in the light of institutional theory. In: Proceedings of the 42nd Hawaii International Conference on System Sciences, pp. 1–9. IEEE (2009)
6. Willson, P., Pollard, C.: Exploring IT governance in theory and practice in a large multi-national organisation in Australia. Inform. Syst. Manage. **26**, 98–109 (2009)
7. Simonsson, M., Ekstedt, M.: Getting the priorities right: literature vs practice on IT governance. In: Technology Management for the Global Future—PICMET 2006 Conference, pp. 18–26. IEEE (2006)
8. Keyes-Pearce, S.: Rethinking the importance of IT governance in the e-World. In: Proceedings of the 6th Pacific Asia Conference on Information Systems, pp. 256–272. AISeL (2002)
9. Winkler, T., Brown, C.V.: Horizontal allocation of decision rights for on-premise applications and software-as-a-service. J. Manage. Inform. Syst. **30**, 13–48 (2014)
10. Ko, D., Fink, D.: Information technology governance: an evaluation of the theory-practice gap. Corp. Govern. **10**, 662–674 (2010)
11. Winkler, T., Goebel, C., Benlian, A., Bidault, F., Günther, O.: The impact of software as a service on IS authority—a contingency perspective. In: Proceedings of the 32nd International Conference on Information Systems, pp. 1–17. AISeL (2011)
12. Yin, R.K.: Case Study Research: Design and Methods. Sage Publications, Thousand Oaks (2008)
13. Ulrich, W., Rosen, M.: The business capability map: the "rosetta stone" of business/IT alignment. Enterp. Archit. **14** (2011)
14. Eisenhardt, K.M., Martin, J.A.: Dynamic capabilities: what are they? Strateg. Manage. J. **21**, 1105–1121 (2000)
15. Swauger, J.: Is it time for an IT governance audit? EDPACS **47**, 1–6 (2013)
16. González-Rojas, O., Lesmes, S.: GovernIT: a software for decision-making support on automated IT governance models. In: Information Systems Development: Advances in Methods, Tools and Management (ISD2017 Proceedings), pp. 12. AISeL (2017)
17. Westerman, G., Hunter, R.: IT Risk: Turning Business Threats Into Competitive Advantage. Harvard Business School Press, Boston, MA, USA (2007)
18. ISACA: COBIT 5: A Business Framework for the Governance and Management of Enterprise IT. ISACA (2012)
19. Cervone, F.: ITIL: a framework for managing digital library services. Digit. Libr. Perspect. **24**, 87–90 (2008)
20. Fonstad, N.O., Robertson, D.: Transforming a company, project by project: the IT engagement model. MIS Q. Exec. **5**, 1–14 (2006)
21. Heart, T., Maoz, H., Pliskin, N.: From governance to adaptability: the mediating effect of IT executives' managerial capabilities. Inform. Syst. Manage. **27**, 42–60 (2010)
22. Gonzalez-Rojas, O., Beltrán, G., Correal, D.: Measurement of current and potential non-financial business value delivery of IT investments. Information **19**, 2869–2874 (2016)
23. Kohnke, A., Shoemaker, D.: Making cybersecurity effective: the five governing principles for implementing practical IT governance and control. EDPACS **52**, 9–17 (2015)
24. ISO: ISO/IEC 38500;2008: Corporate Governance of Information Technology. International Standards Organisation (2008)
25. Jordan, E.: An integrated IT risk model. In: Proceedings of the 9th Pacific Asia Conference on Information Systems: IT & Value Creation, pp. 632–644. AISeL (2005)
26. Caralli, R., Stevens, J., Young, L., Wilson, W.: Introducing OCTAVE Allegro: improving the information security risk assessment process (No. CMU/SEI-2007-TR-012) (2007)
27. Héroux, S., Fortin, A.: Exploring IT dependence and IT governance. Inform. Syst. Manage. **31**, 143–166 (2014)

28. González-Rojas, O.: Governing IT services for quantifying business impact. In: Matulevicius, R., Dumas, M. (eds.) Perspectives in Business Informatics Research. BIR 2015. LNBIP, vol. 229, pp. 97–112. Springer, Cham (2015)
29. González-Rojas, O., Lesmes, S.: Value at risk within business processes: an automated IT risk governance approach. In: La Rosa, M., Loos, P., and Pastor, O. (eds.) Business Process Management. BPM 2016. LNCS, vol. 9850, pp. 365–380. Springer, Cham (2016)

GUI Interaction Interviews in the Evolving Map of Design Research

John Sören Pettersson, Malin Wik and Henrik Andersson

Abstract This chapter presents GUI-ii, Graphical User Interface interaction interview, a method used to remotely discuss, develop and test GUI prototypes with users and stakeholders. Examples of such sessions are presented to demonstrate that the main benefit of GUI-ii is that this way of co-designing allows for interaction-informed discussions around functions and user interfaces, where re-design and hands-on experience can be integrated and efficiently carried out remotely. Using a facilitation tool to enact GUI layout and responses allows participation and evaluation to be mixed in participatory design sessions in a productive way. This form of participatory design is discussed along the dimensions found in Sanders' Map of Design Research. The discussion concludes that GUI-ii facilitates participation by relaxing demands for physical presence and by allowing people to participate from their own work environment while still making it easy for them to directly influence contents, structure and interaction.

Keywords Participatory design · GUI-ii · Interview techniques
Design research

A prior version of this paper has been published in the ISD2017 Proceedings (http://aisel.aisnet.org/isd2014/proceedings2017).

J. S. Pettersson (✉) · M. Wik · H. Andersson
Karlstad University, Karlstad, Sweden
e-mail: john_soren.pettersson@kau.se

M. Wik
e-mail: malin.wik@kau.se

H. Andersson
e-mail: henrik.andersson@kau.se

© Springer International Publishing AG, part of Springer Nature 2018
N. Paspallis et al. (eds.), *Advances in Information Systems Development*,
Lecture Notes in Information Systems and Organisation 26,
https://doi.org/10.1007/978-3-319-74817-7_10

1 Introduction

When conducting interviews face-to-face an interviewer and respondent interact closely and use various combinations of body postures, gestures and facial expressions to enhance their exchange [1]. Body language, facial expressions and hesitations in speech can help the interviewer to understand how certain the respondent is about what he/she is saying and how comfortable, relaxed or tense, someone is during the interview. The interviewer may, by his/her mere presence, affect the interviewee to answer in ways that the interviewee feels obliged to. Conscious or unconscious body signals of the interviewer can also affect the respondent [1].

Telephone interviews are not used so much in qualitative interviewing, but more often for survey research; advantages of telephone interviews are the cost savings, the ability to reach a large population and "hard-to-reach groups" [1] (p. 489). It is also easy to supervise and it reduces biased answers from the respondents as they are less affected by the interviewer [1]. What interviews, either face-to-face or via telephone, are lacking when it comes to supporting the development of interactive systems, is the *interaction* with an *interface*.

We are developing a type of interview-based collaboration technique which we refer to as the GUI interaction interview (GUI-ii). Using half-made prototypes which the respondent can access via web browsers, we ask for help filling empty parts but also probe plain usability issues and encourage immediate remediation by prompts to "let's try to change this in the way you would like it". We contrast this with the UI discussions by high-fidelity color print or screen displays. Such stimuli are known to provoke very narrow comments on specific details [2].

In GUI-ii we use a "wizard" as in the "Wizard of Oz" (WOz) methodology to apply a Participatory Design (PD) approach. PD implies that representative actors directly affected by the system should be part of the development [3]. WOz is normally used for usability testing of interactive systems without the need for programming, and it can also be used for explorative interaction design (e.g. [4]). Our research group developed a system, Ozlab, that supports WOz experimentation and facilitates wizards to control GUI responses in inter-action with a test participant [5]. The most interesting thing is how to make explorative tests in a GUI—wizards will have to be able to articulate themselves in a rather artificial medium. Paper prototyping has long been advocated by user-centered designers, as "a running prototype couldn't be changed immediately" [6] (p. 373). However, in-between the programmed prototypes and the paper mockups there is a toolbox space where Ozlab fits in. Per definition, the WOz method circumvents the need for programming to demonstrate interactivity. Instead, the crucial factor is to have a WOz tool that allows—without much overhead work—for changes in GUI as well as in interaction. At least to some extent Ozlab fulfills these requirements.

Ozlab can also be used in participatory design sessions over a distance. The purpose of the present paper is to discuss *how* by traversing the "Map of Design

Research" by Elizabeth Sanders [7, 8] and the "making, telling, enacting" sequence of activity [9] ("tell" becomes "say" in [10]).

The structure of the chapter is as follows: Sect. 2 explains the ideas behind the interactive prototyping system we used for our GUI-ii sessions and the GUI-ii method itself, while Sect. 3 presents examples of applications of the method. The stage is thereby set for discussing GUI-ii aspects in relations to frameworks for Participatory Design. Section 4 thus highlights and illuminates these aspects in relation to the cardinal directions of Sanders' map and some of the populated locations in it. This discussion is rounded off by explaining some tensions connected to the use of a testing tool for co-design purposes, and also by noting the tension between designing the interactivity in the artefact itself or in a user's interaction with it. Section 5 concludes the paper by summarizing the main points made in the preceding sections.

2 Supporting Development of Interactive Systems in Interactive Sessions

Under the heading "Mimesis and interaction", Brenda Laurel once wrote "The most important distinction between a play and an interface is that an interface is *interactive*, while a play is not. [...] An interface [...] is literally co-created by its human user every time it is used." [11] (p. 73). Obviously, being a hidden actor behind the GUI output, the test manager in a Wizard-of-Oz experiment stages an interactive play, where things are enacted on the display (and sometimes also audible in the air) by both the test user and the manager.

Several authors writing on WOz experiments have mentioned the possibility of using the method not only for *strict testing* of an unimplemented but meticulous specified interaction idea but also for the *explorative* use of what output would facilitate a user's understanding of the user interface under development [12]. "As opposed to assuming a certain dialogue flow, WOz experiments can be used to explore the dialogue space in more detail." [13] (p. 44).

Kelley [14] coined the "OZ paradigm" in the beginning of the 1980s when simulating a language processing components for IBM in two ways. In the first run, "*no* language processing components were in place. The experimenter simulated the system *in toto*." In the second run, "Fifteen participants used the program, and the experimenter intervened as necessary to keep the dialog flowing. As this step progressed, and as the dictionaries and functions were augmented, the experimenter was phased out of the communications loop" [4] (p. 28), [14] (p. 193). The second run yielded fewer and fewer new words for each new participant, and it was succeeded by a *validation* step where a further six participants tested the resulting program to see how it performed. Kelley's use reveals how the Wizard-of-Oz technique can be applied, that is, to develop an interaction design *in interaction*. This is in contrast to merely testing the interaction design.

The possibility to influence the interface elements during explorative interaction sessions are of course dependent on the support for such things provided by the experimental set up. Our system Ozlab is geared to aid in GUI interaction, both for ordinary small-scale usability testing and for explorative sessions. From the very beginning in 2001, we included user groups as designers and testers [15]. During the first few years, it also became apparent that such a tool was quite useful during team-internal demonstrations—the plasticity of the interaction design made it easy to immediately see the implication of different suggestions. After 15 years of various uses, we have now not only toppled the developer—user roles and mixed face-to-face team discussions with interactive GUI expressions, but also started extending the use to GUI-based co-design discussions at a distance.

In 2011, our Wizard-of-Oz prototyping tool Ozlab went from being based on a multimedia production tool called Director to become web-based. While the web environment presents several difficulties [15], it also provides new possibilities for remote interaction. The system runs in the web browser, which means that a person participating in, for example, a test session does not have to install any software on her computer. Instead, she can access the prototype via a URL provided by the designer. Ozlab allows the creation of mockup prototypes from pure graphics with the aid of predefined behaviors which are then accessible during testing, for instance to make objects visible and invisible, to accept text entry or drag-and-drop actions. Such features make a collection of static graphics to appear interactive when a wizard interprets a participant's GUI actions and then responds by further GUI events. Before going into the use of this system in GUI-ii, we will expound a little on what it means to do prototyping.

2.1   Prototypes for Interactive Systems

As we have put forward WOz to include prospective users—these users have been acting as, for example, designers and testers, co-designers, expert reviewers—it is apt to compare it with the three approaches to "making" that Sanders and Stappers identify in a special issue of the journal CoDesign [8]. They mention *probes, toolkits* and *prototypes*. In early design phases, probes can be thrown in by designers to see how stakeholder representatives react: a kind of stimulus for the imagination. When the design work takes on a more directed format, scenarios and storyboards are typically used to visualize the ideas. A participatory-minded designer can serve co-designers with toolkits that allow them to participate in the making of the visualizations. For the third stage, they refer to Stappers' [16] list of roles that prototypes can play in *research through design*:

- Prototypes evoke a focused discussion in a team, because the phenomenon is 'on the table'.
- Prototypes allow testing of a hypothesis.

- Prototypes confront theories, because instantiating one typically forces those involved to consider several overlapping perspectives/theories/frames.
- Prototypes confront the world, because the theory is not hidden in abstraction.
- A prototype can change the world, because in interventions it allows people to experience a situation that did not exist before. [8] (p. 6)

We agree very much with this view, but have noted that programmed prototypes tend to lock in imagination rather early as noted also by others; such as in a textbook in HCI [17] where Bill Verplank is interviewed saying, inter alia: "There is a big push towards prototyping tools that will lead very directly to the product. Almost every computer-based development that I've been part of suffered from a lack of consideration of alternatives" (p. 467).

Now, when extending the WOz to include users as designers and testers (rather than only as test participants), and further, to mix demo and co-design with "testing" into the GUI-ii, we note that this effect in using designs as probes (whether the designs stem from designer or co-designer in a preceding workshop or GUI-ii session) and using designs as prototypes (in more or less all the ways enumerated by Stappers).

2.2 Overcoming Geographic Distance

To overcome geographic distance between users, designers and developers, the designers can send mockups digitally to the user representatives and the developers to receive comments. However, what is missing in sending a fully or partly interactive prototype or a sketch to someone else is the possibility to explore new and unforeseen interactions. To clearly communicate what part of the GUI one is talking about—the functionality offered or the interaction design—is furthermore difficult. Humans are good at interaction, but not at envision it in advance. If a designer or co-designer have the courage to meet various prospective users and other stakeholders through the interface, the Wizard-of-Oz method can be surprisingly productive. WOz can be used in numerous ways to get ideas for developing the interaction design and later to refine ideas or select among ideas, and by the very approach much of this stems from real-use experience and not only from discussions in the team. For the present purpose, we must ask how much of this can be based on distance.

When it comes to ordinary usability testing, Schade [18] argues in an article on the website of the Nielsen Norman group, that a physically present facilitator can more easily time follow-up questions and read the participants' body language. However, if resources are scarce or if timeframes are tight, remotely moderated usability tests can be a good alternative, especially if the users are "geographically dispersed", Schade points out. This calls for attention to another divide: remote user tests can be unmoderated or moderated. Because the facilitator and the participant does not have to schedule a session, the unmoderated remotely conducted user tests can be very time efficient (ibid.). Of course, the system to be tested has to be programmed as it has to run by itself and tasks must be easily understood by the test users. Often completely unmoderated user tests call for too much planning and stress testing of the prototype to be really feasible in iterative design processes where much information on user reactions is wanted almost instantaneously in order to re-design the prototypes. The close encounter of the moderator with the participants is an essential part in participatory design. As will be brought up in the following section, GUI-ii is a close encounter on distance, and it is more co-design oriented than moderated remote testing. At the same time, it should be noted for the three projects mentioned in Sect. 3, that they had already included various sorts of stakeholder discussions and workshops before the GUI-ii sessions.

2.3   A Snapshot of the GUI-ii Workbench

The interviewer, or designer, or Wizard of Oz, in Fig. 1 tacitly controls certain non-implemented functionality of a user interface, which the interlocutor acts upon and also changes, but the participants' direct actions are limited by what the designer has made changeable in the mockup. Sometimes we stop a session and make changes according to expressed suggestions from participants—the WOz method for enacting interfaces allows for quick implementation of rather drastic changes. The paper sheet before the wizard in Fig. 1 is the wizard's interaction script—it can easily be changed if the participant calls for this.

The laptop to the left in Fig. 1 shows a copy of what the participant sees. Screen recording is made there including sound; the round black object is a loudspeaker microphone. Sometimes we record also the wizard's screen, but that is mainly for

Fig. 1 A wizard in front of the prototyping system used during one GUI-ii session

evaluating our WOz system. Schade, in her above-referred discussion about remote moderated usability tests, suggests that the facilitator and the participant communicate via telephone, email, chat or by combining these methods. For GUI-ii, where a wizard is always present to run the interaction (designer-purported or participant-suggested interaction), email and chat are used only by participants to e.g. send documents or links to us. Obviously, the exact arrangements are rather unimportant so long as unconstrained expressions are possible in a normal channel (voice) and GUI (essential for the collaboration exercise).

3 Examples of GUI-ii

For participatory design, Brandt et al. say, "new application of existing tools and techniques is an area ripe for design and research discovery. It is especially important that the exploration of and reflection on the use of the new tools and techniques be situated at all the phases of the design and development process. It is also important that the results of these explorations be published" [19] (p. 176). However, the present presentation is not aiming to give a precise account of explorations made but rather to reflect on how to understand GUI-ii along the dimensions presented by Sanders in her design research map. Nevertheless, a short description of actual GUI-ii practice is in place to explain how it works. In this paper, we profit especially from the experiences of using GUI-ii in three projects with international partners as will be described here.

3.1 Project A: GUI-ii Traits in Walkthrough at a Distance

As an international undertaking, project A yielded important insights about using web-based WOz during remote sessions in addition to some face-to-face sessions. This makes some comparative analysis between remote and in-person sessions feasible. Two of the remote test participants were located in other towns in our country (Sweden) and one in Germany. Think aloud was used during tasks and after the tasks a discussion around the GUI pages took place. This has some traits of GUI-ii. Our findings include:

  i. Usability testing using WOz at a distance can be compared to traditional WOz testing.
 ii. The necessary slow response from the wizard may prompt some people to click repeatedly (if they do not get a quick response their instant feeling of interactivity appears to wane).
iii. A high-quality Internet connection is essential to reduce lag.
 iv. User testing at the mockup stage increased the participants input in the design work.

Of course, this was more of a traditional user test (a demo based on a prototype and tasks to solve) followed by "post-test" discussion of the demonstrated interaction design. But this encouraged us to a more extensive use of what one might call the "participatory potentials" of the GUI dialogues, as shown in the following project.

3.2 Project B: Observing Both Ordinary Interviews and GUI-ii Employment

In project B,[1] participatory design is complicated by not only distance but also two legal systems and two languages: Norwegian and Swedish. The project includes workshops, interviews, and the development of a cross-organization, cross-border web tool for collaboration. The very aim of the project is thus a tool for Computer-Supported Cooperative Work (CSCW [20]), which is why using the Ozlab tool for GUI-ii is quite congenial to the project goal. However, GUI-ii is only one participatory technique among several others used within (and before) project B. Below, we will expound on the observation of face-to-face and GUI-ii interviews held in spring and autumn 2016.

Two methods were used to gather the relevant data for evaluating GUI-ii: observations of face-to-face interviews and recording GUI-ii over Internet (with screen and voice recording). An occasional face-to-face GUI-ii (with recording) gave the interviewer more visual input of the interviewed co-designer but no extra notes needed to be made compared to notes we normally make. 10 GUI-ii sessions were held in the spring and 7 in the autumn. The interviewees were asked to suggest contents in addition to what had been jointly defined in workshops, or to comment on existing content including interaction design. Some text in the GUI were authored by the participant. There were several levels of authoring, from open text spaces for side comments, over instruction texts and specific labels for buttons, drop-down menus, and text fields, and the text fields themselves that our participants could fill in when we walked through the mockup before or after their changes (that is, they acted as "users" of the future CSCW system). Also for drag-and-drop there were actions in the design phase and in the "user" phase.

Interviewer's (Wizard's) Behavior
Thanks to the shared interaction space of the mockup, the wizard could explain the functionality by highlighting changes in the interface by various means, such as displaying a colored emphasis on a list of items. Example: "if you were to click this checkbox [wizard demonstrates by ticking the checkbox], the content matching the selection would be made visible like this [displays colored emphasis]."

[1]Preparing for Future Crisis Management (CriseIT.org), financed under the EU Interreg Sweden-Norway programme (20200721), is the main source for this paper and is also the project that financed writing this paper.

The two main interviewers were quite different in style:

- In the spring series of 10 GUI-iis when the mockup was rather empty, the wizard often waited for the interviewee to find and click on continue buttons, and if the participant asked what to do, he prompted the participant to say what he/she thought was important to do next or suggested to click on the expected button.
- In the autumn series of 7 GUI-iis, when the mockup was rather full and contained some alternatives, the wizard sometimes felt a time pressure to keep within the agreed time (1 h) and had a tendency to click through to other screens in order to be able to demonstrate and redesign all.

The second interviewer had a tendency to use the mouse pointer to encircle the object she spoke about, but the Ozlab system did not show the wizard's mouse pointer as the wizard in WOz tests are meant to be a secret hand behind the purported system's action. Demo pointing had to be done by drag-and-drop icons to be visible to the co-creating participant. Even if this wizard behavior did not really mess up the discussions, we had Ozlab enhanced in 2017 with a switch to make the wizard's pointer visible for the participant.

Observations of Face-to-Face Interviews (Non-GUI-ii Sessions)

In the face-to-face interviews, the respondents used body language and gestures to emphasize their arguments. For example, one respondent said "Everyone uses their smartphones", while taking up his phone to show it, and continued to discuss specific tools and apps he uses while tapping his fingers on the phone. Another respondent used his fingers to count what platforms they had in his organization. After mentioning all platforms, the respondent looked up at the interviewer as if asking "Is the answer enough?" Receiving no spoken feedback, the respondent elaborated the answer by describing the use of the different platforms.

Participant's Behavior in Dialogue in GUI-ii

(a) Participants differs in graphical preferences: When asked how they would like to arrange some crisis exercise activities into a logical workflow (by drag-and-drop), respondents had different preferences about how a flow is graphically organized. One of the respondents organized the workflow top-down, another bottom-up in inverted chronological order, a third from right to left (inverted chronological order), and a fourth organized the workflow diagonally. The prototype contains a label "Place the elements in the area below" and this was also prompted by the interviewer; obviously, few respondents took the word "below" to mean "vertically top-down".

(b) Language barriers can be overcome: Another important consideration is the terminology and language used. Terms used, and taken for granted by some respondents can be difficult to understand for others. Because this project includes Swedish and Norwegian project partners there is potential for even greater language confusion. Using our GUI-ii technique these problems became very evident and confusion was reduced by negotiating alternative terms and concepts.

(c) Real use and real data reveals new problems: Likewise, by asking the participants to actually use the (mockupped) planning system, such as filling out the form with actual data, made it clear whenever the participants struggled to fill out some information in the form. Furthermore, and perhaps even more important, the participants themselves became aware of where the form asked for redundant information or where the labels needed clarifications. As this content had been discussed before in workshops, we dare argue that the participants would not, at least not as easily, reach this insight by just looking at the form instead of interacting with it (just as Beyer and Holtzblatt [6] argue; cf. p. 375).

(d) Designer's ideas can be demoed and replaced: One idea was that each user of the finished system would themselves decide the categories for objects he/she creates (collaborative training material and small educational snippets). During the sessions, however, the interviewees made clear that such a solution would probably result in too many categories. Instead, by checking their files and folders, they filled the boxes with categories that best matched how they today sort and search for the content. Similar in other cases, for instance, even if we provided icons, icons for drag-and-drop could be discussed in several ways: graphic design, symbol meaning, meaning of positioning an icon, number of each icon type.

(e) Sessions with developers can reveal misconceptions: One of the GUI-ii sessions was held with one of the developers of the CSCW program. One scene in the mockup discussed during the session was showing an overview of a crisis training plan in form of a horizontal time-line. Even though the designers already had gathered information from the stakeholders, the developer argued the horizontal presentation manner would be a problem not only programming wise but also usability wise. He held a firm belief that horizontal scrolling would be necessary if items were not simply written in a vertical list, not thinking of that planners draw their timelines on a screen and have no reason to go outside the screen more than they would do on a piece of paper.

Face-to-Face GUI-ii

We found that firewalls sometimes block an easy use of our WOz system via the web. One participant solved this by participating from home.

For another interview session, when the firewall settings caused a problem on the participant's side the interviewer brought two laptops so that participant and wizard both could connect to a wifi present in the building, and thereby connect to the Internet and Ozlab. (As a backup, an interviewer can use a laptop with the Ozlab system installed which could be reached through the laptop's shared hot spot.) For data collection, screen and audio recording software was used on the participants' side. In this single face-to-face GUI-ii session, the respondent was more inclined to comment on "smaller" issues, like incorrect use of tenses, than other respondents had been. This raises the question, did the face-to-face aspects of the interview make the respondent to feel more confident in commenting on details?

3.3   Project C: GUI-ii

Finally, as an example of a more casual GUI-ii employment we can take a series of contact by GoToMeeting with an Italian project partner in yet an international project, here "C". While some project demonstrators needed extensive design, one application area was mainly for back-end IT staff and no user testing was needed. One person delivered scanned sketches and a list of functions to us. We mocked up without regard to graphic design the interaction flow, including some alternatives. By a couple of GUI-ii-based telcos these were walked-through and several minor additional requirements popped up. However, now the project partner expressed an eager to see how the prototype would look like in a review; interest was clearly on hifi graphics while we knew that the parallel demonstrators in this project were not at this stage at all yet. Some months later we again had to bring up issues of exact functions: GUI-ii went fine, but our partners would like to get the whole set of screens—this is not always quickly made in a GUI WOz tool as everything is not "in place" in the mockup but enacted (made visible or invisible) during an interaction session (whether a GUI-ii interview, a GUI-ii group discussion, or simply a test at distance).

3.4   Summary of Lessons Learned from the Three Sources of GUI-ii Experiences

Our observations show that on-screen objects in a GUI-ii constitute a resource for respondents, just as things and fingers do in face-to-face interviews, and that the lack of visual cues from the interviewer's physical presence can promote more elaborate responses, even if different interviewers will have different styles.

Applying GUI-ii at a distance facilitates co-creation of the graphical user interface and the functionality available. Although it might be argued that the GUI-ii is a GUI walk-through [21] we suggest it is not. We are more flexible during the interview; both the interviewer and the respondent can make changes in the mockup during the interview session to try a new design idea. Notably, even the walk-through parts of a GUI-ii session may be dependent on earlier design parts of the on-going session which makes the whole process more of a collaboration exercise than a traditional walk-through. Obviously, also a walk-through approach and not only a GUI-ii approach can utilize input from previous sessions to prepare the next session. However, a growing feeling of ownership is easier to create when one lets the participant walk through what is partly his or her own creation. For instance, in the example above about organizing the workflow, the participants later had to click the activities (labelled buttons) in order to access the corresponding pages (where more co-design activities followed).

We do not use a CSCW system with full-mode interactivity (e.g. GoToMeeting, Skype), because our system is better at handling possibilities and parallel design—the wizard has controls to manage screen content, there are interaction widgets present which makes it easier to demonstrate checkboxes, drop-down menus, and other standard GUI objects. Also, it is easier to enter a use-mode (that is, using the design rather than designing it) without necessarily making the interlocutor think of it and thereby think of it as a test of his/her suggestions. Rather, Ozlab's wizard controls make it possible for the interviewer to just join the interaction if the interviewee tends to act on the objects, which many people tend to do when they have GUI-like images on the smartphone display or computer screen. Had the co-design interview been executed via an ordinary teleconferencing system, the interviewer would have to announce that the interplay now shifts modes, as the interviewee would have to play against the interviewer in the latter's overt role as some form of interactivity crutch.

Nevertheless, just as when using teleconferencing systems, the limits of the technology used will sometimes be all too apparent. Checking the equipment, checking firewalls, and having a relaxed attitude to failures will help as in simpler forms of interviews or co-designing sessions.

4   Framing GUI-ii in the Map of Design Research

Sanders et al. [22] presents a short sketch of "A framework for organizing the tools and techniques of participatory design" with an aim to provide "an overview of participatory design tools and techniques for engaging non-designers in specific participatory design activities." The framework is more elaborate than the map presented by Sanders [7] and further discussed in Sanders and Stappers [8, 10]. On the other hand, the map allows for more discussion rather than classification and therefore, we feel, better suites the presentation of a new PD tool/technique/method such as GUI-ii. Moreover, when going through the tables of Sanders et al. [22], we find that the authors have not ticked table entries in the "on-line" column for any of the techniques listed under "Acting, Enacting and Playing". This makes us wonder if GUI use is excluded from the playing they have in mind. This does not fit with our notion of interaction between people and within groups—computer displays are so prevalent nowadays that trying to hide them from a collaborative session is unnecessary even if one strives to provide a bias-free environment for the discussion. And if GUI is let in, then there is a short step to on-line acting, enacting, and playing. We argue GUI-ii falls under, for example, the category: "Participatory envisioning and enactment by setting users in future situations". But rather than discussing the tables of Sanders et al. [22], we take this remark as a starting point for characterizing GUI-ii techniques in relation to the Map of Design Research [7, 8].

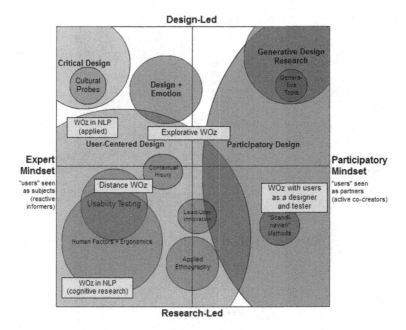

Fig. 2 WOz in the of map of design research. Adapted from Sanders [7]

Sanders [7] presents a map over design practice and design research, with four cardinal directions. Horizontally, one dimension spans from "Expert Mindset" to "Participatory Mindset", and vertically a second dimension goes from "Design-Led" to "Research-Led" (cf. Figs. 2 and 3). "The research-led perspective has the longest history and has been driven by applied psychologists, anthropologists, sociologists, and engineers." (p. 13). While the scientific-led methods have had a gradual extension to the right in the diagram, the "Scandinavian" school took a more decisive step to this end. Methods developed by practitioners in their design work may have a very participatory mind-set but there has also been the opposite mind-set even among practitioners, stressing the designer's special eye for providing critical design questions rather than merely solving design issues [23].

In order to frame GUI-ii in the Map of Design Research, we start by noting that WOz methods take various forms. Explorative WOz is surely more designer oriented; it is about finding good designs, not about establishing a hypothesis of human-computer interaction. Sometime the interaction of a WOz mockup is formed when an interdisciplinary team discusses around it, but as the participants in many other situations may not be aware of the faked interaction, it is hard to ascribe explorative WOz exclusively to the right-hand side of the diagram in Fig. 2. Thus, we let the rectangle "Explorative WOz" stretch from the design expert half into the half representing the participatory mind-set.

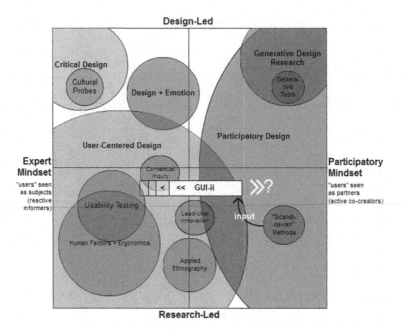

Fig. 3 GUI-ii in the map of design research—extending to the right? Adapted from Sanders [7]

Our own experimentation with users constructing and testing their designs is more firmly rooted in the participatory mindset, and the Ozlab system is quite important to allow refinement cycles and not only fortuitous WOz setups.

Many WOz studies have been within NLP (Natural-Language Processing) and are often oriented quite far to the left in the Map, sometimes led by companies (design-led [4, 24]) rather than conducted primarily to develop corpora of HCI dialogues for a general research and development community [13, 25]. Thus, "WOz in NLP" is put in two different locations in the map.

Our own evaluation in project A of GUIs on distance finds its place within Sanders' Usability Testing circle—except that in project A the renegotiated GUI aspects are brought out and tried within the same session, an act reaffirming the participant as co-designer.

Sanders often refers to the "making, telling, enacting" sequence of activities in design (not necessarily in that order). We think it should be observed that these activities are not automatically allocated to different sessions. Our GUI-ii sessions are often combining four steps: *telling* (around material at hand), *making, telling, enacting*. In order to understand what is "made" during *making* in a GUI-ii session, it is worthwhile to note the shift in the two suites of GUI-ii sessions in the B project: in GUI-ii with pre-prepared mockups, the participants are really interaction designers but much less graphic designers. We suppose this fact might easily go unnoticed by design theoreticians who put a heavy weight on the probes. That the interaction in itself is a co-creation can easily be missed if concrete objects and a lot of storytelling is emphasized.—To Sanders' "thoughts on the curriculum for design" [9], where she writes "We will need to learn from storytellers, performers and sellers" (p. 71), one might add, "and from psychiatrists" as *listening* (observing) is also very important.

It would seem that the thing to do now would be to push GUI-ii as a method further to the participatory mindset edge, as we are trying to get away from ordinary interviews' non-designing and their weak co-creation nature. On the other hand, when looking at the complete development cycle, co-creation activities have already taken place, or, at least, other stakeholders than the designers have set the functional goal for the system. When GUI-ii is brought in, it is not only to entice a host of design suggestions and uncover implicit requirements, but also to refine the ideas for interaction (including graphic) design. The temporal sequence within projects A, B, C runs from a high participatory mindset to a more system expert mindset. The interactive prototypes later piloted are definitively further to the left when the cost of implementation has been given a greater weight.

Therefore, the picture of GUI-ii employment within a project will show a leftward drifting in the Map of Design Research as indicated in Fig. 3, possibly ending in ordinary usability testing, whether based on WOz or programmed interactivity. This means that the employment is very participatory-minded: rather than the process starting further to the left, participants can initially be co-creators of the interaction design. Our previous studies show that a good support for GUI wizardry can facilitate doing explorative interaction design and evaluation. This good support is exploited in GUI-ii, even if the interview format on distance gives a rather clear division of the roles as (expert) designer and (content expert) co-designer.

Participatory design (PD) is normally applied in internal, organizational settings where the development team and the (future) users meet physically [26–30]. However, it is not uncommon that projects span outside of one organizational or even geographical setting because "individuals, stakeholder groups and other entities can be distributed physically, organizationally or temporally" as Gumm et al. explain [31].

PD in itself is not always entirely unproblematic, as teams may face communication problems between the developers, designers and users (for example). When it comes to Distributed Participatory Design [31], however, it has been shown that other problems may occur due to the distribution of the team members and users. We will not go into the problems here, but the face-to-face GUI-ii instance naturally brings up the question whether it is necessary to keep GUI-ii strictly to remote discussions, or should it be used also for what might mistakenly be taken as a prototype walkthrough? Right now, it is most useful for us to use the term GUI-ii for remote co-creation interviews where there is a strong emphasis on actual interaction with the discussed interaction design. For many years, we have used WOz in face-to-face team discussions. Now we need to explore the space for the remote GUI interactions with more or less single participants as this facilitates scheduling and makes every voice heard distinctly. For the latter aspect, confer for example Trischler and co-workers: "in teams where individuals dominate, [...] less collaboration and diminished innovation outcomes are more likely" [32]. Naturally, this can be mitigated by team building processes. Nevertheless, individual suggestions can better be recorded and user-tested if individuals are participating individually after the representatives for the different organizations (especially as in project B) have reached a consensus of a project idea and sketched use scenarios in workshops.

Distance is also important for another reason. Distance means that participants can be in their normal environment, the one they will be in when using the projected system. The correct context of use is important when developing a new system (ISO 9241-210:2010) and it is not surprising that Sanders in her map included Contextual Inquiry, the field interviewing method by Holtzblatt (and further developed into Contextual Design [6]), where the customer, instead of having to explain her work to a designer, the designer goes to the customers' workplace to observe, discuss and gather "data about the structure of work practice" and to "make unarticulated knowledge about work explicit, so designers who do not do the work can understand it" [6] (p. 37). In Sects. 2.3 and 3.2 it was mentioned that participants in GUI-ii sessions refer to material they have on their computer or sometimes they grab a physical folder to check things.

At times, a neutral ground is searched for developers and stakeholders to be on equal footing when the discussions start. Against a PD placement of GUI-ii in the Map of Design Research it can be argued that if the designer prepares the playground (the WOz mockup) both the place and the things in it are biased. However, preliminary workshops outside ordinary workplaces and also at different stakeholders can establish the things (labels, structures, illustrations) to be used. This makes the GUI-ii mockups a *shared* ground (not neutral).

Our impression is furthermore that the fact that co-designers can drag-and-drop things, or re-write labels and other things, makes it obvious that they own the things and the space. Of course, a programmer will tend to think in ease-of-implementation and general-solutions terms, as the example from B demonstrates. This risks over-writing what co-designers propose. In the reported example, the developer met the designers in the GUI-ii, not the co-designers, which suggests that multi-party interviews can be needed (in fact, the reported case took place at three places; one designer had only viewing rights and could only argue by voice. Our system has no restrictions on the number of viewers). However, such a use would approximate telcos and most participants would not really be in the GUI dialogue, hence we leave this option here.

Having mentioned the possibility for co-designers to directly re-design certain features of a GUI under discussion naturally begs the question about the effect of other features, namely features which have to be negotiated with the interviewer before any change can be made: what is the effect on ownership and co-creation in such cases? The answers depend on the tool used, and in particular on the specific version of it used. We will avoid turning the present discussion into a technical manual even if this kind of question directly relates to the method's place in the Map of Design Research. It is worth noting here that Ozlab was built for testing, not co-design, but initially needed no adaptation to our actual use of the system in individual walkthroughs and team discussions. During a live session, not everything can be changed, especially not for the one logging in as participant. In addition, some other features work against us in some GUI-ii situations: for instance, captures of text input can be reused within a running session in other scenes than where the texts were entered, but if the wizard stops a session this memory is lost. This has been a good safety precaution to ensure that fields are empty when a new participant (test subject) enters a test session. But for GUI-ii this is not so convenient because, as mentioned before, the interviewer can swiftly stop and change any aspect of a mockup. Obviously, the clearance of the text memory can in some sessions destroy valuable constructs (if the interviewer does not take time to re-enter them before opening the session again, but that would in most cases not count as a swift change of the mockup). The system is planned to be extended with a permanent memory for text fields. Other features added after cases A, B, and C improve the wizard's work in testing as well as in co-design sessions. However, it would demand an understanding of what GUI-dialogic (that is, 'interactive') interaction design entails in a host of details to really appreciate this mutual support for testing sessions and co-design sessions, which is why an exposé of wizardry widgets is not presented here.

Instead we briefly touch a *making* issue raised by Löwgren: "making," which is programming in his discussion, "is required for explorative design of non-idiomatic interaction" [33] (p. 28). Ozlab will not support many non-idiomatic interaction formats, and obviously, programing is needed to make transformations of graphical objects. Furthermore, Löwgren considers "disposable programming as a major technique for hi-fi sketching" (ibid.), that is, just as for Sanders and others, *making*, is not making the final system but making something to evaluate before continuing with the design efforts. Löwgren stresses the importance of immediate feedback to the designer. Such thoughts are also the basis for both explorative WOz and GUI-ii. For GUI-ii, the feedback is as much to the prospective future user, acting as co-designer, as for the designer. Notably, the immediate feedback, through "rapid-fire rounds of experimental coding," that Löwgren talks about does not necessarily involve "real users" in the loop, but is simply a check for the design team whether the last tweaks improved the look-and-feel or not. Sketching interaction can thus be made in different ways. Even if limited in some dimensions, WOz and GUI-ii necessarily include clients of some kind. This is, in principle, a strength. However, it is also a problem for adoption of these techniques as many designers have a strong wish to see the interaction themselves, rather than to try it out in co-action with prospective users. Then the user is left out of the loop.

5 Conclusion

GUI-ii is a technique that can be used in requirements analysis to deepen the understanding of what required functions really are meant to provide. This technique also facilitates the co-creation of GUIs, to probe usability issues and to pre-evaluate possible extensions.

Interactions between one or several stakeholders and a designer or design team underlie many participatory design activities. However, interview techniques are seldom emphasized in the PD literature which rather focuses collaboration around objects and sketches. Utilizing communication technologies allows for less travelling and might allow more participation, but single-individual interviews make it even easier for people to participate as less scheduling is needed and should be considered for certain participatory design cycles. There is the further good of evaluating lots of design suggestions as one moves from one participant to the next. Even more, if given time as in a one-to-one interview, people in GUI interaction interviews become talkative (or at least interactive), engaged, and can utilize their usual accessories.

The technique itself is as good as the designer/interviewer. The tool supporting the interviews and co-creation sessions have limitations but can also be developed. In addition, when analyzing the multifaceted interaction between two GUI-ii interlocutors, we feel that some sort of notation should be developed for the interaction between Wizard—Wizard's user interface—WOz tool—Participant's user interface—Participant—Ambient resources. From the ISD 2016 conference there is one notable model [34] that might be adapted as a protocol of interview sessions and not only for designing a better WOz tool.

References

1. Bryman, A., Bell, E.: Business Research Methods. Oxford University Press, Oxford (2011)
2. Rettig, M.: Prototyping for tiny fingers.com*. ACM 37(4), 21–27 (1994)
3. Simonsen, J., Robertson, T. (eds.): Routledge International Handbook of Participatory Design. Routledge, New York (2013)
4. Kelley, J.F.: An iterative design methodology for user-friendly natural language office information applications. ACM Trans. Off. Inf. Syst. 2(1), 26–41 (1984)
5. Pettersson, J.S., Wik, M.: The longevity of general purpose Wizard-of-Oz tools. In: OzCHI'15 Proceedings Australian SIG CHI, pp. 422–426. ACM, New York (2015)
6. Beyer, H., Holtzblatt, K.: Contextual Design. Morgan Kaufmann, San Fransisco (1998)
7. Sanders, E.B.N.: An evolving map of design practice and design research. Interactions 15(6), 13–17 (2008)
8. Sanders, E.B., Stappers, P.J.: Probes, Toolkits and Prototypes: Three Approaches to Making in Codesigning. CoDesign Int. J. CoCreation Des. Arts. 10(1), 5–14 (2014)
9. Sanders, E.B.N.: Prototyping for the design spaces of the future. In: Valentine, L. (ed.) Prototype—Design and Craft in the 21st Century, pp. 59–73. Bloomsbury (2013)
10. Sanders, E.B., Stappers, P.J.: Convivial Toolbox—Generative Research for the Front End of Design. BIS Publishers, Amsterdam (2012)
11. Laurel, B.K.: Interface as mimesis. In: Norman, D.A., Draper, S.W. (eds.) User Centered System Design: New Perspectives on Human-Computer Interaction. Lawrence Erlbaum Associates, Hillsdale (1986)
12. Consolvo, S., Harrison, B., Smith, I., Chen, M.Y., Everitt, K., Froehlich, J., Landay, J.A.: Conducting in situ evaluations for and with ubiquitous computing technologies. Int. J. Hum. Comput. Interact. 22(1–2), 103–118 (2007)
13. Schlögl, S., Doherty, G., Karamanis, N., Schneider, A., Luz, S.: Observing the wizard: in search of a generic interface for wizard of Oz studies. In: Proceedings of 4th Irish Human Computer Interaction Conference, pp. 43–50. Dublin City University, Dublin (2010)

14. Kelley, J.F.: An empirical methodology for writing user-friendly natural language computer applications. In: Proceedings of the SIGCHI Conference on Human Factors in Computing Systems (CHI'83), pp. 193–196. ACM, New York (1983)
15. Pettersson, J.S., Wik, M.: Perspectives on Ozlab in the cloud. A Literature Review of Tools Supporting Wizard-of-Oz Experimentation. Karlstad University, Karlstad, Working Paper, urn:nbn:se:kau:diva-33617 (2014)
16. Stappers, P.J.: Prototypes as a central vein for knowledge development. In: Valentine, L. (ed.) Prototype—Design and Craft in the 21st Century, pp. 85–97. Bloomsbury, London (2013)
17. Preece, J., Rogers, Y., Sharp, H., Benyon, D., Holland, S., Carey, T.: Human-Computer Interaction. Addison-Wesley, Wokingham (1994)
18. Schade, A.: Remote usability tests: moderated and unmoderated. NNgroup (2013) https://www.nngroup.com/articles/remote-usability-tests/. Accessed 6 Apr 2017
19. Brandt, E., Binder, T., Sanders, E.B.: Tools and techniques: ways to engage telling, making and enacting. In: Simonsen, J., Robertson, T. (eds.) Routledge International Handbook of Participatory Design, pp. 145–181. Routledge, New York (2013)
20. Olson, G.M., Olson, J.S.: Collaboration technologies. In: Jacko, J.A. (ed.) Human-Computer Interaction Handbook: Fundamentals, Evolving Technologies, and Emerging Applications, 3rd edition, pp. 549–564. CRC Press (2012)
21. Rubin, J., Chisnell, D.: Handbook of Usability Testing. Wiley, Indianapolis (2008)
22. Sanders, E.B., Brandt, E., Binder, T.: A framework for organizing the tools and techniques of participatory design. In: Proceedings of the 11th Biennial Participatory Design Conference, pp. 195–198. ACM, New York (2010)
23. Dunne, A., Raby, F.: Design Noir: The Secret Life of Electronic Objects. Basel (2001)
24. Wirén, M., Eklund, R., Engberg, F., Westermark, J.: Experiences of an in-service wizard-of-Oz data collection for the deployment of a call-routing application. In: Proceedings of the Workshop on Bridging the Gap: Academic and Industrial Research in Dialog Technologies, pp. 56–63, NAACL-HLT 2007. Association for Computational Linguistics, New York (2007)
25. Gould, J.D., Conti, J., Hovanyecz, T.: Composing letters with a simulated listening typewriter. Com. ACM 26(4), 295–308 (1983)
26. Loebbecke, C., Powell, P.: Furthering distributed participative design. Scand. J. Inf. Syst. 21(1), 77–106 (2009)
27. Lukyanenko, R., Parsons, J., Wiersma, Y., Sieber, R., Maddah, M.: Participatory design for user-generated content: understanding the challenges and moving forward. Scand. J. Inf. Syst. 28(1), 37–70 (2016)
28. Mumford, E., Land, F., Hawgood, J.: A participative approach to the design of computer systems. Impact Sci. Soc. 28(3), 235–253 (1978)
29. Mumford, E.: Participative systems design: structure and method. Syst. Objectives Solut. 1, 5–19 (1981)
30. Obendorf, H., Janneck, M., Finck, M.: Inter-contextual distributed participatory design. Scand. J. Inf. Syst. 21(1), 51–76 (2009)
31. Gumm, D.C., Janneck, M., Finck, M.: Distributed participatory design—a case study. In: Proceedings of the DPD Workshop at NordiCHI. ACM, New York (2006)
32. Trischler, J., Pervan, S.J., Kelly, S.J., Scott, D.R.: The value of codesign: the effect of customer involvement in service design teams. J. Serv. Res. Published online: 10 July 2017
33. Löwgren, J.: On the significance of making in interaction design research. Interaction 23(3), 26–33 (2016)
34. Gopalakrishnan, S., Sindre, G.: Activity diagrams with location context: experimental comparison of colour and icon annotations. In: Gołuchowski, J., et al. (eds.) Information Systems Development: Complexity in Information Systems Development (ISD2016 Proceedings). University of Economics, Katowice (2016)

On the Influence of Modification Timespan Weightings in the Location of Bugs in Models

Lorena Arcega, Jaime Font, Øystein Haugen and Carlos Cetina

Abstract Bug location is a common task in Software Engineering, specially when maintaining and evolving software products. When locating bugs in code, results depend greatly on the way code modification timespans are weighted. However, the influence of timespan weightings on bug location in models has not received enough attention yet. Throughout this paper, we analyze the influence of several timespan weightings on bug location in models. These timespan weightings guide an evolutionary algorithm, which returns a ranking of model fragments relevant to the solution of a bug. We evaluated our timespan weightings in BSH, a real-world industrial case study, by measuring the results in terms of recall, precision, and F-measure. Results show that the use of the most recent timespan model modifications provide the best results in our study. We also performed a statistical analysis to provide evidence of the significance of the results.

Keywords Bug location · Model driven engineering · Reverse engineering

A prior version of this paper has been published in the ISD2017 Proceedings (http://aisel.aisnet.org/isd2014/proceedings2017).

L. Arcega (✉) · J. Font · C. Cetina
Universidad San Jorge, Saragossa, Spain
e-mail: larcega@usj.es

J. Font
e-mail: jfont@usj.es

C. Cetina
e-mail: ccetina@usj.es

L. Arcega · J. Font
University of Oslo, Oslo, Norway

Ø. Haugen
Østfold University College, Halden, Norway
e-mail: jfont@usj.es

© Springer International Publishing AG, part of Springer Nature 2018   169
N. Paspallis et al. (eds.), *Advances in Information Systems Development*,
Lecture Notes in Information Systems and Organisation 26,
https://doi.org/10.1007/978-3-319-74817-7_11

1 Introduction

During software evolution, the existing software of a project undergoes modifications to satisfy changes. A change may result in either the addition of a new
software function, the removal of a bug or defect, or the improvement of an existing
software functionality. These maintenance and evolution activities take up to 80%
of the lifetime of a system [1]. Software maintainers spend from 50% up to almost
90% of their time trying to understand a program in order to make changes correctly
[2]. One of the key issues to achieve this goal is finding relevant locations to
address the changes.

Bug Location is one of the most important and common activities performed
during software maintenance and evolution [3]. Currently, research efforts in Bug
Location are concerned with identifying software artifacts associated with bug
descriptions. However, most research on Bug Location targets code [4] as the
software artifact that realizes the feature, neglecting other software artifacts such as
models.

In order to locate bugs in code, the most recent code modifications are regarded
as the most relevant. Bug location results depend greatly on the way in which the
modification timespans are weighted. The consideration of timespans is based on
the Defect Localization Principle. This principle is based on the observation that the
most recent modifications to a project are most likely the cause of future bugs [5, 6].
Considering recent project modifications, it is possible to find relevant code for bug
location [7].

We perform Bug Location in Models (BLiM). To do so, we locate the most
relevant model fragments for a particular bug description. Model fragments are
formed by model elements, and each model element has an associated modification
time. When we apply the Defect Principle to model fragments, we have to decide
how to assign a modification time to the model fragment from the modification time
information on its model elements. The contribution of this work is the design,
application for BLiM, and evaluation of four fitness functions regarding modification timespan weightings. The weightings are the following: (1) the most recent
model modifications (BLiM-recent), (2) the oldest model modifications
(BLiM-oldest), (3) the mean of the modification timespan of the modified model
elements (BLiM-mean), and (4) the sum of the modification timespan of the
modified model elements (BLiM-sum).

In our evaluation, we have applied our approach to the product models from an
industrial partner, BSH. We compare the results of running our BLiM approach
with the different fitness functions. We measure the results using the standard
information retrieval measurements: recall, precision, and the combination of both
(F-measure) [8, 9]. The outcome shows that the use of the most recent modification
timespan of a model element as the modification timespan of a model fragment
(BLiM-recent) provides the best results, and proves that the approach can be
applied in real world environments. The statistical analysis of the results provides
evidence of their significance.

The remainder of the paper is structured as follows: in Sect. 2, we present the Domain Specific Language used by the industrial partner. In Sect. 3, we describe our BLiM approach. In Sect. 4, we evaluate our approach with the data provided by the industrial partner. In Sect. 5, we examine the related work of the area. Finally, we present our conclusions in Sect. 6.

2 Background

The running example and the evaluation of this paper are performed through the products of the industrial partner, BSH. In this section, we present the Domain Specific Language (DSL) used by BSH to formalize their products, called IHDSL. In addition, we present the language used by our approach to formalize the model fragments, the Common Variability Language (CVL).

The newest Induction Hobs (IHs) feature full cooking surfaces, where dynamic heating areas are automatically generated and activated or deactivated depending on the shape, size, and position of the cookware placed on the top. In addition, there has been an increase in the type of feedback provided to the user while cooking. All of these changes are being possible at the cost of increasing the complexity of the software behind IHs.

The Domain Specific Language used by BSH to specify the Induction Hobs (IHDSL) is composed of 46 meta-classes, 47 references among them, and more than 180 properties. However, in order to gain legibility and due to intellectual property right concerns, in this paper we use a simplified subset of the IHDSL (see left part of Fig. 1, IHDSL Metamodel and IHDSL Syntax).

Product Model of Fig. 1 depicts an example of a product model specified with the IHDSL. The product model contains four inverters used to power two different inductors. The upper inductor is powered by a single inverter while the lower inductor is powered by the combination of three different inverters. Power managers act as hubs to perform the connection between the inverters and the inductors.

To formalize the model fragments used by the approach we use Common Variability Language (CVL) [10, 11], given its capabilities to formalize a set of model elements as a model fragment. Right part of Fig. 1 shows an example of a model fragment of the product model. The model fragment includes the three

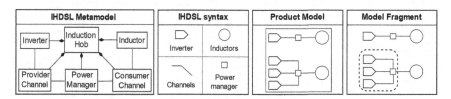

Fig. 1 IHDSL product model and model fragment formalization

inverters in charge of powering the lower inductor along with the three channels and the power manager used to aggregate and manage the power provided by those inverters.

3 Bug Location in Models (BLiM)

This section presents the BLiM approach for bug location. The left part of Fig. 2 shows an example of input for our approach. The approach receives as input a bug description of the bug that the software engineer wants to locate. Typically, these descriptions come from textual documentation of a bug report. Therefore, the query will include some domain specific terms that are similar to those used when specifying the product models. In addition, the software engineer selects a set of product models from the entire family of products that include the bug to be located.

The approach relies on an evolutionary algorithm. The center of Fig. 2 shows a simplified representation of the main steps. The 'Initialize Population' step calculates an initial population of model fragments from the input set of product models. This initial population of model fragments is randomly extracted from the product models. The 'Genetic Operations' produce the new generation of model fragments. First, a selection operation chooses the model fragments that will be used as parents of the new model fragments. The fitness values are used to ensure that the best model fragments are chosen as parents. Then, a crossover operation mixes the model elements of the two parents into a new model fragment. Finally, a mutation operation introduces variations in the new model fragment, in hopes that it achieves better fitness values than its parents. The 'Fitness' step assigns values that assess how good each model fragment is in the following terms: bug description and modification timespan.

As output, the approach provides a list of model fragments that might realize the bug. The output of BLiM (see the right part of Fig. 2) is a ranking of model fragments that realize the target bug. The ranking can be ordered following different criteria, such as the similarity of the model fragments to the bug description, or the model fragment modification timespans.

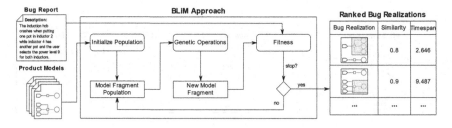

Fig. 2 Overview of the Bug Location Approach in Models: BLiM

3.1 Genetic Operations of the BLiM Approach

The generation of model fragments is performed by applying genetic operators adapted to work on model fragments. In other words, new fragments are generated from existing ones through the use of two genetic operators: the crossover operator, and the mutation operator. We use the crossover and mutation operations presented in [12].

The crossover operation takes a model fragment from a first parent model and the whole product model from a second parent model, generating a new individual that contains elements from both parents and thus preserving the basic mechanics of the crossover operation.

The mutation possibilities of a given model fragment are driven by its associated product model. Each model fragment is associated to a product model, and the model fragment mutates in the context of its associated product model. In other words, the model fragment will gain or drop some elements, but the resulting model fragment will still be part of the referenced product model. For more details about these genetic operations see [12].

3.2 Fitness of the BLiM Approach

In evolutionary algorithms, the fitness step is used to imitate the different degrees of adaptation to the environment that different individuals have. Following this idea, our fitness step is used to determine the suitability of each model fragment to the problem. The input of this step is a population of model fragments, and the produced output is a set with each model fragment from the input population, accompanied by two fitness values: similarity to the feature description, and most recent model fragment modifications.

Model Fragment Similarity to the Bug Description
To assess the relevance of each model fragment in relation to the bug description provided by the user, we apply methods based on Information Retrieval (IR) techniques. Specifically, we apply Latent Semantic Analysis (LSA) [13] to analyze the relationships between the description of the bug provided by the user and the model fragments. There are many IR techniques, but most research efforts show better results when applying LSA [14–16].

LSA constructs vector representations of a query and a corpus of text documents by encoding them as a term-by-document co-occurrence matrix, (i.e., a matrix where each row corresponds to a term and each column corresponds to a document, with the last column corresponding to the query). Each cell holds the number of occurrences of a term (row) inside a document or the query (column). LSA provides good results when applied to source code [14–16]. We use the LSA technique applied to models in the same way as [12].

The documents are text representations of model fragments. The text of the document corresponds to the names and values of the properties and methods of each model fragment (e.g. a model element of the class inductor will contain some properties related to its coil manufacturer and heat potential). The query is constructed from the terms that appear in the bug description. If the textual terms used for the model and the bug description differ too much, the LSA will not work. Therefore, the text from the documents (model fragments) and the text from the query (bug description) are homogenized by applying Natural Language Processing techniques (tokenizing [14], Parts-of-Speech Tagging [17], and Lemmatizing [8]) to eventually reduce this gap. The union of all the words extracted from the documents (model fragments) and from the query (bug description) are the terms (rows) used by our LSA fitness.

We normalize and decompose the matrix into a set of vectors using Singular Value Decomposition (SVD) [13]. One vector that represents the latent semantics of the document is obtained for each model fragment and for the query. Finally, the similarities between the query and each model fragment are calculated as the cosine between the two vectors. The fitness value that is given to each model fragment is the one that we obtain when we calculate the similarity, obtaining values between -1 and 1. For more details see [12].

Timespan Weightings

In this proposed fitness step, the modifications of the model over time are taken into consideration in order to extract the most relevant model for the target bug. In this section, we define the four timespan weighting functions used in our work.

These functions are based on the timespan between the last modification of a model element and the usage day. A recently modified model element (i.e. a short timespan) has a lower timespan value than another model element that was modified farther in the past. As a model fragment is composed by a set of model elements the timespan weighting of the model fragment depends on the timespan weightings of the model elements that compose it.

The timespan is based on the number of days and can therefore be very large when the model fragment was modified a long time ago. To normalize the timespans, mathematical solutions can be used. We used square roots because it has achieved good results in other works that use time differences [11]. The use of square root is more suitable and more effective for the proposed approach.

We devised four objective functions to capture the timespan weightings for the model fragments. Next, we define each of these functions:

The most recent model modifications (recent): this function expresses the concern of capturing primarily the model fragments with the model elements that have the lowest modification timespans. That is, model elements that have been recently modified. Then, the value of the model fragment will be the value of the most recently modified model element. In the example of Fig. 3, the value of the model fragment is 7 days, that means a square root of 2.646.

The oldest model modifications (oldest). This function expresses the concern of capturing primarily the model fragments with the model elements that have the

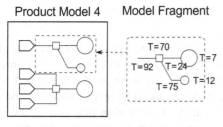

T : timespan from the last modification in days

Approach	Timespan
BLiM-recent	7 days
BLiM-oldest	92 days
BLiM-mean	44.667 days
BLiM-sum	280 days

Fig. 3 Timespan of the modifications of the model elements of a fragment

highest modification timespans. That is, model elements that have not been modified for a long time, longer than most other elements. Then, the value of the model fragment will be the value of the model element less recently modified model element. In the example of Fig. 3, the value of the model fragment is 92 days, that means a square root of 9.592.

To avoid taking into account only the extremes (oldest and most recent modifications), we also define these two objective functions:

The mean of the timespan of the modified model elements (mean). This function expresses the concern of capturing primarily the model fragments with the model elements that have the lowest mean timespan. Then, the value of the model fragment will be the value of the mean of the timespan of the modified model elements. In the example of Fig. 3, the value of the model fragment is 46.667 days, that means a square root of 6.831.

The sum of the timespan of the modified model elements (sum). This function expresses the concern of capturing primarily the model fragments with the model elements that have the lowest timespan sum. Then, the value of the model fragment will be the value of the sum of the timespan of the modified model elements. In the example of Fig. 3, the value of the model fragment is 280 days, that means a square root of 16.733.

4 Evaluation: Bug Location in BSH

This section presents the evaluation of our approach: the experimental setup, a description of the case study where we applied the evaluation, the obtained results, the performed statistical analysis, and the threats to validity. To evaluate the approach, we applied it to an industrial case study from our partner, BSH: a leading manufacturer of home appliances in Europe.

4.1 Experimental Setup

The goal of this experiment is the evaluation of the different timespan weighting objective functions as fitness for our BLiM approach. In addition, we compare the BLiM approach with a baseline [18]. The baseline is the approach used in BSH for bug location. It is an evolutionary algorithm guided by textual similarity, however the baseline does not take into account the modification timespan of the model elements. Although it was designed having a more general purpose in mind (Feature Location), it is the best they have for Bug Location in Models.

To evaluate our BLiM approach with the different objective functions (BLiM-recent, BLiM-oldest, BLiM-mean, and BLiM-sum) and the baseline approach, we run each of the approaches and obtain a ranking of model fragments that we can compare with an oracle in order to check accuracy. The inputs of the evaluation process, which are the product family, and bug reports, were provided by BSH.

The oracle is the ground truth, and is used to compare the results provided by the BLiM approach and the baseline. To prepare the oracle, BSH provided us with the bug reports that have occurred in the product models. These bug reports contain natural language bug descriptions and the approved bug realizations. In said bug reports, each bug description is mapped to a single model fragment. A Model fragment is a subset of elements of a model, specified with the model fragment formalization capacities of the CVL [10]. In other words, for each bug, we know which is the associated model fragment that implements it.

The baseline approach is a Single-Objective Evolutionary Algorithm (SOEA), whereas BLiM is Multi-Objective Evolutionary Algorithm (MOEA). The works in [19] shows that common MOEA measures such as hypervolume [20] are not necessarily suitable for comparing solutions by MOEAs (our BLiM approach) with solutions by SOEAs (baseline in this work). Therefore, in order to compare the baseline approach with BLiM, we first take the best solution of the baseline approach for its single-objective (the similarity with the bug description), and then we take the best solution of BLiM with regard to the objective of the baseline approach (the similarity with the bug description), as described in [19]. Finally, these solutions are compared to the bug realization of the oracle in order to get a confusion matrix.

A confusion matrix is a table that is often used to describe the performance of a classification model (in this case both BLiM-X and the baseline) on a set of test data (the solutions) for which the true values are known (from the oracle). In our case, each solution outputted by the approaches is a model fragment composed of a subset of the model elements that are part of the product model (where the bug is being located). Since the granularity is at the level of model elements, each model element presence or absence is considered as a classification. The confusion matrix distinguishes between the predicted values and the real values classifying them into four categories:

True Positive (TP): values that are predicted as true (in the solution) and are true in the real scenario (the oracle).
False Positive (FP): values that are predicted as true (in the solution) but are false in the real scenario (the oracle).
True Negative (TN): values that are predicted as false (in the solution) and are false in the real scenario (the oracle).
False Negative (FN): values that are predicted as false (in the solution) but are true in the real scenario (the oracle).

Then, some performance measurements are derived from the values in the confusion matrix. In particular, we create a report including three performance measurements (recall, precision, and F-measure), for each of the test cases for both BLiM-X and the baseline.

Recall measures the number of elements of the solution that are correctly retrieved by the proposed solution and is defined as follows:

$$Recall = \frac{TP}{TP + FN} \tag{1}$$

Precision measures the number of elements from the solution that are correct according to the ground truth (the oracle) and is defined as follows:

$$Precision = \frac{TP}{TP + FP} \tag{2}$$

F-measure corresponds to the harmonic mean of precision and recall and is defined as follows:

$$F\text{-}measure = 2 * \frac{Precision * Recall}{Preecision + Recall} = \frac{2 * TP}{2 * TP + FP + FN} \tag{3}$$

Recall values can range between 0% (which means that no single model element from the realization of the bug obtained from the oracle is present in any of the model fragments of the solution) to 100% (which means that all the model elements from the oracle are present in the solution).

Precision values can range between 0% (which means that no single model fragment from the solution is present in the realization of the bug obtained from the oracle) and 100% (which means that all the model fragments from the solution are present in the bug realization from the oracle). A value of 100% precision and 100% recall implies that both the solution and the bug realization from the oracle are the same.

The approach has been implemented within the Eclipse environment. We used the Eclipse Modeling Framework [21] to manipulate the models and CVL to manage the model fragments. The evolutionary algorithm was built using the Watchmaker Framework for evolutionary Computation [22], which allowed us to implement our own genetic operators. The IR techniques that were used to process the language were implemented using OpenNLP [23] and the English (Porter2) [24]. The LSI was implemented using the Efficient Java Matrix Library [6].

4.2   Case Study

The case study where we applied our evaluation process is the Induction Hob Product Family of BSH (already presented in Sect. 2 as the running example). The oracle is composed of 46 induction hob models, which are on average composed of more than 500 elements. BSH provided us with documentation of 37 bug reports and the approved bug realizations. For each of the 37 bugs, we created a test case that includes the set of product models where that bug was manifested and a bug description, both obtained from the documentation.

For this case study, we executed 30 independent runs for each of the 37 test cases for BLiM with all the different timespan weightings, and with the baseline (as suggested by [25]), i.e., 37 (bugs) × 5 (approaches) × 30 repetitions = 5550 independent runs.

4.3   Results

In this section, we present the results obtained by both BLiM (with the four fitness functions) and by the baseline approach, for the case study. The 5550 fragments obtained in the executions (one fragment obtained in each execution) had an average size of 52 model elements. Each model element has appeared at least one time in the model fragments.

Table 1 shows the mean values of recall, precision and F-measure of the graphs for both BLiM-X (with the four fitness functions) and the baseline, for the case study. BLiM-recent obtains the best results in recall and precision, providing an average value of 79.10% in recall and 73.26% in precision. The next best results are obtained by BLiM-mean, providing an average value of 71.43% in recall and 64.91% in precision. The third best values are obtained by BLiM-sum, providing an average value of 60.61% in recall and 45.69% in precision. BLiM-oldest obtains the worst value in precision, 27.99%, while the baseline approach obtains the worst

Table 1 Mean values and standard deviations for Recall, Precision and F-measure

	BLiM-recent	BLiM-oldest	BLiM-mean	BLiM-sum	Baseline
Recall ± σ	79.10 ± 11.75	51.21 ± 12.58	71.43 ± 11.18	60.61 ± 11.56	44.25 ± 14.79
Precision ± σ	73.26 ± 9.44	27.99 ± 7.74	64.91 ± 9.57	45.69 ± 12.45	29.04 ± 9.47
F-measure ± σ	76.07 ± 8.34	36.20 ± 7.46	68.02 ± 7.54	52.10 ± 8.26	35.07 ± 9.00

value in recall, 44.25%. In terms of recall and precision, BLiM-recent outperforms the rest of the approaches.

From the results, we can see that there are some bugs (around 24% on average) that are not properly located by the approach. This happens because the fitness function that guides the search is not giving high fitness values to the model fragments realizing those bugs. This can happen due to differences between the language used in the bug descriptions and the product models, or in cases where there are few differences in the modification timespan among the different model fragments.

4.4 Statistical Analysis

To properly compare our BLiM approach (with the four fitness functions) and the baseline approach, all of the data resulting from the empirical analysis was analyzed using statistical methods following the guidelines in [25]. The goals of our statistical analysis are: (1) to provide formal and quantitative evidence (statistical significance) that BLiM-recent does in fact have an impact on the comparison metrics (i.e., that the differences in the results were not obtained by mere chance); and (2) to show that those differences are significant in practice (effect size).

Statistical significance

To enable statistical analysis, all of the algorithms should be run a large enough number of times (in an independent way) to collect information on the probability distribution for each algorithm. A statistical test should then be run to assess whether there is enough empirical evidence to claim (with a high level of confidence) that there is a difference between two algorithms (e.g. A is better than B). In order to do this, two hypotheses, the null hypothesis H_0 and the alternative hypothesis H_1 are defined. The null hypothesis H_0 is typically defined to state that there is no difference among the algorithms, whereas the alternative hypothesis H_1 states that at least one algorithm differs from another. In such a case, a statistical test aims to verify whether the null hypothesis H_0 should be rejected.

The statistical tests provide a probability value, *p-value*. The *p-value* obtains values between 0 and 1. The lower the *p-value* of a test, the more likely that the null hypothesis is false. It is accepted by the research community that a *p-value* under 0.05 is statistically significant [25], and so the hypothesis H_0 can be considered false.

The test that we must follow depends on the properties of the data. Since our data does not follow a normal distribution in general, our analysis requires the use of non-parametric techniques. There are several tests for analyzing this kind of data;

Table 2 Holm's post hoc *p-value* and $\hat{A}_{12}$ statistic for each pair of algorithms

	Holm's		$\hat{A}_{12}$	
	Recall	Precision	Recall	Precision
Recent versus oldest	4×10^{-12}	$\ll 2 \times 10^{-16}$	0.9437546	1
Recent versus mean	0.0434	0.019	0.6775018	0.7319211
Recent versus sum	1.1×10^{-6}	7.6×10^{-10}	0.8699781	0.9466764
Recent versus baseline	$\ll 2 \times 10^{-16}$	$\ll 2 \times 10^{-16}$	0.9656684	1
Oldest versus mean	5.8×10^{-7}	$\ll 2 \times 10^{-16}$	0.1278305	0
Oldest versus sum	0.0416	1.4×10^{-6}	0.2885318	0.1022644
Oldest versus baseline	0.0527	0.939	0.6449963	0.4598247
Mean versus sum	0.0078	9.1×10^{-5}	0.7465303	0.8663258
Mean versus baseline	2.7×10^{-11}	$\ll 2 \times 10^{-16}$	0.9181885	1
Sum versus baseline	8.7×10^{-5}	1.3×10^{-6}	0.7991234	0.8363769

however, the Quade test shows that it is the most powerful when working with real data [26]. In addition, according to Conover [27], the Quade test is the one that has shown the best results when the number of algorithms is low (no more than 4 or 5 algorithms).

The *p-value* obtained in the test are $\ll 2 \times 10^{-16}$ for recall and precision, the statistics value obtained are 32.628 and 62.196 for recall and precision respectively. Since the *p-value* are smaller than 0.05 for recall and precision, we reject the null hypothesis. Consequently, we can state that there exist differences among the algorithms (BLiM-recent, BLiM-oldest, BLiM-mean, BLiM-sum, and the baseline) for the performance indicators of recall and precision.

However, with the Quade test, we cannot answer the following question: Which of the algorithms gives the best performance? In this case, the performance of each algorithm should be individually compared against all other alternatives. In order to do this, we perform an additional post hoc analysis. This kind of analysis performs a pair-wise comparison among the results of each algorithm, determining whether statistically significant differences exist among the results of a specific pair of algorithms.

Table 2 shows the *p-value* of Holm's post hoc analysis for the case study and the performance indicators for the five algorithms (BLiM-recent, BLiM-oldest, BLiM-mean, BLiM-sum, and the baseline). The majority of the *p-value* shown in this table are smaller than their corresponding significance threshold value (0.05), indicating that the differences of performance between the algorithms are significant. However, when comparing BLiM-oldest and the baseline (seventh row), the values are greater than the threshold, indicating that the differences between those algorithms could be due to the stochastic nature of the algorithms and are not significant.

Effect size

When comparing algorithms with a large enough number of runs, statistically significant differences can be obtained even if they are so small as to be of no practical value [25]. Then it is important to assess if an algorithm is statistically better than another and to assess the magnitude of the improvement. Effect size measures are needed to analyze this.

For a non-parametric effect size measure, we use Vargha and Delaney's $\hat{A}_{12}$ [20, 26]. $\hat{A}_{12}$ measures the probability that running one algorithm yields higher values than running another algorithm. If the two algorithms are equivalent, then $\hat{A}_{12}$ will be equal to 0.5.

For example, $\hat{A}_{12} = 0.7$ means that we would obtain better results in 70% of the runs with the first algorithm of the pair that have been compared, and $\hat{A}_{12} = 0.3$ means that we would obtain better results in 70% of the runs with the second algorithm of the pair that have been compared. Thus, we have an $\hat{A}_{12}$ value for every pair of algorithms.

Table 2 shows the values of the size effect statistics. In general, the largest differences were obtained between BLiM-recent and the baseline, where BLiM-recent achieves better recall than the baseline 96% of the times and better precision almost all the times. When comparing BLiM-recent and BLiM-mean the differences are not so big, with BLiM-recent outperforming BLiM-mean in recall 67% of the times and in precision 73% of the times.

BLiM-recent obtained the best performance results among the five evaluated approaches (see Table 1). The performed statistical analysis indicated that BLiM-recent outperforms the rest of the approaches in terms of recall and precision (around 70% of the times when compared to BLiM-mean, 90% of the times when compared to BLiM-sum and almost all the times when compared to BLiM-oldest and the baseline). Overall, these results confirm that the use of BLiM-recent against the baseline approach has an actual impact.

4.5   Threats to Validity

In this section, we present some of the threats to the validity of our work. We follow the guidelines suggested by de Oliveira et al. [28] to identify those applicable to this work.

Conclusion validity threats: To address the *not accounting for random variation* threat, we considered 30 independent runs for each bug with each algorithm. As we used the approach that BSH uses for bug location as a comparison baseline, the *lack of a meaningful comparison baseline* threat is addressed. In this paper we employed standard statistical analysis following accepted guidelines [25] to avoid the *lack of a formal hypothesis and statistical tests* threat. For avoid the *lack of a good descriptive analysis* threat, we have used the precision, recall, and F-measure measurements to analyze the confusion matrix obtained from the experiments; however, other measurements could be applied.

Internal validity threats: To address the *poor parameter settings* threat, we used standard values for the algorithms. As suggested by Arcuri and Fraser [25], default values are good enough to measure the performance of location techniques in the context of testing. Nevertheless, we plan to evaluate all the parameters of our algorithm in a future work. As we have evaluated our work in an industrial case study the *lack of real problem instances* threat is addressed.

Construct validity threats: To address the *lack of assessing the validity of cost measures* threat, we performed a fair comparison among BLiM-X and the baseline by generating the same number of model fragments and using the same number of fitness evaluations.

External validity threats: The *lack of a clear object selection strategy* and the *lack of evaluations for instances of growing size and complexity* threats are addressed by using an industrial case study, BSH. Our instances are collected from real world problems. In addition, regarding the generalization of our approach, the set of models where the bugs have to be located are conforming to MOF (the OMG metalanguage for defining modeling languages), and the bug reports must be provided using natural language. Then, our evaluation does not rely on the particular conditions of our domain. Nevertheless, the evaluation should be replicated in other domains before assuring their generalization.

5 Related Work

Saha et al. [15] presented BLUiR, which uses a baseline "TF.IDF model". They believe that code constructs improve the accuracy of bug localization. They syntactically parse the source code into four document fields: class, method, variable, and comment. The summary and the description of a bug report are considered as two query fields. Textual similarities are computed for each of the eight-document field-query field pairs and then summed up into an overall ranking measure. Kim et al. [29] propose both a one-phase and a two-phase prediction model to recommend files to fix. In the one-phase model, they create features from textual information and metadata of bug reports, apply Naïve Bayes to train the model using previously fixed files as classification labels, and then use the trained model to assign multiple source files to a bug report. In the two-phase model, they first apply their one-phase model to classify a new bug report as either "predictable" or "deficient", and then make predictions only for "predictable" reports. Unlike us, all of these approaches do not take into account the modification timespan of the retrieved source locations. Furthermore, these approaches target code while our approach targets models to locate the bug realizations.

Zamani et al. [30] proposed an approach that included weighting and ranking the source code locations based on both the textual similarity with a change request and the use of the time metadata. This approach gives better results than IR techniques. However, their approach is applied at the source code level, while we use a Multi-Objective Evolutionary Algorithm to address the location of bugs in models.

In addition, other approaches use genetic algorithms to locate features in models, Font et al. [12, 18] propose two approaches to locate features in a model. However, these works do not take into account the modification timespan of the model elements. Our work, in contrast, is focused on searching bug realizations, hence, the timespan weighting is an important piece of the approach in order to obtain accurate results.

6 Conclusion

Bug Location is a significant maintenance activity. In this paper, we have proposed four approaches for bug location in models (BLiM-recent, BLiM-oldest, BLiM-mean, BLiM-sum) and compared them with a baseline. Our BLiM-X approaches, in order to guide our bug location evolutionary algorithm, consider: (1) the similitude to the bug description, and (2) the modification timespan weightings of the models.

We evaluate which approach produces better results in terms of precision, recall and F-measure. To do so, we applied the five approaches in an industrial domain, BSH, that has a model based product family (firmware of Induction Hobs). We report our evaluation, including: experimental setup, results, statistical analysis, and threats to validity.

The results show that the application of the Defect Localization Principle that has achieved good results in bug location in code leads to a significant improvement when it has applied to bug location in models compared to the baseline approach. The findings of our work are:

- The application of the Defect Localization Principle using the most recent modification timespan of a model element (BLiM-recent) provides the best results in our study.
- Results also show that our approach can be applied in real world environments. Nevertheless, we need further experiments that involve the final users of our approach in order assure that can be applied in all real world environments.

In addition, this work presents a statistical analysis of the results. This analysis provides evidence of the significance of results obtained, and we can state that they were not obtained by mere chance.

Acknowledgements This work has been partially supported by the Ministry of Economy and Competitiveness (MINECO) through the Spanish National R+D+i Plan and ERDF funds under the project Model-Driven Variability Extraction for Software Product Line Adoption (TIN2015-64397-R).

References

1. Lehman, M.M., Ramil, J.F., Kahen, G.: A paradigm for the behavioural modelling of software processes using system dynamics. Citeseer (2001)
2. Antoniol, G., Gueheneuc, Y.-G.: Feature identification: an epidemiological metaphor. IEEE Trans. Softw. Eng. **32**(9), 627–641 (2006)
3. Dit, B., Revelle, M., Gethers, M., Poshyvanyk, D.: Feature location in source code: a taxonomy and survey. J. Softw. Maint. Evol. Res. Pract. (2011)
4. Rubin, J., Chechik, M.: A survey of feature location techniques. In: Reinhartz-Berger, I., Sturm, A., Clark, T., Cohen, S., Bettin, J. (eds.) Domain Engineering, pp. 29–58. Springer, Berlin (2013)
5. Hassan, A.E., Holt, R.C.: The top ten list: dynamic fault prediction. In: 21st IEEE International Conference on Software Maintenance (ICSM'05), pp. 263–272 (2005)
6. Efficient Java Matrix Library, https://ejml.org. Accessed: April 07, 2016 (2016)
7. Sisman, B., Kak, A.C.: Incorporating version histories in Information Retrieval based bug localization. In: 2012 9th IEEE Working Conference on Mining Software Repositories (MSR), pp. 50–59 (2012)
8. Plisson, J., Lavrac, N., Mladenic, D.: A rule based approach to word lemmatization. In: Proceedings of the 7th International Multi-Conference Information Society IS 2004. pp. 83–86 (2004)
9. Vargha, A., Delaney, H.D.: A critique and improvement of the CL common language effect size statistics of McGraw and Wong. J. Educ. Behav. Stat. **25**(2), 101–132 (2000)
10. Haugen, Ø., Møller-Pedersen, B., Oldevik, J., Olsen, G.K., Svendsen, A.: Adding standardized variability to domain specific languages. In: Proceedings of the 2008 12th International Software Product Line Conference, pp. 139–148. IEEE Computer Society, Washington, DC, USA (2008)
11. Zimmermann, T., Weisgerber, P., Diehl, S., Zeller, A.: Mining version histories to guide software changes. In: Proceedings of the 26th International Conference on Software Engineering, pp. 563–572. IEEE Computer Society, Washington, DC, USA (2004)
12. Font, J., Arcega, L., Haugen, Ø., Cetina, C.: Feature location in model-based software product lines through a genetic algorithm. In: 15th International Conference on Software Reuse, Limassol, Cyprus (2016)
13. Landauer, T.K., Foltz, P.W., Laham, D.: An introduction to latent semantic analysis. Discourse Process **25**(2-3), 259–284 (1998)
14. Manning, C.D., Schütze, H.: Foundations of Natural Language Processing. Reading, 678 (2000)
15. Saha, R.K., Lease, M., Khurshid, S., Perry, D.E.: Improving bug localization using structured information retrieval. In: 2013 28th IEEE/ACM International Conference on Automated Software Engineering (ASE), pp. 345–355 (2013)
16. Salton, G., McGill, M.J.: Introduction to Modern Information Retrieval. McGraw-Hill Inc., New York, NY, USA (1986)
17. Hulth, A.: Improved automatic keyword extraction given more linguistic knowledge. In: Proceedings of the 2003 Conference on Empirical Methods in Natural Language Processing, pp. 216–223. Association for Computational Linguistics, Stroudsburg, PA, USA (2003)
18. Font, J., Arcega, L., Haugen, Ø., Cetina, C.: Feature location in models through a genetic algorithm driven by information retrieval techniques. In: Proceedings of the ACM/IEEE 19th International Conference on Model Driven Engineering Languages and Systems, pp. 272–282. ACM, New York (2016)
19. Ishibuchi, H., Nojima, Y., Doi, T.: Comparison between single-objective and multi-objective genetic algorithms: performance comparison and performance measures. In: 2006 IEEE International Conference on Evolutionary Computation, pp. 1143–1150 (2006)
20. Zitzler, E., Thiele, L.: Multiobjective optimization using evolutionary algorithms—a comparative case study. In: Eiben, A.E., Bäck, T., Schoenauer, M., Schwefel, H.-P. (eds.)

Parallel Problem Solving from Nature—PPSN V: 5th International Conference Amsterdam, The Netherlands September 27–30, 1998 Proceedings. pp. 292–301. Springer Berlin Heidelberg, Berlin, Heidelberg (1998)

21. Steinberg, D., Budinsky, F., Paternostro, M., Merks, E.: Eclipse Modeling Framework, 2nd edn. Addison-Wesley Professional (2009)
22. Dyer, D.W.: The watchmaker framework for evolutionary computation (evolutionary/genetic algorithms for Java) (2006)
23. Apache OpenNLP: Toolkit for the processing of natural language text. http://opennlp.apache.org/. Accessed: April 07, 2016 (2010)
24. The English (Porter2) stemming algorithm. http://snowball.tartarus.org/algorithms/english/stemmer.html, Accessed: April 07, 2016 (2002)
25. Arcuri, A., Fraser, G.: Parameter tuning or default values? An empirical investigation in search-based software engineering. Empir. Softw. Eng. **18**(3), 594–623 (2013)
26. García, S., Fernández, A., Luengo, J., Herrera, F.: Advanced nonparametric tests for multiple comparisons in the design of experiments in computational intelligence and data mining: experimental analysis of power. Inf. Sci. (NY) **180**(10), 2044–2064 (2010)
27. Conover, W.J.: Practical Nonparametric Statistics, 3rd edn. Wiley, New York (1999)
28. de Oliveira Barros, M., Dias-Neto, A.C.: 0006/2011-Threats to validity in search-based software engineering empirical studies. RelaTe-DIA 5(1) (2011)
29. Kim, D., Tao, Y., Kim, S., Zeller, A.: Where should we fix this bug? A two-phase recommendation model. IEEE Trans. Softw. Eng. **39**(11), 1597–1610 (2013)
30. Zamani, S., Lee, S.P., Shokripour, R., Anvik, J.: A noun-based approach to feature location using time-aware term-weighting. Inf. Softw. Technol. **56**(8), 991–1011 (2014)

Product Traceability in Ceramic Industry 4.0: A Design Approach and Cloud-Based MES Prototype

João Barata, Paulo Rupino da Cunha,
Anand Subhashchandra Gonnagar and Mateus Mendes

Abstract We propose a customer-focused approach to design product traceability for Industry 4.0. Our design-science research includes a review of traceability technologies and participative enterprise modeling in the ceramic industry. We find benefits in combining Business Process Modeling Notation and Goal-oriented Requirements Language representations to (1) promote reflection by experts with different backgrounds, (2) reach consensus with a solution that addresses the goals of multiple stakeholders, and (3) ensure that customers' needs are a priority in traceability design. The resulting model combines technologies in different stages of the product lifecycle and is implemented in a cloud-based MES (Manufacturing Execution System) prototype. Depending on each stage and strategic intention, the identification code can be embedded in the product, transport, or package. Our contribution can assist managers in the creation of cloud-based MES to support traceability integration at (1) technological, (2) vertical, and (3) horizontal levels that are required in the fourth industrial revolution.

Keywords Traceability · Ceramic industry · BPM · GRL · Manufacturing execution system · Industry 4.0

A prior version of this paper has been published in the ISD2017 Proceedings (http://aisel.aisnet.org/isd2014/proceedings2017).

J. Barata (✉)
CTCV - Technological Center for Ceramics and Glass, Coimbra, Portugal
e-mail: barata@dei.uc.pt

J. Barata · P. R. da Cunha
CISUC, University of Coimbra, Coimbra, Portugal
e-mail: rupino@dei.uc.pt

J. Barata · A. S. Gonnagar · M. Mendes
ESTGOH, Polytechnic Institute of Coimbra, Oliveira do Hospital, Coimbra, Portugal
e-mail: mia166901@estgoh.ipc.pt

M. Mendes
Institute of Systems and Robotics of the University of Coimbra, Coimbra, Portugal
e-mail: mmendes@estgoh.ipc.pt

© Springer International Publishing AG, part of Springer Nature 2018   187
N. Paspallis et al. (eds.), *Advances in Information Systems Development*,
Lecture Notes in Information Systems and Organisation 26,
https://doi.org/10.1007/978-3-319-74817-7_12

1 Introduction

The fourth industrial revolution (or Industry 4.0) is changing the landscape of manufacturing at a global scale. Production flexibility and decentralization, resource efficiency, and the emergence of new information systems have the "potential to turn around the industrial practice comprehensively" [1].

Manufacturing execution systems (MES) is one type of plant information systems that handles industry operations, process supervision and control [2, 3]. To take advantage of Industry 4.0 models and technologies, modern cloud-based MES have to deal with product traceability in distributed manufacturing, for example "where workflows of multiple factories are coordinated centrally to provide plant managers with real-time tracking, visibility, and control across several plants". Cloud-based MES have been proposed to address this challenge, integrating different information from suppliers in the supply chain, order tracking, real-time data, materials tracking and complete product information [4].

Product traceability is defined by ISO 8402 as "the ability to retrace the history, the use or location of an article or an activity, or similar articles or activities, by means of recorded identification" [5]. Current concerns of industrial managers include preventing errors in the supply chain (e.g. incorrect product selection, or misidentification of customers' requirements); managing risks of product use (e.g. identification of components, origins of materials, and counterfeit products); obtaining efficiency in inspections; and improved control of quality, inventory, manufacturing, and logistics [6]. The importance of traceability is also present in the popular quality management standard ISO 9001:2015 [7], which highlights this requirement in Sections 8.5.2 (identification and traceability) and 8.6 (people responsibilities). Additionally, [6] mentions the need to consider the goals of stakeholders that are internal and external to the firm and distinct phases of product lifecycle. Namely, product development, production, use, and disposal. Still, according to [8], it is necessary to consider different traceability technologies in industry "because of changes in material properties and various operations in process stages. Therefore, suitable traceability methods need to be identified for different process sections". Also, [9] suggests that it is necessary to integrate various mechanisms for traceability, because each one has its strengths and weaknesses. Despite all this, in some sectors of the economy, product traceability is still in initial stages of development. The millenarian production of ceramics that we addressed in this study is one of those sectors.

In this paper, we focus on the table and ornamental ware ceramic sub-group characterized by concurrent production of many different products. For example, a tableware product line can include different models (e.g. cup, jar, and dish) with multiple decorations. Product diversity, aggressive environmental conditions (e.g. kiln firing temperatures above 1000 °C; dusty production environments that make reading and sensing difficult), and the multiple operations in the production line make product traceability a major challenge in ceramics. The company participating in our research is implementing a cloud-based MES for distributed manufacturing, which requires extensive traceability requirements for the entire lifecycle of the ceramic product.

We posit that designing traceability systems can be addressed by enterprise modeling, "*an activity where an integrated and commonly shared model describing different aspects of an enterprise is created*" [10]. It can be carried out with the participation of the system stakeholders to improve the quality of the proposed solution, obtain consensus, and commitment from the users [10, 11]. The need to include traceability in the agenda of ceramic production and the need to identify potential technologies and implementation methods motivated us to formulate three research objectives:

1. Model ceramic product traceability systems involving multiple stakeholders;
2. Identify traceability technologies that can be used in table and ornamental ceramic production;
3. Create a cloud-based MES prototype that implements the traceability model for distributed manufacturing in ceramic industry.

The remainder of this paper is organized as follows. Section 2 introduces our design-science research approach, that involved a ceramic producer and a national technological center for ceramic and glass industries. Next, we explore studies addressing traceability technologies and application cases in distinct sectors of the economy. Section 4 details our traceability model. In Sect. 5, we present a cloud-based MES prototype for the ceramic sector. Afterward, Sect. 6 discusses results and we conclude in Sect. 7, stating study limitations and opportunities for future work.

2 Method

Design-science has its foundations in the work of [12] and seeks to produce innovations, and create and evaluate artifacts aiming to solve specific organizational problems [13]. In our research we adopt the broad definition of Information System (IS) artifact suggested by [14] that integrates "information artifact", "technology artifact" and "social artifact". According to the authors, "technology artifacts (such as hardware and software), information artifacts (such as a message) and social artifacts (such as a charitable act) are different kinds of artifacts that together interact in order to form the IS artifact" [14].

Our research follows the phases proposed by [15] namely, (1) problem identification and motivation, (2) definition of the objectives for a solution, (3) design and development, (4) demonstration, (5) evaluation, and (6) communication.

The motivation to study traceability in table and ornamental ware emerged in a technological center with the mission to support ceramic industry development in Portugal. This country is one of the top exporters of these products: the first in the European Union and the second worldwide [16]. Consequently, public and private organizations are joining efforts to evolve the ceramic IS support and achieve competitive advantages towards Industry 4.0. First, we conducted a review of relevant literature, presented in Sect. 3. Based on the identified cases and technologies and in contacts with ceramic experts, we constructed a holistic model for traceability in table and ornamental ware production that implements a manufacturing execution system and, to external stakeholders, provides real time information (e.g. results from quality tests during production of ceramic products). Design and development (step 3, according to [15]) was inspired by participative approaches to modeling in Information System Development (ISD) [10, 11].

The preliminary results of our research (regarding objectives 1 and 2) were presented and discussed at the ISD 2017 conference that was held in Larnaca, Cyprus. In this revised and extended version of the paper we present the recently developed cloud-based MES prototype that implements our product traceability model. This software is being deployed in a Portuguese ceramic company, that provided positive feedback. We concluded our design research with a joint assessment of the results by researchers and practitioners, documenting and publishing the findings.

3 Literature Review

In Sect. 3.1 we describe the concept of traceability design and the opportunities to advance in this area. Section 3.2 summarizes the most relevant technologies for product identification and traceability in industry. In Sect. 3.3, we discuss the implementation of these technologies in different sectors of the economy.

3.1 Traceability Design

Product traceability can have a strategic purpose, going beyond the mere identification of where products are [17]. There are also design principles to build traceability systems that suggest considering multiple actors and elements of the supply chain [18]. Other researchers have proposed different solution for traceability design. For example, [19] proposes a mathematical model for product recall. Other authors, for example [20] addressed graphical solutions to model traceability in manufacturing using graphs. According to these authors, a "gozinto graph represents a graphical listing of raw materials, parts, intermediates and subassemblies, which a process transforms into an end product, through a sequence of operations" [20]. The study presented by [21] adapts the axiomatic design method combining both modeling techniques: graphical and mathematical. The authors start by the identification of traceability functional requirements and graphically map them to the physical processes. Their proposal extends traceability design to different areas of the supply chain.

These studies give important contributions for traceability design in industrial contexts. However, mathematical models have limited use in the initial stages of traceability design, involving multiple experts in the process. The graphical approach suggested by [20] provides detailed information of the operations and the elements involved. Yet, existing models do not address strategic aspects of traceability, namely, (1) the contrasting perspective of multiple stakeholders, (2) the list of possible technologies and the priorities of their implementation, and (3) the participative approach to modeling. There are opportunities to test different modeling techniques to design product traceability in industries.

3.2 Technologies for Traceability

There are multiple technologies available to implement traceability in industrial processes. Examples of popular identification technologies include barcode, Quick Response (QR) code, and Radio Frequency Identification (RFID). Their main purpose is to identify a specific product or group of products (e.g. production lot), but many other technologies can be used individually or even combined for traceability.

Linear barcodes, namely the Universal Product Code (UPC) and European Article Number (EAN) variants, are amongst the most used identification technologies, for example, in the food sector [22]. Barcodes encode product data such as part number, serial numbers, supplier numbers, and more. Barcode scanners allow accurate reading and enable companies to track product information in multiple phases of the supply chain, reducing human errors that are common in manual data entry. Barcodes are a popular way of identification affixed in most products available in supermarkets, but they also suffer from limitations of applicability in industry due to the nature of the materials typically used. For example, in the wood industry the "barcode traceability system is simple and low cost, however, it is difficult to be massively applied in wood trade and traceability, because of the nature of wood" [23].

QR codes are two-dimensional codes that provide high speed reading [24]. Its graphical image stores information vertically and horizontally, thus providing a higher data density when compared to linear barcodes. One of the possible uses of QR codes is to protect consumers and retailers from counterfeit products and they can contain Uniform Resource Locators (URLs), texts, and geo co-ordinates, among other possibilities. Examples of QR code use include advertising campaigns, linking to company websites and contest sign-up pages. More recently, QR codes are being tested in the metalworking industry to identify metal parts [25]. According to the authors, QR codes can be engraved in the products overcoming the problems of detaching that are common in labels.

RFID is another popular identification solution, having its foundations in the work of the physicist Léon Theremin during the last century. It was developed and used by the military to identify and differentiate friendly and foe aircrafts.

Since then, it has been used also in commercial airplanes, as well as in many other industry sectors. Nowadays, RFID's are used in laptops, mobiles, building access systems, passports, car keys, and ID cards. An RFID tag can store more information when compared to linear barcodes, for example, adding the production date or the expire date to the product identification code [26]. Another advantage is that it does not require line-of-sight scanning because it uses radio waves to communicate with the reader. The RFID tags are classified as active (using battery to emit radio waves, readable from larger distances) and passive (generating the required power from the scanner's interrogating radio waves) as per the need in the business.

The list of traceability technologies is vast and includes many other options, some of them associated with the emerging topic of Industry 4.0, a priority for Europe and for the entire globe [27]. Wireless solutions, communication technologies such as 4G/5G, mobile devices including smartphones/PDAs/Tablets, Near Field Communications (NFC), Indoor/Outdoor GPS and Cloud platforms are now available to tackle the challenges of traceability in modern supply chains [28]. In fact, Industry 4.0 design principles of interconnection, decentralized decisions, and information transparency [29] require real-time identification of products and their production stages. The priority to reduce lot sizes, individualize production [30], and ensure individualized trace data, call for a combination of technologies and new competencies for the industry [31].

Popular as they are, there are common limitations to traceability tags such as RFID, barcodes, and QR codes, for example, in highly adverse environments such as the case of high temperature processes. Exposures to temperatures of around 1000 °C require solutions that do not require direct contact with the product. Possibilities include computer vision to count/identify specific products. However, in spite of the potential of this technology in quality inspection of defects [32], these types of systems have not yet been tested in the table and ornamental ware ceramic sector, where there are significant challenges posed by the hundreds or even thousands of possible product formats.

3.3   Application Cases: Solutions and Opportunities

Multinational companies are investing in traceability solutions. For example, Hitachi provides solutions targeting the beef and the steel industries [33]. Examples of internal and external traceability solutions in construction, food, and manufacturing are described by [6], accounting for backward and forward traceability. The former providing information about product history and production details (e.g. responsibilities), with the latter describing what will happen to the product in the supply chain [6].

Traceability in the wood industry can use a combination of techniques such as punching, painting, barcodes, QR Codes, micro-wave sensors, DNA-fingerprinting, and RFID [23]. On one hand, the sector is evolving from traditional punching and barcodes to digital systems that involve QR Codes and genetic technologies. On the other hand, some authors identify that "few countries in the forest sector and generally the wood industry are using IT methods of wood traceability" [23], and it would be interesting to develop a standard traceability method to assist this traditional sector of the economy.

The food industry is one of the most critical for human safety and, consequently, for traceability requirements: procedures and systems for the identification of outsourced production; product identification; producer data; and destination of all supplied products. The importance of tracking technologies using carriers tags (e.g. RFID and barcode) in food manufacturing is explained in [34]. However, the authors also state that "data carriers alone do not establish traceability. The use of RFID facilitates chain information management because it eases the automated data capture process, but it does not establish traceability itself. Traceability requires association of identifiers with locations and processes, and following such identifiers through the chain from their emergence until their obliteration" [34].

The healthcare sector is making important investments in mobile technologies and the use of QR codes, for example, for medicine prescriptions [35]. Moreover, barcodes are commonly used in pharmaceutical products. The initiatives for mobile health using remote monitoring are creating opportunities for the use of healthcare applications with mobile devices.

Benefits of product traceability in the cases described are extensive, including the possibility of obtaining complete information for the customer, trace suppliers' production and logistics, identify quality issues, enhance product visibility, inventory control, certification, counterfeit goods protection, or ethical and legal responsibilities [6, 25, 36]. But in spite of the many existing applications, applications in ceramic industry are scarce. In fact, a Google Scholar search with the keyword combination "product traceability" AND "ceramic manufacturing" returns a single result about current trends in ceramic. Extending the scope of our search criteria (e.g. "traceability" AND "ceramic" AND "RFID") we found a master thesis directly related to sanitaryware traceability [37]. von Sivers and Sjögren [37] compared different technologies and suggested the use of (product engraved) Datamatrix 2D codes, consisting of black and white modules, usually arranged in a square pattern, which are similar to QR codes but more usual in industrial settings. However, the author focused on internal traceability techniques, not addressing the design method and external stakeholders' involvement in the system design, such as end customers' goals.

The lack of solutions for our target ceramic sub-group and the possible benefits of combining technologies reinforced our decision to continue the research with participative enterprise modeling, as described in Sect. 4.

4   Modeling Product Traceability in Table and Ornamental Ceramic Industry

Our participative approach involved experts in ceramics, IT, and electronics. After reviewing potential traceability technologies, we visited a ceramic company and interviewed an expert in the ceramic process from a private research and development institute. The simplified process of table and ornamental ceramic production is presented in Fig. 1, using Business Process Modeling and Notation (BPMN).

The sequence of activities in the ceramic process and the simultaneous production of multiple product references pose specific challenges for traceability design, as illustrated in Fig. 2.

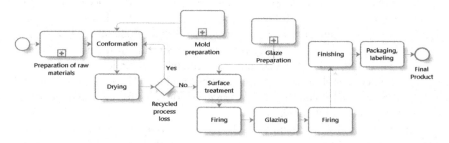

Fig. 1 Ceramic production model. Adapted from [38]

Fig. 2 Ceramic product mix: a complex scenario for traceability design

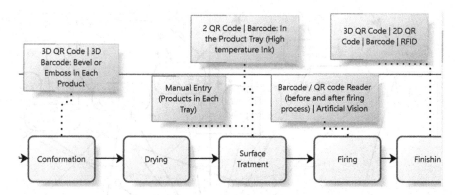

Fig. 3 Business process model for traceability identification (extract for production activities)

Figure 2 shows the several references in the production line. The fragile consistency of the ceramic material in all the production stages and the low cost of each unit limits the use of some traceability options, such as (proportionately expensive) RFID tags. Moreover, this case revealed a highly manual process that is mostly supported by paper records. Process participants may be internal (e.g. customer service, sales, marketing, production) or external to the company (e.g. the customers, partners, and material suppliers), each one demanding an analysis of the most applicable traceability technology. Figure 3 presents a mapping of selected traceability technologies according to the manufacturing process activity.

We highlight (1) QR codes, barcodes, or 2D Datamatrix embedded in the ceramic product at conformation stage, (2) high temperature ink to make the codes readable during/after firing above 1000 °C (there are multiple intrusive/ non-intrusive marking techniques available that are out of the scope of our paper, such as laser marking, dot pen or ink jet), and the possible use of computer vision for automatic product count in areas of difficult access. The automatic reading of trays before and after the firing process will allow real time identification of the product under fire and ready for the finishing activity.

The process model of Fig. 3 is useful, but does not explain why the technology was needed or used in each activity. Therefore, we could not establish priorities and clarify the comparative interest of the specific technology. For example, if an activity could use barcode and QR code, which one was best for that activity and for the overall traceability purpose? So, in a second stage, we created goal models with the jUCMNav Eclipse plug-in [39] to understand the needs of each stakeholder of the traceability system.

Figure 4 presents an extract of the GRL model we developed for the customers.

Goal models can be useful for communication in the initial modeling process, identifying requirements and the main goals of the system actors. There are recent studies adopting GRL in participative enterprise modeling [40]. Figure 4 includes two main traceability technologies that the design team found more valuable for the customer of table and ornamental ware: barcode and QR code (represented as GRL

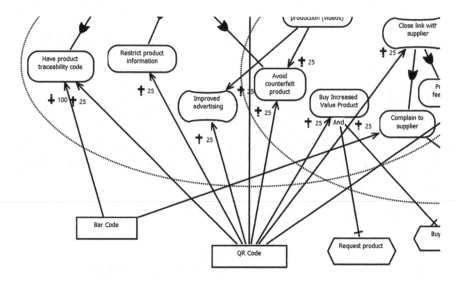

Fig. 4 Goal model for traceability identification (extract for customers: reseller and end user)

resources in the bottom-left of Fig. 4). The modeling team connected the resources with the goals of the actors and considered barcodes useful for only two goals (two contribution arrows—to "Have a product traceability code" and to support "Complains to supplier"). QR codes could address eight goals and/or soft goals of the customers, which suggests that it was preferable to the actors in this scenario. After completing our models we established the most important traceability technologies for each actor and process activity (represented as tasks in the bottom-right of Fig. 4). In our goal model, resources (traceability technologies) are connected with goals, not tasks, but we can identify the link of resources and tasks via contribution arrows. Moreover, in this model we can identify why the technologies are used (e.g. in support of the identified goals of the actors), thus adding information that was not available in the BPMN model.

Figure 5 shows the traceability landscape for table and ornamental ceramic.

This model suggests that QR codes are strategic for internal processes and to customer use. For example, the end customer (reseller or end user) can access a web page to see a video about the product or the production. However, external partners such as suppliers and vendors/retailers need barcodes for lot checking and sales process (e.g. in supermarket points-of-sale). Due to its higher cost, RFID is an option for high-value products only, for example, with intensive manual finishing or historical value, but it can be used in the future to track transport cars. For this classification of traceability technologies, we got our inspiration in the McFarlan strategic grid [41], detailed in Fig. 6, for the ceramic production stage.

The grid presented in Fig. 6 is created for each actor of the system—the example is for ceramic production, but it can be extended to the end user, vendors, and other actors. According to [41], strategic solutions (on the top left of Fig. 6) are important to

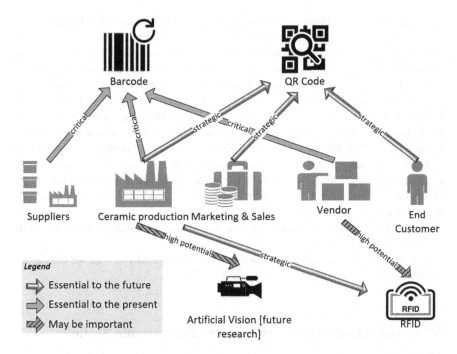

Fig. 5 Product traceability landscape: model for table and ornamental ceramic

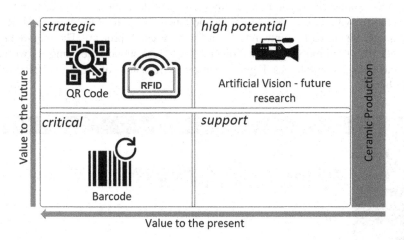

Fig. 6 Product traceability: technological portfolio—production. Adapted from [41]

the company future; critical solutions (bottom left) are important to the present; and high potential solutions (top right) may be important to the future, but it is uncertain. The design team considered QR codes as strategic to provide increased value to the customer and contextualized information during production stages, RFID as strategic to identify transport cars location in the factory, and computer vision as high potential for product traceability that requires additional field testing. We also found an opportunity to identify product moulds with barcodes to improve traceability of the tools used in the process (e.g. how many products were made by each ceramic mould).

We discussed our approach with a medium sized ceramic company that agreed to participate in a European Union co-funded project to develop and validate the integrated traceability system in a new cloud-based MES. According to the company manager, this model can provide the foundations to build a comprehensive cloud-based MES for table and ornamental ceramic, supported by traceability technologies, and integrating multiple actors of the ceramic production supply chain, particularly useful in distributed manufacturing scenarios that occur in the company. The manager stated that "nowadays, (…) product traceability is needed for different parts of the supply chain (…). The product history is as important as the price tag […and] information must be available at all stages of cradle-to-cradle or cradle-to-grave design".

The next section describes the cloud-based MES prototype that we developed using the proposed model for traceability.

5 Cloud-Based MES Prototype for the Ceramic Sector

The cloud-based MES aims to support the entire lifecycle of table and ornamental ceramic production, including requirements of distributed manufacturing and integration with three traceability technologies: barcode, QR code, and RFID (computer vision will be integrated in a future research project). The requirements include the use of mobile information systems [42] to support the company workers via tablets and smartphones. Figure 7 presents screenshots of the cloud-based MES dashboard.

Fig. 7 Cloud-based MES prototype—Dashboard

The cloud-based MES was designed for mobile devices, allowing the production team, production managers, and the external partners to share data about each production order, product characteristics, and responsibilities in the process. Traceability data is critical in the cloud-based MES for (1) automatic data input, (2) data quality check, and (3) output generation (e.g. QR code labels) tailored for each stakeholder in the process. Inputs include data obtained by barcode readers (e.g. suppliers' material) and product logistics in the plant area—provided by the RFID system. The data obtained by sensors is then compared with the data directly inserted via tablets/smartphones in each process phase (e.g. good/bad parts and rework) to show discrepancies to the production manager. Finally, the cloud-based MES also prints the required barcode and QR code labels to use in the different stages of the product lifecycle, for example, the final packaging QR code and the dynamically generated webpage for the product information (accessible via QR code to the end customer). Another area of our prototype is presented in Fig. 8—material traceability reports.

The solution developed for the ceramic company enables tracing the final products, product parts, and materials. Figure 8 presents an example of production report with multiple criteria, providing a traceability analysis for each product stage, material used, or product part. The traceability components of RFID, barcodes, and QR codes provide inputs to the cloud-based MES (e.g. stock movement) but also a complementary confirmation of data quality. For example, contrasting product stock levels recorded in each department with the information obtained by the RFID readers enables the identification of potential problems in the process flow (e.g. wrong quantity input, defects, rework, delays in specific departments) and more precise identification of the stage of each product in the required production plant/line. Figure 9 present the main modules of the cloud-based MES.

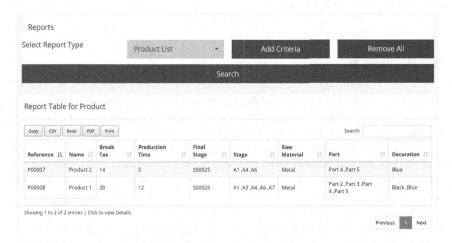

Fig. 8 Cloud-based MES prototype—Material traceability

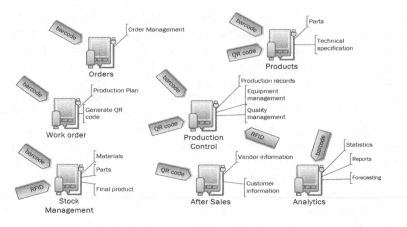

Fig. 9 Cloud-based MES prototype—Modules

The Products module includes all the information required for each product, such as parts, materials, production time (adjusted automatically), and partners information. The Orders module is where the production cycle begins, providing the data for work order generation (for each factory). The Production control module includes a mobile interface and support for automatic data input from the traceability layer (e.g. RFID readers). Our cloud-based MES also includes a Stock management module, the After Sales module, that dynamically generates the web pages for vendors and end customers (via QR code) and the Analytics module. Other modules, under development, were omitted for sake of simplicity, such as ERP integration, maintenance management, and energy management. For each module, in Fig. 9 we represent the most relevant traceability technology (e.g. QR code for the after sales module).

6 Discussion

In spite of the different options available for product traceability in ceramic production we did not find a single technology that could be used throughout the entire product lifecycle and address the needs of internal and external stakeholders. QR codes are interesting for consumer information, while linear barcodes are low-cost and efficient for tray identification during a production process. RFID can also be used for transport cars identification and for more expensive products, but has several limitations for being used during production in aggressive environments such as those we can find in the ceramic industry.

To deal with the problem of selecting a suitable mix of traceability technologies for the particular industry in our study, we found benefits in using multiple representations of the production system with participative enterprise modeling.

First, the contrast of different models—BPMN and GRL—improved the reflection about traceability challenges amongst experts of different domains. BPMN clarifies the sequence, interactions, and elements of the supply chain, while GRL explores the "why" of the system actors, their requirements, beliefs, goals, and resources. Second, it helped in the construction of a consensual perspective for the next steps that includes sourcing the traceability system aligned with the company strategy. On one hand, RFID has several advantages for storing data and reading at a distance, but it was not compatible with high temperatures, and it is proportionately expensive when compared to the low average price of ceramic products. Also, it is not practical to provide extra features to the end consumer. On the other hand, QR codes provided advantages for multiple goals of stakeholders (e.g. consumer) and to develop online web services (thanks to the ability to encode full URLs), but we can't simply eliminate linear barcodes because retailers need them (e.g. in point-of-sales in supermarkets).

The use of multiple modeling techniques helped us move the focus from technology to the requirements for our cloud-based MES platform. When the team started this project, the goal was to identify candidate technologies for product traceability. Then we shifted our attention to the goals of the different stakeholders included in BPMN and GRL models. We agree with [43] in that the operational backbone of the organizational IS must be complemented with digital services targeting different stakeholders. Traceability in the context of Industry 4.0 requires supply chain integration increasing the need to use multiple models, accessible to different experts and ensuring a strategic focus [41].

Cloud, wireless, and mobile can provide "the glue" for traceability information in cloud-based MES for distributed manufacturing. The information traced in the product line can be available to customers or to specific partners/suppliers to plan deliverables of raw material and final product components according to the plan. The use of smartphones in the production line also opens possibilities for future research, taking advantage of QR/barcodes in products, and trays. For example, for quality control, embedded QR codes can simplify product recall (e.g. the same product model can have problems in a single production lot while the others conform to specifications).

According to the company managers, the cloud-based MES prototype was able to integrate traceability requirements from multiple stakeholders, rather than staying restricted to those of internal operations. This benefit is particularly relevant for small and medium sized companies that struggle with (1) the lack of human resources for production control tasks, (2) the need to share information between multiple elements of the supply chain, and (3) the flexibility needed for constant changes in the production plan and real-time information requested by their partners and end-customers.

7 Conclusions

We presented an approach to model product traceability that integrates multiple technologies and stakeholders' viewpoints. The ceramic industry provided the setting that includes adverse environmental conditions for traceability technologies. An overall model for product traceability landscape is proposed, inspired by the classification of [41] and a prototype for cloud-based MES implementing the model was created. Our results suggest that a multi-model approach has the potential to contribute to team learning and creativity in complex scenarios that involve distributed manufacturing and require the participation of multiple stakeholders in ISD. We confirmed previous studies pointing to the benefits of enterprise modeling for achieving consensus in ISD [10] and found new opportunities to use traceability technologies and promoted debate amongst team participants using the models. Our approach extends the work of [4] by (1) proposing an approach to model traceability requirements and (2) implement a sectorial cloud-based MES prototype.

As for limitations, first, the technologies and application cases identified in our literature review are restricted to those found in the consulted literature databases. Second, we restricted the modeling artifacts to BPMN and GRL models, because the design team was already familiar with BPMN tools and recent research suggested benefits of GRL for participative enterprise modeling [40]; other modeling methods and languages can be used. Third, in spite of our participative approach to enterprise modeling, traceability in ceramic production is highly complex and the environmental conditions (e.g. temperature and dust) present challenges to system implementation that require additional research. Nevertheless, our project identified opportunities to use mobile devices and automatic tracking in traditional product lines, including product, transport, and package identification codes. Fourth, although we already found a company that validated our initial model with a cloud-based MES prototype, the system is still under development and we do not have experimental evidence of the benefits for efficiency and effectiveness in the production. These are opportunities to address in upcoming phases of our research that may be extended to other sectors of the economy.

Currently, we are implementing the cloud-based MES in the company and testing the distributed manufacturing of products combining ceramic and cork - a specific model of lamp that is produced in parallel by two distinct companies, one responsible for the cork parts and the other for the ceramic parts, assembly, and packaging. The main contribution of the present project is a graphical approach to design traceability integrating multiple stakeholders' viewpoints in cloud-based MES with requirements of distributed manufacturing. Moreover, our design-science research evaluates existing artifacts (BPMN and GRL) concluding for their positive synergy in the development of product traceability. For managers, we identify traceability technologies and suggest digital innovations in the context of table and ornamental ceramic.

Acknowledgements This work has been partially supported by Portugal 2020 and European Union, European Regional Development Fund (ERDF), POCI-01-0247-FEDER-024541.

References

1. Lasi, H., Fettke, P., Kemper, H.G., Feld, T., Hoffmann, M.: Industry 4.0. Bus. Inf. Syst. Eng. **6**, 239–242 (2014)
2. Valckenaers, P., Van Brussel, H.: Holonic manufacturing execution systems. CIRP Ann. Manuf. Technol. **54**, 427–432 (2005)
3. Banker, R.D., Bardhan, I.R., Chang, H., Lin, S.: Plant information systems, manufacturing capabilities, and plant performance. MIS Q. **30**, 315–337 (2006)
4. Helo, P., Suorsa, M., Hao, Y., Anussornnitisarn, P.: Toward a cloud-based manufacturing execution system for distributed manufacturing. Comput. Ind. **65**, 646–656 (2014)
5. ISO: ISO 8402:1994 Quality management and quality assurance—vocabulary. International Organization for Standardization, Geneva (1994)
6. Terzi, S., Panetto, H., Morel, G., Garetti, M.: A holonic metamodel for product traceability in Product Lifecycle Management. Int. J. Prod. Lifecycle Manag. **2**, 253 (2007)
7. ISO: ISO 9001:2015 Quality management system—Requirements. International Organization for Standardization, Geneva (2015)
8. Zhang, J., Feng, P., Wu, Z., Yu, D.: Automatic identification-enabled traceability in supply chain management. In: WiCOM'08. 4th International Conference on Wireless Communications, Networking and Mobile Computing. IEEE, New York (2008)
9. Zhang, X., Zhang, J., Liu, F., Fu, Z., Mu, W.: Strengths and limitations on the operating mechanisms of traceability system in agro food, China. Food Control **21**, 825–829 (2010)
10. Stirna, J., Persson, A., Sandkuhl, K.: Participative enterprise modeling: experiences and recommendations. In: Advanced Information Systems Engineering, pp. 546–560. Springer, Berlin (2007)
11. Pankowska, M.: User participation in information system development. In: International Conference on Information Society (i-Society), pp. 396–401 (2012)
12. Simon, H.: The Sciences of the Artificial, 3rd edn. MIT Press, Cambridge (1996)
13. Hevner, A.R., March, S.T., Park, J.: Design science in information systems research. MIS Q. **28**, 75–105 (2004)
14. Lee, A.S., Thomas, M., Baskerville, R.L.: Going back to basics in design science: from the information technology artifact to the information systems artifact. Inf. Syst. J. **25**, 5–21 (2015)
15. Peffers, K., Tuunanen, T., Rothenberger, M.A., Chatterjee, S.: A design science research methodology for information systems research. J. Manag. Inf. Syst. **24**, 45–78 (2007)
16. APICER: Ceramic Tableware, http://www.ceramica.pt/en/setor.php?s=decorativa [2018-02-23]
17. Alfaro, J.A., Rábade, L.A.: Traceability as a strategic tool to improve inventory management: a case study in the food industry. Int. J. Prod. Econ. **118**, 104–110 (2009)
18. Ngai, E.: Building traceability systems: a design science approach. In: Proceedings of the 16th Americas Conference on Information Systems (2010)
19. Dai, H., Tseng, M.M., Zipkin, P.H.: Design of traceability systems for product recall. Int. J. Prod. Res. **53**, 511–531 (2015)
20. Jansen-Vullers, M.H., Van Dorp, C.A., Beulens, A.J.M.: Managing traceability information in manufacture. Int. J. Inf. Manage. **23**, 395–413 (2003)
21. Dai, H., Ge, L., Zhou, W.: A design method for supply chain traceability systems with aligned interests. Int. J. Prod. Econ. **170**, 14–24 (2015)
22. Lehmann, R.J., Reiche, R., Schiefer, G.: Future internet and the agri-food sector: State-of-the-art in literature and research. Comput. Electron. Agric. **89**, 158–174 (2012)
23. Tzoulis, I., Andreopoulou, Z.: Emerging traceability technologies as a tool for quality wood trade. Procedia Technol. **8**, 606–611 (2013)

24. Soon, T.J.: QR Code. Synthesis J., 59–78 (2008)
25. Ventura, C.E.H., Aroca, R.V., Antonialli, A.Í.S., Abrão, A.M., Rubio, J.C.C., Câmara, M.A.: Towards part lifetime traceability using machined quick response codes. Procedia Technol. **26**, 89–96 (2016)
26. Prater, E., Frazier, G.V., Reyes, P.M.: Future impacts of RFID on e-supply chains in grocery retailing. Supply Chain Manag. Int. J. **10**, 134–142 (2005)
27. Smit, J., Kreutzer, S., Moeller, C., Carlberg, M.: Industry 4.0—Study for the ITRE Committee. (2016)
28. Barata, J., Cunha, P.R.: Mobile supply chain management: moving where? In: Proceedings of the 13th European, Mediterranean and Middle Eastern Conference on Information Systems (EMCIS), pp. 1–13. Krakow, Poland (2016)
29. Hermann, M., Pentek, T., Otto, B.: Design principles for Industrie 4.0 scenarios. In: Proceedings of the 49th Hawaii International Conference on System Sciences (HICSS), pp. 3928–3937. Grand Hyatt, Kauai (2016)
30. Brettel, M., Friederichsen, N.: How virtualization, decentralization and network building change the manufacturing landscape: an Industry 4.0 perspective. Int. J. Mech. Aerosp. Ind. Mechatron. Manuf. Eng. **8**, 37–44 (2014)
31. Prifti, L., Knigge, M., Kienegger, H., Krcmar, H.: A competency model for "Industrie 4.0" employees. In: 13th International Conference on Wirtschaftsinformatik, pp. 46–60. St. Gallen, Switzerland (2017)
32. Cubero, S., Lee, W.S., Aleixos, N., Albert, F., Blasco, J.: Automated systems based on machine vision for inspecting citrus fruits from the field to postharvest—a review. Food Bioprocess Technol. **9**, 1623–1639 (2016)
33. Moriyama, S., Tanabe, H.: Traceability and identification solutions for secure and comfortable society. Hitachi Rev., 50–54 (2004)
34. UNESCAP: Information management in Agrifood Chains: towards an integrated paperless framework for agrifood trade facilitation. United Nations (2015)
35. Mira, J.J., Guilabert, M., Carrillo, I., Fernández, C., Vicente, M.A., Orozco-Beltrán, D., Gil-Guillen, V.F.: Use of QR and EAN-13 codes by older patients taking multiple medications for a safer use of medication. Int. J. Med. Inform. **84**, 406–412 (2015)
36. Zarei, S.: RFID in mobile supply chain management usage. Int. J. Comput. Sci. Technol. **1**, 11–20 (2010)
37. von Sivers, R., Sjögren, A.: Traceability in a sanitary ware production system–a case study at Ifö Sanitär (2013)
38. Quinteiro, P., Almeida, M., Dias, A.C., Araújo, A., Arroja, L.: The carbon footprint of ceramic products. In: Assessment of Carbon Footprint in Different Industrial Sectors, pp. 113–150. Springer Singapore (2014)
39. Amyot, D., Rashidi-Tabrizi, R., Mussbacher, G.: Improved GRL modeling and analysis with jUCMNav 5. In: Proceedings of the 6th International i* Workshop (iStar 2013), CEUR, vol. 978. pp. 137–139 (2013)
40. Barata, J., Cunha, P.R.: Mending the patchwork of requirements from multiple standards using participative goal modelling: a case in the food industry. Requir. Eng. (in press), pp. 1–17 (2017)
41. McFarlan, F.W.: Information technology changes the way you compete. Harv. Bus. Rev., May–June, 98–103 (1984)
42. Barata, J., Cunha, P.R., Stal, J.: Mobile supply chain management in the industry 4.0 era: an annotated bibliography and guide for future research. J. Enterp. Inf. Manag. 31, 173–192 (2018)
43. Andersen, P., Ross, J.W.: Transforming the LEGO Group for the Digital Economy. In: ICIS 2016 Proceedings. Dublin, Ireland (2016)

User Evaluations of an App Interface for Cloud-Based Identity Management

Farzaneh Karegar, Daniel Lindegren, John Sören Pettersson
and Simone Fischer-Hübner

Abstract Within a project developing cloud technology for identity access management, usability tests of the mock-up of a mobile app identity provider were conducted to assess Internet users' consciousness of data disclosures in consent forms and their comprehension of the flow of authentication data. Results show that using one's fingerprint for giving consent was easy, but most participants did not have a correct view of where the fingerprint data is used and what entities would have access to it. Familiarity with ID apps appeared to aggravate misunderstanding. In addition, participants could not well recall details of personal data releases and settings for disclosure options. An evaluation with a confirmation screen improved the recall rate slightly. However, some participants voiced a desire to have control over their data and expressed a wish to manually select mandatory information. This can be a way of slowing users down and make them reflect more.

Keywords Cloud computing · Identity management · Data disclosure
Usable privacy · Smartphone

A prior version of this paper has been published in the ISD2017 Proceedings (http://aisel.aisnet.org/isd2014/proceedings2017).

F. Karegar (✉) · D. Lindegren · J. S. Pettersson · S. Fischer-Hübner
Karlstad University, Karlstad, Sweden
e-mail: farzaneh.karegar@kau.se

D. Lindegren
e-mail: dlindegren93@gmail.com

J. S. Pettersson
e-mail: john_soren.pettersson@kau.se

S. Fischer-Hübner
e-mail: simone.fischer.huebner@kau.se

1 Introduction

On the Internet, people often need to prove their rights to access services by digitally authenticating themselves. They also need to provide personal information in that context. Helping service providers to trust users' information and users to trust that their personal information is not used for other purposes than they intend when providing it, is an important matter for our information society. In addition, usability issues arise with growing information and security demands.

CREDENTIAL[1] is an EU-funded Horizon 2020 project that involves developing, testing and presenting cloud-based services for storing, managing and sharing digital identity information and personal data with a higher level of security than existing technology.

The CREDENTIAL *Wallet* is the central component of the tools developed within the project. It offers a set of security and application services providing, among others, authentication and authorization mechanisms combined with novel cryptographic technologies like proxy re-encryption and malleable signatures. Some specific pilot cases are developed within the project to demonstrate how the CREDENTIAL technology can be deployed in diverse contexts.

In order to display the CREDENTIAL *Wallet* solution, the demonstrated system has to be equipped with user interfaces (UIs). Besides the pilot-specific user interfaces, there must also be some general user interfaces to demonstrate the functionality. The present study covers a set of three user tests ($n = 3 \times 20$ participants) made of the core functions of authorization and authentication to which the general user interfaces of the *Wallet* will give access. UI mock-ups were inserted in interactive prototypes in order to evaluate ordinary Internet users' management and consciousness of data disclosures in consent forms in a mobile app as well as to analyze their mental models of the flow of authentication data. The results are of general interests as they demonstrate the users' preferences, doubts, and misunderstandings of a type of identity management technology that could possibly be a facilitator in the ever-more digital economy of the world.

This presentation is structured in the following way. Section 2 gives an overview of the project from which this study stems. In Sect. 3, existing work on protecting users' privacy by improving permission dialogues and users' perceptions of data flow in the context of digital identity providers are described, and we point to lacunas in the body of previous studies. The questions that our user tests were addressing are presented in Sect. 4. Section 5 then elaborates on the set-up of the three tests. The results and related discussions, respectively, come in Sects. 6 and 7. Finally, Sect. 8 contains our concluding remarks and suggestions for future work.

---

[1]https://credential.eu/

2   Background to the Present Study: The CREDENTIAL Project

The goal of the CREDENTIAL project is to enable an information sharing network for cloud-based identity information in which *even the identity provider (IdP) cannot access the data in plain-text*; hence, the CREDENTIAL technology protects the data owner's right to define the right to access her/his personal data [1, 2]. This is achieved by using a proxy re-encryption (as defined by [3]), which enables the data encrypted by a user's private key to be transformed by a third party to data that can be decrypted by a recipient's private key with the help of a re-encryption key provided to the third party by the user.

CREDENTIAL's basic architecture [4] integrates cryptographic mechanisms for users, the *Wallet* (the third party acting as the IdP), and data receivers (web shops, cloud services, etc.).

- The User owns the data that are stored securely in encrypted form and can be shared with other account-holders in the CREDENTIAL *Wallet*. An application in the user's smartphone (and other devices) handles cryptographic operations involving the user's private key, such as encrypting the data, signing, or generating a re-encryption key.
- The *Wallet* is a cloud-based data storage and sharing service ensuring constant availability of the data on the Internet, scalability, and cost effectiveness. It uses multi-factor authentication and authorizes access to the data it stores. When a re-encryption key is available for some specific set of data as specified by the user, these data can be shared with specified receivers even if the user or his/her client application is not available.
- The Data Receiver, who can be either another person or a service provider, accesses data stored in the CREDENTIAL *Wallet* or authentication assertions issued by the *Wallet*.

The user authenticates to the *Wallet* to get read and write permissions to her *Wallet* account, which are used to upload signed and encrypted data. Upon a data request from, e.g., a website, the user provides the *Wallet* with a re-encryption key towards this data receiver and defines a "policy" specifying which data may be disclosed. These disclosure rules are stored in the *Wallet*, which uses the re-encryption key to re-encrypt the data. A receiver will thus receive encrypted data according to the disclosure rules and is able to decrypt the data (and to verify any digital signature on the disclosed data).

Within the project, three different pilots in the eGovernment, eHealth and eBusiness domains are developed [1, 4]. Some core functionalities will appear to any user of the CREDENTIAL technology; the personal *Wallet* account is important and accessed through an app on the data owner's smartphone (several access devices can be defined). The user interfaces of this app can be used to evaluate not only people's ability to use such an app but also for important general questions concerning people's understanding of consent-giving to data-disclosure and their appreciation of more privacy-friendly Single Sign-On (SSO) solutions than what is presently offered to the general public. Only a fraction of these user interfaces has been utilized here; the next section will present other studies within the field to highlight identified problems as well as lacunas in the research in order to explain our motivation in undertaking this study. In Sect. 4, we elaborate on the precise research questions we address in this paper.

3   Previous Studies

CREDENTIAL *Wallet*, acting as an identity provider (IdP) and a data access manager, supports users with its functionalities through a mobile application. As mentioned in Sect. 1, prototyping for a mobile app providing the authentication and authorization functionalities, we aimed at investigating people's understanding of the concept of signing up for and signing in to a service provider using an IdP providing its services via a mobile app and their perceptions of the data flow between entities when users share their personal information from the *Wallet* and give their consents via authorization dialogues.

Researchers have investigated users' comprehensions and attitudes towards using identity providers (e.g., OpenID or different social network identity providers) on the desktop enumerating some misconceptions and problems regarding understanding the data flow.

The most common in-use identity providers nowadays are social network SSO systems like Facebook in the first place and Twitter and Google the second [5]. Hence, the work on understanding people's information sharing is mainly focused on Facebook acting as an IdP. Besmer et al. [6] show that people are not aware of data sharing, its risks and implications using Facebook SSO. Robinson et al. [7] in line with Egelman [8] show that people have quite good general understanding of the information sharing using an IdP. However, it can be improved by designing better interfaces and help them to understand the exact information being shared. Also, Bauer et al. [9] conclude that people are somewhat aware of the range of attributes passed by the IdP to the service provider but aligned with Egelman's work [8] they emphasize the fact that due to habituation, people do not pay attention to the exact content of the consent forms and have some preconceptions about what is shared.

The number of mobile apps available has exploded over the past few years; many of them request permissions to access private data and resources, like user accounts or location. Users, however, are often unaware of this kind of access even though they must grant the required permissions upon app installation or updating processes. There have been studies on the app permission dialogues which investigate the effects of dialogues on people's decision-making and comprehensions and give new suggestions to improve the users' privacy [10, 11]. However, to the best of our knowledge, there is no previous work on the effectiveness of identity providers' authorization dialogues on mobile devices to help people understand what they are sharing with which entity, and the users' perceptions of data flow when they use a mobile application as an intermediary to sign up for a service provider.

Considering the problem of sharing information and giving the consent without a proper level of knowledge about what is shared in the context of identity providers, some researchers tried to improve front solutions to protect users' privacy by proposing more privacy-friendly designs. For example, Javed and Shehab [12, 13] utilize eye-tracking techniques and animation to enforce and grab users' attention towards permissions. Wang et al. [14, 15] propose new interfaces for Facebook authorization dialogue to eliminate the previous problems of the interfaces and improve the awareness and users' control over their personal data.

Besides lack of attention to and understanding of what is shared, people have incorrect mental models of the achieved security when they use an IdP. Studies by Sun et al. [16] and Arianezhad et al. [17] show that people believe their identity provider's passwords are shared with service providers. In the CREDENTIAL *Wallet* app, giving consent is done by entering a pin code or a single touch on the Touch ID to scan the fingerprint (only the latter was used in user tests reported below). That is, not only for signing in to the IdP but also for giving consent and confirming the information sharing shown in the authorization dialogue, users should scan their fingerprints (or enter the pin code) as this assures the identity of the user who gives the consent.

This paper reports, thus, on investigations into the users' consciousness of data disclosures in consent forms and the users' perception of the flow of authentication data.

4 Evaluation Goals

Even if a usability study can be thought of as aiming for a swiftly functioning service which users mindlessly can safely use, minimizing task completion times is not an aim in this study, but rather to find what are obstacles for users, especially as concerns their ideas—their mental models—of the solutions developed within the project.

The research focus was twofold:

- User's consciousness of data disclosures in consent forms
- User's mental models of the flow of authentication data.

More specifically, some auxiliary questions were developed before tests but also between them, namely:

i. Do users find this novel solution manageable and attractive?
ii. Does familiarity with an existing authentication application affect attractiveness?
iii. What are users' preferences for selection of mandatory data in consent dialogues?

iv. Do users pay attention to what data they consent to share? (Here: Do users pay enough attention to what data they consent to share to remember these after a few minutes?)

v. Would an extra confirmation page help them to pay attention?

vi. What are users' mental models and preferences for authentication method?

For this first evaluation of the CREDENTIAL UIs, we have made three user tests with users recruited outside of the project [18]. Task completion and duration were used as performance indicators. The SUS scale, i.e., System Usability Scale [19], was used for participants' estimation of how manageable and attractive they found the represented functionality. The SUS scale consists of 10 statements such as:

I think that I would like to use this system frequently.

I found the various functions in this system were well integrated.

The respondents comment by a Likert scale from *Strongly disagree* to *Strongly agree*.

In order to address questions of preferences, experience, and understandability, our usability tests were accompanied by also other questionnaires than the SUS scale.

User Test 1 was designed for the above general goals and participants were by convenience limited to people in Sweden familiar with the Swedish Mobile BankID[2] (17 out of 20 actually used the Mobile BankID and three others used Desktop BankID) which has the authentication capability of the CREDENTIAL app and is generally used.

User Test 2 paralleled Test 1: as the participants in Test 1, in general, liked the idea of the *Wallet* and had no problems in using the app, a second test was conducted where all participants had to be non-Swedish and unfamiliar with solutions like Swedish BankID. In order to simplify recruitment, the test was again conducted in and around our university, but with exchange students and visiting parents, and guest professors and newly arrived staff.

User Test 3 was also initiated based on the results from the first test. This time the prototype had an additional screen where participants had to re-confirm which data they authorized the *Wallet* to disclose to a certain receiver. Would this make people more likely to remember disclosure options? (We simplified the test to not include a second task present in Test 1 and 2 where participants were instructed to re-enter a website and simply sign in, i.e. "authenticate".)

---

[2]https://www.bankid.com/en/

5 User Test Design

5.1 Recruitment of Participants

The participants were recruited to create a sample that was evenly distributed in regard to age and sex—we did not analyze gender or age influence, but we balanced the sample to neutralize such effects. We set out to find participants with a wider age range than the ordinary students, which otherwise constitute a varied recruitment ground, why we included both students and personnel of our university in the sample (thus, age was balanced between young adults and mature adults). Most participants were pursuing their higher education or they had their higher education degrees already, and none of them were from Computer Science and Information Systems Departments but two in User Test 2 had basic computer science knowledge. For each test, 20 participants were recruited, equally distributed between men and women. For age, see Table 1.

The participants were recruited by the authors and internships (see the Acknowledgement section). Each participant was offered a coupon valid at one of the university canteens.

As the most widely used identity providers among Internet users are the SSO solutions provided by social networks, we asked the participants about their familiarity and experience in this context. All of the participants of the first and second user studies stated that they had seen social login buttons previously, and more than half of these 40 participants expressed that they use the social login buttons on websites like Spotify, Airbnb, SoundCloud and online TV providers. For the third study, this was not interrogated into as that study was meant to see the effect of the confirmation page on participants' ability to remember what data they ticked for sharing.

5.2 Test Procedure

The user tests were conducted using the screens for authentication and authorization (to data sharing) made interactive in Axure[3] (Test 1 and 3) and Ozlab[4] (Test 2) on an Android mobile phone and a prototype of a fictitious website for which the

Table 1 Age distribution in the three user tests

Age group	Test 1	Test 2	Test 3
Age 20–29	11	13	9
Age 30–39	3	2	1
Age 40–49	5	3	7
Age 50–70	1	2	3
Average	32.2	31.0	36.1

---

[3]https://www.axure.com/
[4]https://www.kau.se/en/ozlab/

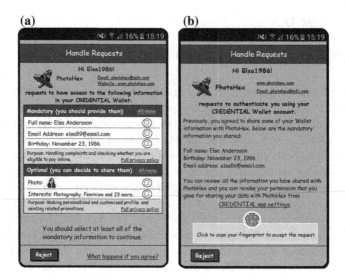

Fig. 1 **a** Authorization screen, and **b** authentication screen

participants were asked to pretend they wanted to sign up. Procedures were standardized to avoid bias of moderators/interviewers [20]. Authorization and authentication screens used in Test 1 and 2 are shown in Fig. 1, and Fig. 2 presents the confirmation screen in Test 3.

Participants were given a persona with a pre-defined set of personal information showing up in the CREDENTIAL app; by this, participants could feel secure that they were not compromising their own personal details for taking part in the study.[5] Moreover, it allowed full control of what each participant encountered, assuring a standard experience that can be compared between participants [21]. Thus, users were instructed to perform security-related tasks as the primary (and unreal) task of interaction, but the lack of ecological validity is not severely affecting the comparisons between the different tests as the premises remained the same.

Each session took 20–40 min and included an introduction and consent signing, a registration task, a questionnaire about this task including SUS grading, an authentication task (for Test 1 and 2) also followed by a questionnaire, and finally a general questionnaire with demographic data and follow-up questions about using

---

[5]No Ethical Approval was required by our IRB. Because we used personas, no personal data were used during the test and the data collected in the interviews were anonymous and included no sensitive data. Participation was completely voluntary with the option to withdraw at any time; informed consent was obtained from each participant. Therefore, under these conditions the Swedish *Etikprövningslagen* does not require any ethical approval.

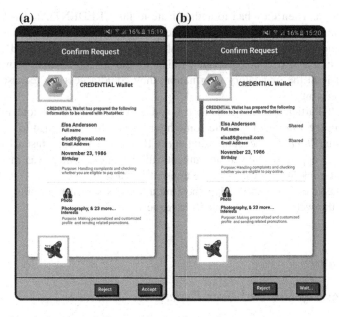

Fig. 2 Confirmation screen: **a** before, and **b** after the user's acceptance

fingerprint and data sharing. One moderator/interviewer and one note keeper were present during each session.

Besides the SUS form, the questionnaires aimed at investigating if participants paid attention to what personal information they shared with the website from the CREDENTIAL account during the authorization task. We asked about 14 different personal information types including the mandatory and optional information and fingerprint pattern. Moreover, we investigated to what extent the participants noticed the informative links in the UI to receive more information about what happens if they share their data with the website from their CREDENTIAL *Wallet*. Also, we were interested to see to what extent the participants' mental models and the way they think are compatible with what is happening nowadays when they use an IdP to share their data with other parties.

5.3 Description of Interactive Tasks

For more reproductions of the user interfaces, see [22] where data from User Test 1 is reported in detail (the same user interfaces were used in User Test 2 and 3, while an additional re-confirmation page was used in the app mock-up in the last test).

Task 1: Participants were asked to sign up (register) to the (fictitious) website *PhotoHex* using the CREDENTIAL button instead of the Facebook button and manual alternative shown on the same web page. They entered the user name of their persona. Then they had to authenticate to the CREDENTIAL *Wallet* app on the mobile phone and received the request from *PhotoHex* for their name, email address and birthday, and also (optional) profile photo and interest data (in the mock-up of the app "Photography, Feminism, and 23 more" were shown). After ticking at least the mandatory information, they could accept the request by using their fingerprint.

Task 2: Participants in User Test 1 and 2 were furthermore told to imagine re-entering the *PhotoHex* website some hours later. Now, they had to sign in (log in) to their *PhotoHex* account using the CREDENTIAL app. Instead of a data request, the app now showed an authentication request, which was made with a fingerprint click again, just as in the consent in Task 1.

Both tasks ended with the app showing a success screen informing the user to return to the webpage that initiated the request.

6   Results

6.1   Ease of Use and User Experience Metrics

Almost all 60 participants managed to complete the tasks given to them. In each of the first two user tests, two and three persons had a problem in Task 1 to find out how to continue; in the third test, there was a "Continue" button which no one missed. As for completion time, the tests with two tasks showed a clear decrease in completion time between the two tasks (on average from 100 to 57 s in Test 1; from 62 to 44 s in Test 2). During the study, some participants mentioned that it is always hard when one is using an app for the first time. This show that users are expecting some initial efforts in order to be soon rewarded by a more fluent and quicker use.

Also, the SUS values in Table 2 reflect this: compared to two of the grading scales presented in [23] that are based on a high number of answers from different studies, the CREDENTIAL app in its mock-up dress was perceived as "Good" which definitively is within the "Acceptable" range. However, other responses showed participants confusing data disclosed with other data. In fact, as User Test 1 demonstrated these good SUS values, the evaluation went further to not only

Table 2 SUS scores after each task

Test	Test 1		Test 2		Test 3
Task	Task 1	Task 2	Task 1	Task 2	Task 1
Aver.	75.88	81.98	78.19	85.86	78.25
St. Dev.	11.74	11.69	13.98	12.29	18.24
Min.	47.50	57.50	50.00	47.50	35
Max.	95.13	97.50	100.0	100.0	100

balance BankID users/non-users (Test 2) but also to see the effects of a separate confirmation screen in which selected data were listed (Test 3).

6.2 Expressed Preference for Data Selection

When asked in the questionnaire after the first task whether they preferred to have to manually tick checkboxes ("i.e., an interface as in the current task") or to have all the mandatory information selected by default, a majority of the participants in the three tests wanted to select the mandatory information manually (15 in Test 1, and 13 in each of Test 2 and 3). This puts the time and SUS values in perspective: speed is not the top priority for many users.

6.3 Recall of Consents to Data Disclosure

In line with other studies (Sect. 3), we found that people do not pay sufficient attention to details of data releases and settings for disclosure policies.

Only two of the 60 participants could correctly identify in a list of fourteen items what information was shared from the CREDENTIAL app with the website. In the UI prototype of the app, the mandatory information consisted of full name, birthday and email address. All participants accepted the request in the authorization task so all of them shared the information with the website (*PhotoHex* in the study). However, in Test 1 and 2, a few participants ticked "no" when asked to state if they shared the full name, email address, and birthday. Interestingly, some did not seem to notice that when they shared their birthdays, they implicitly shared their ages (the screen showed the date with year number): some participants did not have consistent answers for their birthdates and ages. A handful in each test ticked "no" for age but many, especially in Test 2, showed uncertainty and chose "not sure". In Test 1, two participants, who were not sure if the birthday was shared, ticked that the age was shared.

For optional information, some selected to share all the optional information when doing the authorization tasks but not all of them remembered properly what they shared. In Test 2, 12 people shared "interest" but only 3 remembered having done so. Also, some of the people who did *not* share the optional information did not remember correctly if they shared a photo or their interests. Photo sharing was more remembered than sharing interests. For instance, in Test 1, regarding the photo, just two participants answered incorrectly but for sharing the interests five participants were not successful to correctly answer the questions. As an example of test results, Table 3 shows the numbers of participants in User Test 1 who ticked "yes", "no" or "not sure" for each piece of information.

In the list of information types, we included items that were not on the authorization screen of the app, such as hometown, credit card number and educational

Table 3 Distribution of "yes", "no", and "not sure" answers in user Test 1

Information	Yes		No		Not sure	Sum
	Correct	Incorrect	Correct	Incorrect		
Your post address	N/A	4	9	N/A	7	20
Your full name[a]	15	N/A	N/A	4	1	20
Your email address[a]	17	N/A	N/A	1	2	20
Your educational background	N/A	0	16	N/A	3	19[c]
Your fingerprint pattern	N/A	17	2	N/A	1	20
Your home town	N/A	1	11	N/A	8	20
The city in which you live	N/A	1	11	N/A	8	20
Your birthday[a]	14	N/A	N/A	3	3	20
A photo of yours[b]	6	2	12	0	0	20
Your phone number	N/A	2	12	N/A	5	19[c]
Your interests[b]	4	2	10	3	1	20
Your credit card number	N/A	1	16	N/A	3	20
Your age ([a]by implication)	14	N/A	N/A	3	3	20
Your mobile device model	N/A	1	10	N/A	9	20

N/A not applicable
[a]Mandatory information ("birthday" included year number in the mock-up)
[b]These were presented in the UI as optional choices. Six participants chose to share both photos and interests and one participant shared only the interests. The remaining thirteen selected just the mandatory data
[c]One participant forgot to answer

background. Interestingly, some people incorrectly stated that some of this information was shared with the website. Among all the information being asked that was shared or not, people were most successful at remembering about sharing the photo and were most unsuccessful at understanding if they shared the fingerprint with the website.

Would people fare better if a separate confirmation page was shown in order to reinforce the impression of the selected data? User Test 3 was designed for this comparison. Before calculating ratios of successful mentioning of the correct pieces of information, it is important to realize that the ratios are dependent on how many alternatives our questionnaire contained. To better report the awareness of participants of personal data being shared we measured the relevance of responses using precision and recall. Ronen et al. [24] used these measurements to report people's awareness of data exposures when using a federated identity provider to sign in to websites. Ronen and co-workers defined the precision (P) as the ratio between the number of data types a participant named correctly and the number of data types the participant named, and defined the Recall (R) as the ratio between the number of

Table 4 Precision and recall values excluding "age" (values for method one in brackets)

Test	Test 1		Test 2		Test 3	
	Precision	Recall	Precision	Recall	Precision	Recall
Avg.	0.80 (0.68)	0.79	0.75 (0.72)	0.70	0.80 (0.68)	0.86
St. Dev.	0.14	0.22	0.18	0.17	0.14	0.18
Min.	0.46	0.33	0.33	0.40	0.58	0.50
Max.	1.00	1.00	1.00	1.00	1.00	1.00

data types a participant named correctly and the number of data types that were actually transferred to the website.

In order to better see people's degree of certainty, we let them tick either "yes", "no", "not sure" for *every* data type. The self-expressed uncertainty averaged to 21, 30 and 22% in the three tests, i.e. rather high which is interesting and speaks for solutions like the Data Track presented in [21]. The option to tick "not sure" instead of what sometimes might have been "yes" made us calculate precision in two ways. Method One was as Ronen's calculation by interpreting "not sure" as "no"; thus only "yes" answers were counted. Method Two calculated precision as the proportion of all correct "yes" *and* "no" to *all* "yes" and "no" per person.

In Table 4, the related average, standard deviation, minimum and maximum for recall and precision are reported with brackets around Method One values. "Age" was removed from the table as some respondents might have thought of explicit consent rather than what "Birthday" implies. (Two participants in Test 1 did not answer all the questions for data being shared; their responses are excluded from these calculations.)

Although the average numbers are not very low, the distribution figures show that many had a rather limited awareness of the data types being transferred. The average recall rate for the 38 participants included in Table 4 for Test 1 and 2 is 0.74, while Test 3, with its extra confirmation page, had a notably higher Recall rate. Recall rates did not correlate with age ($R^2 = 0.006$ counted on all 58 participants).

The prototype contained the very common multi-layered approach to present the necessary data for informed consent (for instance, a multi-layered approach is argued by the Art. 29 Working Party [25]). The only participant who actually opened the full information did not show any remembrance of this when answering the questionnaire afterwards.

6.4 Mental Model and Preference for Authentication via an App

In User Test 1, most participants seemed to understand that they used the CREDENTIAL *Wallet* mock-up to authenticate, but this could depend on their previous experience with a similar solution as explained in Sect. 4. That would bias the conclusion about the acceptability of this technology if not other subjects, for instance from other countries, are included. The User Test 2, however, showed that inexperience of this type of authentication did not affect the SUS values (cf. Table 2). User Test 3 merely confirmed previous results.

Nonetheless, some participants were worried about the security and thereby also the privacy because they could not really figure out how it worked. The single point of failure (as it is called in the literature, that is, if the one and only IdP malfunctions, the user is at a loss) could be a cause of the worries but in fact, only a handful participants mentioned this: either that hacking gives wide access to users' information or that dropping the phone inhibits users' access to the CREDENTIAL app.

Using the fingerprint for giving consent (at the same screen requesting for the personal information in authorization dialogue, for example) was from a simple usability perspective not a problem, but from the post-task questions it is obvious that most of the participants did not know that the pattern is processed only locally. Table 3 shows that in User Test 1, almost all participants (17 out of 20) thought the fingerprint pattern was forwarded to the web service requesting some data. In Test 2, seven people thought so. The mistaken view of authentication data disclosure is reflected in the answers to the last questionnaire in the user tests which included a question "Where do you think that your fingerprint is stored and processed?" Table 5 lists the number of respondents that selected one or several of three alternatives.

On a question "What do you think about using your fingerprint to agree to share your personal data?" four participants in User Test 1 and thirteen in Test 2 expressed that they did not like to use their fingerprints and said they prefer passwords. One explained that it was not pleasant to give the consent with the fingerprint because it might be saved and used in unwanted ways. Others thought it could be hacked.

Table 5 Perceived storage and processing location for fingerprint

Where is the fingerprint stored?	Test 1	Test 2	Test 3
Mobile device (correct answer)	4	9	5
CREDENTIAL app	11	6	8
Mobile and app	2	2	5
App and website	2	0	0
Mobile, app, website	1	2	1
Website	0	1	1

7 Discussion

Like our study, Bauer et al. [9] demonstrated that participants' precise under-standing of what is sent is not significantly affected by the consent dialogues (instead, as that study indicates, it is affected by their privacy concern level and that they have some preconceptions about what is going to be sent). Egelman [8] also showed that participants did not read the authorization dialogues and they did not pay attention to the details of the dialogues during the test.

Interestingly, the extra step of being confronted with a confirmation screen, which simply repeated what had already been agreed to, made the recall value rise in Test 3 as well as the minimum values. The recall rate of 0.86 can be compared with 0.74 which is the average for the 38 persons from Test 1 and 2 included in Table 4. As neither of these two tests included the confirmation screen, it seems that there are reasons to evaluate the impact of confirmation screens also in future studies, and possibly leave it as the default option when requests concern several data types, even if users may be able to switch it off.

As mentioned in Sect. 6.2, when asked in the questionnaire after the first task, a majority of the participants in the three tests wanted to select the mandatory information manually. This can be a way of slowing users down and thus make them reflect more. We do not mean that people should feel obstructed, but the design should make people more actively see or choose the data to be disclosed and the conditions for the disclosure. Nevertheless, the results in Sect. 6.3 show that in spite of the selection that our test participants had to do, they had in fact rather vague ideas of what they had "consented" to share with *PhotoHex*. This principle could be pursued further (as we will do) to see if a more explicit action of data selection, such as drag-and-drop, would instill a better impression on users' short-term memory.

Even if the data in Table 5 is not consistent with the numbers on the "finger-print" row of Table 3 (which covers Test 1, but similar results were obtained in the other tests), it is anyhow obvious that many people do not understand how "local" this authentication is. The results concerning the fingerprint are in agreement with the studies by Sun et al. [16] and Arianezhad et al. [17] which show people have incorrect mental models about the achieved security when using IdPs to sign up. Nevertheless, more investigations are needed to see if the problem is related to using the fingerprint for giving consent or in general it relates to the lack of knowledge about how fingerprint works on the mobile phones. There are a few works on users' experiences, attitudes, and adoption decisions scanning the fin-gerprint to unlock their mobile devices [26]. Recently, in parallel to our study, Javed et al. [27] investigated the users' comprehension and risk perception of Apple's Touch ID technology. They conducted some user studies to assess users' perceptions of Touch ID authentication process for third party applications and fingerprint access and storage. Javed's et al. [27] findings show that Touch ID users are unaware of the Touch ID authentication process for signing into mobile apps on their phones, and have incorrect perceptions regarding the storage and access of their registered fingerprint before and after Touch ID authentication. However, there seems to be no research on people's understanding and perceptions of the fingerprint when it is used in the context of identity providers to give consent.

The Swedish respondents in Test 1 and 3 seem to be more ill-informed than the foreign visitors to Sweden in Test 2.[6] This was not really why we conducted the tests, but the results raise intriguing questions. Can the cause be the Mobile BankID? Do the users trust the app that the banks trust? Whatever the cause for the misunderstanding, the implication can be seen in answers to other questions. For example, the data briefly accounted in the last paragraph of Sect. 6.4 point to a hesitance to embrace the fingerprint method. There is an immediate remedy: in order to follow the Android standard, the UI should contain alternatives, for instance a pin code. Of course, this can be elaborated further: will users think that the pin code is sent to web services?

While comprehension is most important, ease of use is of interest as it too will affect adoption [2, 29]. Ruoti et al. [30] have studied the usability of seven authentication systems including federated SSO systems like Google OAuth 2.0 and Facebook Connect. In their study, they defined three groups of authentication techniques and the method which won in each group was also compared and tested for SUS score with the winners of the two other groups. In the final analysis, Google OAuth was the winner between different technologies with the SUS score of 75. Our average SUS scores for the CREDENTIAL app, both for authentication and authorization task, align with Ruoti's study.

Finally, a limitation of our study is that inferential statistics results have not been sought. This is a natural outcome of a project which still produces tentative user interfaces for several alternative ways of making data selection in authorization dialogues (we intend to contribute to Privacy Pattern research [31]). Testing of new alternatives makes the total numbers of participants being big enough for some inferential statistics. In a later study, it was possible by summing up over several different modes of selection to reach statistically significant results concerning, e.g., young adults being quicker than mature adults while no significant difference was found in recall rates between age groups. These results cannot be summarized here as the different selection modes deserve a more elaborate treatment in order to make explicit what has been subject to evaluation. Likewise, not every aspect needs to be analyzed by inferential statistics: while the interesting difference between BankID users and non-users is significant, similar calculations for data types requested in authorization dialogues would be based on the individual data types (such as "Your post address") and this is not of a general interest and, furthermore, not within the scope of this study.

---

[6]Despite the non-random sampling, attempting an hypothesis test comparing proportions π of persons answering correctly with H_0: $\pi_{BankID} - \pi_{no} = 0$ and H_1: $\pi_{BankID} - \pi_{no} < 0$, one gets at a significance level $p < 0.05$ that the proportion of non-BankID users answering only "Mobile Device" is larger than the proportion of BankID users doing that [28].

8 Conclusions: A Way Forward for Identity Access Management GUI Design

In sum, further evaluation is required concerning how people would understand what data are needed, how to select these, and what data are actually sent. Our results suggest that a confirmation screen can be a default option in authorization (consent) dialogues.

The desire expressed by many to select the mandatory information manually can be explored as a way of slowing users down and make them reflect more.

Also, user evaluation should be conducted for more compound data disclosure from cloud-based wallets. Projections as in the CREDENTIAL project [22] to use secure data sharing also for authorization requests concerning file-based data (documents such as signed documents and health records), will need careful design to avoid that users select wrong files, especially if data are not directly visible in an app for the identity access management.

Fears of the single point of failure and other misconceptions are clearly a problem. While the fact that data are only stored in encrypted (i.e. protected) form in the *Wallet* in the cloud could be communicated to the user with stronger emphasis, informing the user about the remaining privacy issues in regard to the meta information that the cloud provider is gaining about the user's usage of services remains a challenge (see also [2]). The comparison of BankID users with others indicates that trust is trust in an actor (bank), not in the system, which can possibly lead to a skewed mental model of what should be trusted. This calls for educating the general public besides designing usable user interfaces.

Acknowledgements This work has received funding from the European Union's Horizon 2020 research and innovation programme under grant agreement number 653454. The authors want to thank Caroline Kayser and Manuel Gawert who conducted the data collection for the second user test (Farzaneh Karegar and Daniel Lindegren made the original prototypes and conducted the first user test, and Lindegren conducted the third user test), Charlotte Bäccman who reviewed a project report and helped with an initial set of participants, and Dan Larsson who discussed how to compare proportions.

References

1. Hörandner, F., Krenn, S., Migliavacca, A., Thiemer, F., Zwattendorfer, B.: CREDENTIAL: a framework for privacy-preserving cloud-based data sharing. In: 11th International Conference on Availability, Reliability and Security (ARES), pp. 742–749 (2016)
2. Karegar, F., Striecks, Ch., Krenn, S., Hörandner, F., Lorünser, T., Fischer-Hübner, S.: Opportunities and challenges of CREDENTIAL. Towards a metadata-privacy respecting identity provider. In: Lehmann A., et al. (eds.) Privacy and Identity 2016, IFIP AICT 498, pp. 76–91. Springer, Berlin (2016)
3. Blaze, M., Bleumer, G., Strauss, M.: Divertible protocols and atomic proxy cryptography. In: Nyberg, K. (eds.) EUROCRYPT'98, vol. 1403 of LNCS, pp. 127–144. Springer, Berlin (1998)

4. Kostopoulos, A., Sfakianakis, E., Chochliouros, I., Pettersson, J.S., Krenn, S., Tesfay, W., Migliavacca, A., Hörandner, F.: Towards the adoption of secure cloud identity services. In: Proceedings of the 12th International Conference on Availability, Reliability and Security (ARES'17), Article 90, 7 p. ACM (2017)
5. Vapen, A., Carlsson, N., Mahanti, A., Shahmehri, N.: Information sharing and user privacy in the third-party identity management landscape. In: IFIP International Information Security Conference, pp. 174–188. Springer International (2015)
6. Besmer, A., Lipford, A.H.: Users' (mis)conceptions of social applications. In: Proceedings of Graphics Interface 2010, pp. 63–70. Canadian Information Processing Society (2010)
7. Robinson, N., Bonneau. J.: Cognitive disconnect: understanding facebook connect login permissions. In: Proceedings of the Second ACM Conference on Online Social Networks, pp. 247–258. ACM (2014)
8. Egelman, S.: My profile is my password, verify me!: the privacy/convenience tradeoff of Facebook connect. In: Proceedings of the SIGCHI Conference on Human Factors in Computing Systems, pp. 2369–2378. ACM (2013)
9. Bauer, L., Bravo-Lillo, C., Fragkaki, E., Melicher, W.: A comparison of users' perceptions of and willingness to use Google, Facebook, and Google+ single-sign-on functionality. In: Proceedings of the 2013 ACM Workshop on Digital Identity Management, pp. 25–36. ACM (2013)
10. Liccardi, I., Pato, J., Weitzner, D.J., Abelson, H., De Roure, D.: No technical understanding required: helping users make informed choices about access to their personal data. In: Proceedings of the 11th International Conference on Mobile and Ubiquitous Systems: Computing, Networking and Services, pp. 140–150. ICST (2014)
11. Van Kleek, M., Liccardi, I., Binns, R., Zhao, J., Weitzner, D.J., Shadbolt, N.: Better the devil you know: exposing the data sharing practices of smartphone apps. In: CHI'17. ACM (2017) (forthcoming)
12. Javed, Y., Shehab, M.: Investigating the animation of application permission dialogs: a case study of Facebook. In: International Workshop on Data Privacy Management, pp. 146–162. Springer International Publishing (2016)
13. Javed, Y., Shehab. M.: Look before you authorize: using eye-tracking to enforce user attention towards application permissions. Proc. Priv. Enhancing Technol. 2017(2), 23–37 (2017)
14. Wang, N., Grossklags, J., Xu, H.: An online experiment of privacy authorization dialogues for social applications. In: Proceedings of the 2013 Conference on Computer Supported Cooperative Work, pp. 261–272. ACM (2013)
15. Wang, N., Xu, H., and Grossklags, J.: Third-party Apps on Facebook: privacy and the illusion of control. In: Proceedings of the 5th ACM Symposium on Computer human Interaction for Management of Information Technology, p. 4. ACM (2011)
16. Sun, S.-T., Pospisil, E., Muslukhov, I., Dindar, N., Hawkey, K., Beznosov, K.: What makes users refuse web single sign-on?: An empirical investigation of OpenID. In: Proceedings of the Seventh Symposium on Usable Privacy and Security, pp. 4:1–20. ACM (2011)
17. Arianezhad, M., Jean Camp, L., Kelley, T., Stebila, D.: Comparative eye tracking of experts and novices in web single sign-on. In: Proceedings of the Third ACM Conference on Data and Application Security and Privacy, pp. 105–116. ACM (2013)
18. Rubin, J., Chisnell, D.: Handbook of Usability Testing: How to Plan, Design and Conduct Effective Tests. Wiley, NJ (2008)
19. Brooke, J.: SUS: a "quick and dirty" usability scale. In: Jordan, P.W., Thomas, B., Weerdmeester, B.A., McClelland, I.L. (eds.) Usability Evaluation in Industr, pp. 189–194. Taylor and Francis, London (1996)

20. Onwuegbuzie, A.J., Leech, N.L.: Validity and qualitative research: an oxymoron? Qual. Quant. **41**(2), 233–249 (2007)
21. Karegar, F., Pulls, T., Fischer-Hübner, S.: Visualizing exports of personal data by excercising the right of data portability in the data track—are people ready for this? In: Lehman, A., et al. (eds.) Privacy and Identity Management. Facing up to Next Steps, pp. 164.181. Springer, Berlin (2016)
22. D3.1 UI Prototypes V1.: Deliverable from the project CREDENTIAL (2017). Available at: credential.eu/publications/deliverables/d3-1-ui-prototypes-v1/
23. Bangor, A., Kortum, P., Miller, J.: Determining what individual SUS scores mean: adding an adjective rating scale. J. Usability Stud. **4**(3), 114–123 (2009)
24. Ronen, S., Riva, O., Johnson, M., Thompson, D.: Taking data exposure into account: how does it affect the choice of sign-in accounts? In: Proceedings of the SIGCHI Conference on Human Factors in Computing Systems CHI'13, pp. 3423–3426. ACM (2013)
25. Art. 29 Data Protection Working Party: Opinion 10/2004 on More Harmonised Information Provisions. (November 25th, 2004). 11987/04/EN WP 100. European Commission (2004)
26. Bhagavatula, C., Ur, B., Iacovino, K., Kywe, S.M., Cranor, L.F., Savvides, M.: Biometric authentication on iPhone and Android: usability, perceptions, and influences on adoption. In: Proceedings of USEC 2015 (2015)
27. Javed, Y., Shehab, M., Bello-Ogunu, E.: Investigating user comprehension and risk perception of Apple's touch ID technology. In: Proceedings of the 12th International Conference on Availability, Reliability and Security (ARES'17). Article 35, 6 p. ACM (2017)
28. Lind, D., Marchal, W., Wathen, S.: Two-sample tests about proportions. In: Statistical Techniques in Business & Economics, 17th ed., pp. 550ff. McGraw-Hill (2017)
29. Davis, F.D.: Perceived Usefulness, perceived ease of use, and user acceptance of information technology. MIS Q. **13**(3), 319–339 (1989)
30. Ruoti, S., Roberts, B. Seamons, K.: Authentication melee: a usability analysis of seven web authentication systems. In: Proceedings of the 24th International Conference on World Wide Web (Republic and Canton of Geneva, Switzerland), WWW'15, pp. 916–926. International World Wide Web Conferences Steering Committee, (2015)
31. Lenhard, J., Fritsch, L., Herold, S.: A literature study on privacy patterns research. In: 43rd Euromicro Conference on Software Engineering and Advanced Applications, pp. 194–201 (2017)

User-Friendly and Extensible Web Data Extraction

T. Novella and I. Holubová

Abstract Creation of web wrappers is a subject of study in the field of web data extraction. Designing a domain-specific language for a web wrapper is a challenging task, because it introduces tradeoffs between expressiveness of a wrapper's language and safety. In addition, little attention has been paid to execution of a wrapper in a restricted environment. In this paper we present a new wrapping language—Serrano—that has three goals: (1) ability to run in a restricted environment, such as a browser extension, (2) extensibility to balance the tradeoffs between expressiveness of a command set and safety, and (3) processing capabilities to eliminate the need for additional programs to clean the extracted data. Serrano has been successfully deployed in a number of projects and provided competitive results.

Keywords Web data extraction · Safe execution · Restricted environment
Web browser extension

1 Introduction

Since the dawn of the Internet, the amount of available information has been steadily growing every year. Email, social networks, knowledge bases, discussion forums—they all contribute to the rapid growth of data. These data are targeted for human consumption, therefore, the structure tends to be loose. Although humans can easily make sense of unstructured and semi-structured data, machines fall short

A prior version of this paper has been published in the ISD2017 Proceedings (http://aisel.aisnet.
org/isd2014/proceedings2017).

T. Novella · I. Holubová (✉)
Charles University, Prague, Czechia
e-mail: holubova@ksi.mff.cuni.cz

T. Novella
e-mail: tomasnovella@gmail.com

© Springer International Publishing AG, part of Springer Nature 2018   225
N. Paspallis et al. (eds.), *Advances in Information Systems Development*,
Lecture Notes in Information Systems and Organisation 26,
https://doi.org/10.1007/978-3-319-74817-7_14

and have a much harder time doing so. Automation of data extraction therefore gives companies a competitive edge: instead of time-consuming and tedious human-driven extraction and processing, they become orders of magnitude more productive, which leads to higher profits and more efficient resource usage. With the advent of new web technologies, such as AJAX [1], and the rise of the Web 2.0 [2], simple raw manipulation of HTML [3] proved no longer sufficient. As a result, extraction tools have started being bundled with an HTML layout rendering engine, or have been built on top of a web browser to be able to keep up with modern standards. Extraction tools have evolved to be more user-friendly; many came with a wizard—an interactive user interface—that allowed for convenient generation of wrappers. All this evolves in the direction to increase wrapper maintainability, which helps to take on incrementally larger tasks. Major challenges facing the tools available currently on the market are as follows:

• Data manipulation Tools, even the recent ones, provide only a restricted way of data manipulation, such as data trimming and cleaning. These tasks are often delegated to separate tools and modules, which may be detrimental to wrapper maintenance, considering it leads to unnecessary granularization of a single responsibility, since there have to be additional programs that process the data that are pertinent to the given wrapper.
• Extensibility With the rapid evolution of web technologies, many tools soon become obsolete due to the inability to easily extend the tool to support modern technologies.
• Execution in restricted (browser) environment New execution environments have emerged, which gives rise to novel applications of data extraction. Examples include web browser extensions (in-browser application), which help to augment the user browsing experience. These environments are restricted in terms of programming languages they execute and system resources. Besides, script execution safety is another concern.

In this paper we propose a novel data extraction language, Serrano, which deals with all the three mentioned problems. In Sect. 2 we overview the related work. In Sect. 3 we introduce the Serrano language. Section 4 showcases the user stories, Sect. 5 discusses the advantages of Serrano and Sect. 6 concludes.

2 Related Work

Inspired by [4] in this paper we define a web wrapper as a procedure for seeking and finding data, extracting them from web sources, and transforming them into structured data. The exact definition of a wrapper varies and it is often interchanged with the definition of the extraction toolkit [5], a software extracting, automatically and repeatedly, data from websites with changing contents, and that delivers extracted data to a database or another application. Toolkits are often equipped with a GUI that features an internal WebView that represents a tab in a browser to facilitate wrapper generation. Typically, a user manipulates with the web inside the WebView in order to obtain the desired data. User actions are recorded as DOM [6] events, such as form filling, clicking on elements, authentication, output data identification, and a web wrapper is generated. This wrapper can run either in the toolkit environment, or separately packaged with a wrapper execution environment. After the execution additional operations may be implemented, such as data cleaning [7], especially when information is collected from multiple sources. Finally, extracted data are saved in a structured form in a universal format, such as XML [8], JSON [9], or into a database.

One of the first endeavors to classify Web Data Extraction toolkits [4] proposed a taxonomy for grouping tools based on the main technique used by each tool to generate a wrapper. Tools were divided into six categories: languages for wrapper development (e.g., TSIMMIS [10]), HTML-aware tools (e.g., W4F [11]), NLP-based tools (e.g., RAPIER [12]), wrapper induction tools (e.g., WIEN [13]), modeling-based Tools (e.g., NODoSE [14]) and ontology-based tools (e.g., DIADEM [15]). Most wrappers combine two or three of underlying techniques for locating data in the documents to compensate for their deficiencies. We can distinguish regular expression-based approaches (e.g., W4F), tree-based approaches (e.g., OXPath [16]), declarative approaches (e.g., Elog [17]), spatial reasoning (e.g., SXPath [18]), and machine-learning based approaches (e.g., RAPIER). In [19], the authors identify and provide a detailed analysis of 14 enterprise applications of data extraction.

3 Serrano Language

This section examines and explains why Serrano was designed the way it was. For a complete in-depth specification, the reader is referred to the official language specification.[1] The source codes as well as playground projects can be found on Github[2] and are written in Javascript.

Gottlob [20] presented four desiderata that would make an ideal extraction language:

1. Solid and well-understood theoretical foundation Serrano uses jQuery[3] selectors, a superset of CSS selectors, for locating elements on the web page. These technologies have been studied in depth along with their limitations and computational complexity. Serrano wrapper is a valid JSON and every command corresponds to a Javascript command.

---

[1]https://github.com/salsita/Serrano/wiki/Language-Spec.

[2]https://github.com/salsita/Serrano/tree/master/serrano-library.

[3]https://jquery.com/.

2. A good trade-off between complexity and the number of practical wrappers that can be expressed One of Serrano's cornerstones is extensibility. Currently, the language can only locate elements by CSS selectors and simulate mouse events. Nevertheless, the command set can be easily extended so that a larger range of wrappers can be expressed.
3. Gentle learning curve Many Serrano commands have the same name and arguments as their Javascript counterparts.
4. Suitability for incorporation into visual tools Selector identification is a task already handled by browsers in the Developer Tools extension. There is no obvious obstacle that would prevent us from incorporating selected Serrano commands into a visual tool.

In order to make a language easy to integrate with Javascript, we leveraged JSON. In contrast to other data transmission formats, such as XML, JSON has been strongly integrated into Javascript, which eliminates the need of additional helper libraries for processing. In Serrano, both the wrapper and the result are valid JSON objects. This makes them convenient to transform and manipulate: they can be passed around via AJAX, or altered via Javascript directly, since they are represented by a built-in object type.

Moreover, Javascript libraries such as Lodash[4] further extend object manipulation capabilities. To deal with extensibility, Serrano has separated the command set and allows to create custom commands. Examples of such extension are commands for document editing which makes Serrano, to the best of our knowledge, the first data extraction as well as data editing language used in the browser. With a simple extension of a command set, we can allow Serrano to manipulate the native Javascript window object, manage user credentials[5] or change the page location. This offers expressive power and control beyond the range of most extraction tools. Wrapper maintainability is another design goal. Powerful commands, such as conditions and type checks, make it possible to write verification inside the wrapper.

3.1 Type System

Serrano type system inherits from the Javascript type system. It supports all types that are transferable via JSON natively; that is *number, string, boolean, undefined, null* and *object* as well as some additional Javascript types, such as *Date* and *Regexp*.

---

[4]https://lodash.com/.

[5]http://w3c.github.io/webappsec-credential-management/.

3.2   Scraping Directive

The basic building block is called a scraping directive. It represents a piece of code that evaluates to a single value. There are 3 types of scraping directives: *command, selector* and *instruction.*

Command

Commands are the core control structure of Serrano. As such, they appear similar to functions in common programming languages; in that they have a name and arguments. However, their use is much broader. Serrano has commands such as !if for conditions, logical commands such as !and, !or, commands for manipulation with numbers and arrays of numbers, such as !+, !-, !*, !/ etc. Elevating the strength of commands and making them the central control structure is the cornerstone of flexibility and extensibility: all control structures are of the same kind and adding/ removing these structures is a part of an API. Although some languages, such as Selenium IDE,[6] make it possible to write plugins and extensions of default command sets,[7] we did not find any wrapping language that allows to add and remove any command control structure arbitrarily.

Syntactically, a command is a JSON array, where the first element has a string type denoting the command name followed by arguments (the rest of the array).

Below, we present an example of the !replace command with three string arguments.

```
["!replace", "hello world", "hello", "goodbye"]
```

In this example, !replace is the command name, which has three arguments, namely hello world, hello and goodbye. This command returns a new string based on an old string (supplied as a first argument) with all matches of a pattern, be it a string or a regular expression (second argument) replaced by a replacement (third argument). Finally, the command returns the string goodbye world.

Raw arguments

Command arguments, unless stated explicitly otherwise, have implicit evaluation. That means, when an argument of a command is another scraping directive, it is first evaluated and only then the return value supplied. However, this behavior is not always desired. Because of this, the command specification determines which arguments should be raw (not processed). An example of such a command is the ! constant command, that takes one raw argument and returns it. Had the argument not been specified as raw, the constant command would return a string "hello mars".

---

[6]https://addons.mozilla.org/en-US/firefox/addon/selenium-ide/.

[7]http://www.seleniumhq.org/docs/08_user_extensions.jsp##chapter08-reference.

```
["!constant", ["!replace", "hello world", "world", "mars"]] ⇒ ["!replace", "hello
world", "world", "mars"]
```

Implicit foreach

By default, commands have a so-called implicit foreach. That means, when the first argument of the command is an array, the interpreter engine automatically loops through the array, and applies the command to each element, returning a list of results. It is also known as the map behavior. Conversely, when a command does not have an implicit foreach, the first argument is passed as-is, despite being an array.

An example illustrates two commands. Command !upper has the implicit foreach enabled. Thus, it loops through the array of strings and returns a new array containing the strings in upper case. The second command !at has the implicit foreach functionality disabled; therefore is selects the third element in the array. (Had it been enabled for !at, the command would return the third letter of each string, namely the following array ["e", "o", "r", "u"].)

```
//implicit foreach enabled for !upper
["!upper", ["!constant", ["hello", "world"] ] ] ⇒ ["HELLO", "WORLD"]
//implicit foreach disabled for !at
["!at", ["!constant", ["one", "two", "three", "four"] ], 2] ⇒ "three"
```

Selector

A selector is used for extracting specific elements from the web page. It is denoted as a single-item array, containing only one element (of type string) that is prefixed with one of the characters $, =, ~ and followed by a string indicating the selector name. This selector name is treated as a CSS selector (more precisely, a jQuery selector[8]).

From the low-level perspective, a selector is syntactic sugar for the !jQuery command (which takes one or two arguments and evaluates them as a jQuery selector command[9]) and the different kinds of selectors are syntactically "desugarized" as follows:

- **Dollar sign** This is the basic type of selectors. ["$selector"] is treated as ["!jQuery", "selector"] which internally invokes the $("selector") jQuery method.
- **Equal sign** Selectors that start with this sign, i.e., ["=selector"] are treated as an instruction [["$selector"], [">!call", "text"]]. The important thing is, that after selecting specific elements, the text value of the selector is returned, which internally corresponds to invoking a jQuery text() method on the result.

---

[8]https://api.jquery.com/category/selectors/.

[9]http://api.jquery.com/jquery/.

- **Tilde sign** This sign infers that type conversion of a selector result to a native Javascript array is imposed. By definition, [" ~ selector"] is treated as [["$selector"], [">!arr"]].

Most wrapping languages (including Selenium IDE language and iMacros[10]) enable to target elements by CSS selectors. Those languages also support other forms of element addressing such as XPath queries. SXPath language enables addressing elements by their visual position. Serrano does not support those additional methods and in the first version we decided to implement the support for CSS selectors, since they are more familiar to web stack developers than other methods. Nevertheless, we consider adding further methods of element addressing a valuable future prospect.

Instruction

An instruction is a sequence of commands (and selectors), that are stacked in an array one after another. Similarly to the UNIX pipe (|), the output of the previous command can be supplied as the first argument of the following. This functionality is enforced by the addition of an optional greater than sign at the beginning of a command name or a selector. In that case, the supplied argument is called the implicit argument. Otherwise, the result of the previous command is discarded. The example below illustrates three examples of upper casing the hello string. The first directive is an instruction that constructs a hello string and passes it to the !upper command. The second directive is a direct command and the third one first constructs the goodbye string, but because the !upper method is not prefixed with the greater than sign, it is discarded and the command runs only with its explicitly stated hello argument. The last directive throws an error, since the !upper command is expecting one argument and zero arguments are supplied.

```
[["!constant", "hello"], [">!upper"]]
["!upper", "hello"]
[["!constant", "goodbye"], ["!upper", "hello"]]
⇒ "HELLO"
[["!constant", "goodbye"], ["!upper"]] ⇒ Error
```

3.3   Scraping Query and Scraping Result

Scraping directives are assembled into a higher logical unit that defines the overall structure of data we want to extract. In other words, a scraping query is a

---

[10]http://imacros.net/.

finite-depth key-value dictionary where for each key, the value is the scraping directive or another dictionary. The example below showcases a scraping query.

```
{
title: [["$h2"], [">!at", 2], [">!lower"]],
time: {
start : [["$. infobar [itemprop='datePublished ']"], [">!attr", "content"],
[">!parseTimeStart"]]
end: //another scraping directive }
}
```

Once the Serrano interpreter starts interpretation of a scraping query, it recursively loops through all the keys in an object and replaces the scraping directive with respective evaluated values. E.g., if the interpreter runs in context of a fictional movie database page, scraping query above will evaluate to a *scraping result* that looks like this.

```
{
title: "The Hobbit",
time: {
start: "8:00pm" end : "10:41pm"
}
}
```

The structure provides two main advantages over wrappers in other languages: (1) The pivotal part of the Serrano wrapper are the data, and a quick glance at a scraping query reveals what data are being extracted and what the instructions that acquire them are. Wrapping languages such as internal Selenium IDE language or iMacros are instruction-centric, that is, the wrapper is described as a sequence of commands, where some commands happen to extract data. Languages, such as Elog also do not reveal immediately the structure of the extracted data. (2) A scraping query consists of scraping directives. If one directive throws an error, it can be reported, and the processing continues with the following directive in the scraping query. In tools, such as Selenium IDE, the data-to-be-extracted are not decoupled, so a failure at one point of running the wrappers halts the procedure.

3.4 Scraping Unit

A *scraping unit* roughly corresponds to the notion of a web wrapper. It is a higher logical unit that specifies when the scraping is to begin as well as what actions need to be executed prior to data extraction. The reason is that often scraping cannot start immediately after the page loads. When scraping from dynamic web pages, we might be awaiting certain AJAX content to load, some elements to be clicked on etc. These waits are referred to as *explicit waits*.

Some languages, such as TSIMMIS, do not expect that some content is not ready immediately after the page has loaded. Other languages, such as iMacros, also consider the page ready right after the load[11] but also provide a command to wait for a given period of time.[12]

We have separated the waiting prescription into the scraping unit instead of mixing it with the wrapper itself to make the wrapper more clear and separate the tasks. A certain disadvantage of our approach might be the fact, that for more complex wait instructions (e.g., scraping intertwined with waiting) we also have to mix them, which creates a disorderly wrapper.

Because the execution can be delayed or ceased (if the element we are waiting for will not appear), interpretation of the scraping unit returns a Javascript Promise. A Promise is an object that acts as a proxy for a result that is initially unknown, usually because the computation of its value is yet incomplete.

3.5 Page Rules

Sometimes we want to execute different wrappers and run actions on a single web page. *Page rules* is an object, that associates scraping units and scraping actions with a web page. To our best knowledge, no wrapping language has this functionality and users have to manage the wrappers and actions manually. Thus Serrano also has the role of a "web data extraction manager", where it manages which wrapper should be executed on a given page.

The page rules object has two properties, *scraping* and *actions*, that serve for specification of scraping units and actions, respectively. A valid rules object must have at least one of these properties non-empty. The scraping property contains either a single scraping unit, or a key-value pair of scraping units and their names. Serrano then enables the user to execute the scraping unit by the name. Similarly, an action can either be a scraping action (which is a special type of a scraping directive) or a key-value pair of named actions.

---

[11]http://wiki.imacros.net/FAQ##Q:_Does_the_macro_script_wait_for_the_page_to_fully_finish_loading.3F.

[12]http://wiki.imacros.net/WAIT.

3.6   Document Item and Global Document

Each page rules object needs to be associated with the respective URL or a set of URLs so that, at the visit of a web page in the browser, Serrano is able to find the most suitable rules object. The associating object is called a *document item* and it has the following four properties: the *domain*, then either a *regexp* (a regular expression) that matches the URI, or a *path* which is the URN, and finally the *rules* object. Multiple document items may match the given URL. In that case, we select the match with the highest priority.

The priority is given to every document. The most important criterion is the "length" of a domain. This is determined by the number of dots in the URL. E.g., scholar.google.com has a higher level of specification than google.com and thus it has higher priority. The next criterion for priority is determined by other fields. The *regexp* field has higher priority than the *path* field. Both fields are optional and they cannot be used in a single document item simultaneously. The lowest priority has a document item with the domain attribute set to *. This domain item is also referred to as the *default domain item* and matches all URLs.

Finally, an array of document items forms a *global document* and it is the top-level structure that encapsulates all the data in Serrano. With the Serrano API, we usually supply this global document and the engine chooses the matching page rules.

3.7   Command Set

One of the leading ideas behind Serrano is to create an extensible language that extracts and processes the extracted data. The aim is to completely eliminate the need for middleware processing that is dependent on a given wrapper. Therefore, we consider extraction and subsequent data processing as one responsibility and find valuable to couple these tasks together. As a consequence, Serrano wrapper creators are capable of extracting and cleaning the data, all in one script. To accomplish this, the resulting command set must be rich—the extracted data often undergo complex transformations in order to be unified. These commands constitute the core library of Serrano.

The rest of this section provides an overview of most important commands and illustrates useful use cases. The full list can be found in the Language Specification.[13]

Conditions and Logical Predicates
Ability to change the control flow is one of the distinguishing features of Serrano. Using conditions, Serrano can decide which information to scrape and how to

---

[13]https://github.com/salsita/Serrano/wiki/Language-Spec.

transform it during runtime. Commands that contribute to this category are divided into:

- *Branching commands.* The main representative is the !if command with optional *else* branch. The first argument is a predicate, which is a scraping directive that returns a Boolean result.
- *Existence tests* Commands, such as !exists or !empty and their logical negations !nexists, !nempty enable us to test if a given structure exists (is not undefined or null) and whether the array contains any elements, respectively.
- *Comparison tests* serve for comparing two integers. Commands in this category are: !lt, !gt, !le, !ge, !eq, !neq and are directly translated to <, >, <=, >=,==, !==, respectively.
- *Compound conditions* include !and and !or commands and their !all and !any aliases. They help to group multiple single predicates into compound predicates.
- *Result filtering* is a means for reducing an array of results to only those items that pass a filtering criterion. For this purpose we define the !filter command that takes an argument in the form of an array and on each array item it evaluates the *partial condition* that is the second argument to !filter command. By partial condition we mean that the condition which is the argument of the !filter command should use argument chaining, i.e., should be evaluated on each tested item of the filtered array.

Arithmetics

Arithmetics is especially useful when we need to add offsets to dates, or do other minor calculations. There are four commands !+, !-, !*, !/ that cover the basic operations with numbers. The commands have two operands and work on both numbers and arrays of numbers. If both operands are arrays of the same length, the operation is executed "per partes". Otherwise, NaN is returned.

Text Manipulation

Among the myriad of commands, we list the most important ones: !lower, !upper, !split, !trim, !replace, !join, !concat, !splice, and !substr. The behavior is identical to their Javascript counterparts; details are provided by the official specification.

DOM Manipulation

Serrano has been recently enriched with DOM manipulation capabilities on top of data extraction. To manipulate the DOM we can use !insert, !remove and !replaceWith commands, which are identical to their jQuery counterparts.

The !insert command takes three arguments: first one has to be a selector, followed by the string "before" or "after" to denote where the insertion is to be done, and the final argument is the text to be inserted.

```
["!insert", ["$p:first" ], "before", " < h2 > Hello John! </h2 > " ]
```

The third variable may also be a template string enclosed by {{ and }}. Names of interpreted variables are either plain names, or refer to nested properties using standard Javascript dot notation. The object with template values is supplied when the scraping is initiated.

```
["!insert", ["$p:first"], "before", " <h2> Hello {{person.name}}!</h2>"]
```

The !remove command takes one argument—the selector that is to be removed from the DOM. Finally, !replaceWith is used for replacing selected elements with a new content. It takes two arguments, the selector and the HTML definition of a new content.

4   User Stories

Serrano has proven its applicability in a number of real-world projects. Below, we pick three and discuss how Serrano has benefited them.

4.1   Magneto Calendar

Magneto[14] is a cloud-based calendar system that enables creation of meetings and to-dos from any web page and adding them to Google or Microsoft Exchange calendar. It also extracts key information for the corresponding events and stores it with the items. If the user visits a website that contains information suitable for a calendar event and clicks on the Magneto button (see Fig. 1), a browser action window appears with extracted information of the event. To achieve this goal, Magneto uses custom-page wrappers, along with the default wrapper.

There were two main reasons for rewriting the rules in Serrano: (1) As the project expanded, the number of web sites and their respective wrappers became harder to maintain and manage. (2) Updating the whole extension every time a single wrapper is updated is stultifying to the user and bandwidth-consuming.

Separation and outsourcing the rules into Javascript would run into several problems, most important of which is *safety*. Javascript is a general-purpose language and allowing to execute arbitrary Javascript code in the extension would create a potential security hole. Furthermore, downloading and executing remote Javascript violates the conditions of the most application stores, for the same reason. Hence, the application could not be placed there. Usage of an-other wrapping language would also be problematic. Wrappers that were already written in

---

[14]https://magneto.me/welcome/about-us.html.

Fig. 1 Magneto interface, when user clicked on the Magneto browser action button

Javascript involved processing of the scraped information, such as cleaning of the selected data from HTML tags, date processing etc.

When rewriting wrappers into Serrano, we identified common functionality across the wrap- pers and created new commands, including !convert12hTo24 h which was used to convert the time of an event into a 24-h clock, since some web sites use a 12-h format. Further helper commands include !textLB (LB stands for line break) that appends a new line symbol after specific tags, such as <div>, <p>, <br>, <hr>. Another command was !cleanupSel for removing the tags and the superfluous white spaces from the selected text.

Next, we identified parts of the wrappers that required higher expressive power than Serrano had. We created commands that encapsulate this functionality and they work as black boxes. That is, the functionality that requires higher expressive power is encapsulated within the commands without granting the language higher expressive power. These constructs include while loops, exceptions etc.

Another challenge for Serrano was understanding of the date of an event on Facebook. Facebook, for user convenience, describes dates in various formats depending on when it is going to occur. Valid descriptions of a date include: *May 24, next Thursday, tomorrow* etc. Our workaround involved creating a !parseFacebookDate command, which was a raw copy and paste of the complex function featuring in the former Javascript wrapper. After some time, Facebook coupled additional microdata [21] with the event, so this command was removed.

After the replacement[15] of Javascript wrappers with Serrano scraping units, both maintainability and maintenance were increased.

---

[15]https://github.com/salsita/Serrano/tree/master/magneto/scraping-units.

Effective Java (Java Series): Amazon.co.uk: Joshua Bloch ...
https://www.amazon.co.uk/**Effective-Java**-Joshua-Bloch/dp/0201310058 ▾
Effective Java (Java Series) Paperback – 5 Jun 2001. ... Start reading **Effective Java** Programming Language Guide on your Kindle in under a minute. ... Josh Bloch is one of the **Java** core architects and in **Effective Java** Programming Language Guide provides a **Java** master class.

◥MyPoints˙ Earn 2 Points per dollar at eBay!
Java: Effective Java by Joshua Bloch (2008, Paperback) - eBay
www.ebay.com › Books › Textbooks, Education ▾
★★★★★ Rating: 5 - 2 votes - $22.67 to $50.41
Find great deals for Java: **Effective Java** by Joshua Bloch (2008, Paperback). Shop with confidence on eBay! ... **Effective Java** 2nd Edition. $23.97 **Buy** It Now.

Fig. 2 Excerpt of the search results for "Effective Java" augmented by MyPoints extension

4.2 MyPoints

MyPoints[16] is a shopping rewards program that runs affiliate programs with 1900 + stores. It motivates people to make a purchase at associated stores to earn points, which can be then transformed into discount coupons and subsequently redeemed. Serrano was used in beta version of the extension. On websites with search results of a search engine, MyPoints extension injects a text informing the potential shopper about the amount of points they can earn, as shown in Fig. 2. Moreover, when the user proceeds to a checkout in the store, it automatically fills in the input field with an available coupon. To serve this purpose, the commands for DOM manipulation[17] were added.

4.3 Video Downloader

In this case, an extension was built into a modified version of Opera browser.[18] The purpose of Video Downloader (VD) is to facilitate download of a currently played video and to enable one to eventually watch it offline. To accomplish this, VD identifies videos on the websites—either by recognizing the domain, or the player if the video is embedded—and attaches a small button that is displayed when user hovers over the video. VD applies Serrano rules for both player element and player content identification. Specifically, an instruction for player identification returns a player element, which is then supplied to the second Serrano instruction for download address identification.

---

[16]http://mypoints.com/.

[17]https://github.com/salsita/Serrano/wiki/Language-Spec##dom-manipulation.

[18]The browser vendor wishes to remain undisclosed.

During the implementation of the extraction rules we encountered two challenges. The first was that the video player element only needed to be extracted when it had a class attribute with off-screen value. This was achieved by extending the command set with !if. The second challenge was caused by the fact that some players use different forms of video embeddings. For example, Youtube uses both <object> and <embed> tags for embedding a video in an external source. However, Serrano was able to deal with this by conflating these elements in one selector.

5 Discussion

In this part we explain the motivation behind choosing Serrano in the above-mentioned projects. In all the projects we were limited to extraction within a browser extension which had to be safe and able to extract the required data. Along with Serrano we considered two alternatives: pure Javascript and in-browser wrappers such as iMacros/Selenium. These tools were primarily designed for writing UI tests, hence we refer to them as *testing tools*.

In Table 1 we compare the technologies in terms safety, learning curve and extensibility. Regarding safety, executing arbitrary Javascript code poses a serious security risk. Testing tools are safe depending on the capabilities of their default command set. In terms of a learning curve for web developers, Javascript is the best option followed by Serrano, which uses CSS selectors and has very similar functions to Javascript. Testing tools have a very specific API suited for the scope they were designed for. Extensibility-wise, Javascript is a Turing-complete language with no need for extension of capabilities. Serrano has an expressive power determined by the command set. The basic set only supports CSS selectors but it can be theoretically extended to support everything Javascript does (by e.g., addition of an !eval command which would evaluate pure Javascript). Wrapping languages of testing tools are not extensible to the best of our knowledge.

In Table 2, we discuss the feasibility of the technology with regard to the scope of the task. For easy tasks with minimum scraping logic, both Serrano and testing tools score well, thanks to a built-in library of functions that make scraping easy, as opposed to native Javascript which requires a lot of code and libraries. In medium complexity tasks, Javascript is closing in due to its expressiveness. And very complex tasks are impossible to manage with testing tools since their command sets

Table 1 Key attributes of the technology	Technology	Simple tasks	Medium tasks	Hard tasks
	Serrano	Easy	Medium	Very hard
	Javascript	medium	Medium	Hard
	Testing tools	Easy	Medium/ Hard	Impossible

Table 2 Suitability of the technology for a given project scope

Technology	Safety	Learning curve	Extensibility
Serrano	Volatile	Gentle	Good
Javascript	Low	None	Not needed
Testing Tools	Fixed	Steep	None

are impossible to extend. Writing very complex wrappers is admittedly more difficult in Serrano than in Javascript, but it is not impossible, since the command set can be extended to arbitrary expressive power.

6 Conclusion

The aim of our research was to create a web data extraction tool that could work in a restricted environment. We implemented a novel language, Serrano, which championed extensibility of the command set and separation of concerns. That helped to eliminate the need for any accompanying software further transformating and processing of the extracted data. Extensibility also works the other way—the command set can be reasonably restricted so that the wrappers will only be able to extract and process data to the extent they are allowed to. Deployment in real-world projects has proven the durability of the language as well as significance of the goals. Each project we faced contributed to broadening of the command set confirming its extensibility.

Despite the advantages, there still remain a few steps that can be taken to further improve the language. E.g., creation of a toolkit with a GUI, outsourcing wrapper creation and then dynamically downloading and updating them, or building a database of command sets so that the users of Serrano could find appropriate commands to personalize the language functionality.

Acknowledgements This work was supported by project SVV 260451.

Bibliography

1. *AJAX*. Mozilla Developer Network, 2017. https://developer.mozilla.org/en/ajax
2. G. Cormode, B. Krishnamurthy: Key differences between Web 1.0 and Web 2.0. First Monday **13**(6) (2008)
3. A vocabulary and associated APIs for HTML and XHTML, 2016. https://www.w3.org/TR/html5/
4. Laender, A.H., Ribeiro-Neto, B.A., da Silva, A.S., Teixeira, J.S.: A brief survey of web data extraction tools. ACM Sigmod Record **31**(2), 84–93 (2002)
5. R. Baumgartner, W. Gatterbauer, G. Gottlob. Web data extraction system. In Encyclopedia of Database Systems, pp. 3465–3471. Springer, Berlin (2009)

6. *Document Object Model (DOM)*. W3C, 2005. http://www.w3.org/TR/REC-DOM-Level-1/ cover.html
7. Rahm, E., Do, H.H.: Data cleaning: problems and current approaches. IEEE Data Eng. Bull. **23**(4), 3–13 (2000)
8. Extensible Markup Language (XML) 1.0 (Fourth Edition), 2006. http://www.w3.org/XML/
9. D. Crockford. The application/json Media Type for JavaScript Object Notation (JSON). JSON.org (2006)
10. J. Hammer, J. McHugh, H. Garcia-Molina. Semistructured Data: the TSIMMIS Experience. In: *ADBIS '97*, p. 22 (1997)
11. Sahuguet, A., Azavant, F.: Building intelligent web applications using lightweight wrappers. Data Knowl. Eng. **36**(3), 283–316 (2001)
12. Califf, M.E., Mooney, R.J.: Bottom-up relational learning of pattern matching rules for information extraction. JMLR **4**, 177–210 (2003)
13. Kushmerick, N.: Wrapper induction: efficiency and expressiveness. Artif. Intell. **118**(1), 15–68 (2000)
14. B. Adelberg: NoDoSE—a tool for semi-automatically extracting structured and semistructured data from text documents. ACM Sigmod Record 27(2):283–294 (1998)
15. T. Furche, G. Gottlob, G. Grasso, O. Gunes, X. Guo, A. Kravchenko, G. Orsi, C. Schallhart, A. Sellers, C. Wang: DIADEM: domain-centric, intelligent, automated data extraction methodology. In: WWW '12, pp. 267–270. ACM, New York (2012)
16. T. Furche, G. Gottlob, G. Grasso, C. Schallhart, A. Sellers: OXPath: a language for scalable data extraction, automation, and crawling on the deep web. VLDB J. **22**(1), 47–72 (2013)
17. R. Baumgartner, S. Flesca, G. Gottlob: The Elog web extraction language. In: LPAR, pp. 548–560. Springer, Berlin (2001)
18. E. Oro, M. Ruffolo, S. Staab: SXPath: extending XPath towards spatial querying on web documents. In: Proc. VLDB Endow. **4**(2), 129–140 (2010)
19. E. Ferrara, P. De Meo, G. Fiumara, R. Baumgartner. Web data extraction, applications and techniques: a survey. Knowl. Based Syst. **70**, 301–323 (2014)
20. G. Gottlob, C. Koch: Monadic datalog and the expressive power of languages for web information extraction. JACM **51**(1), 74–113 (2004)
21. I. Hickson: HTML microdata, 2011. http://www.w3.org/TR/microdata/

Printed in the United States
By Bookmasters